D.H. LAWRENCE: CENTENARY ESSAYS

D. H. LAWRENCE:

CENTENARY ESSAYS

EDITED BY
MARA KALNINS

BRISTOL CLASSICAL PRESS

Printed in Great Britain

First published (1986) by

BRISTOL CLASSICAL PRESS
Department of Classics
Wills Memorial Building
Queens Road
BRISTOL BS8 1RJ

British Library Cataloguing in Publication Data

Kalnins, Mara
  D.H. Lawrence: centenary essays.
  1. Lawrence, D.H. — Criticism and interpretation
  I. Title
  823'.912   PR6023.A93Z/

  ISBN 0–86292–181–3
  ISBN 0–86292–180–5 Pbk

Printed and bound in Great Britain by
Short Run Press Ltd, Exeter

Contents

Editor's Preface

The plaque commemorating D.H. Lawrence in Westminster Abbey and installed in this, the centenary year of his birth, has inscribed on it his own words, which are a fitting epitome of his life and art: 'Homo sum! the adventurer'. The controversial writer whose books were censored, expurgated and banned in his lifetime and whose writings were as often vilified as praised (as Hardy's had been a generation earlier) has finally been awarded this tribute to his genius, fifty-five years after his death. Those years have seen a dramatic reversal and re-appraisal of his achievement from comparative neglect in the two decades following his death in 1930 to a revival of his reputation in the mid-1950's and the increasingly wide recognition since then of, as F.R. Leavis has put it, 'the insight, the wisdom, the revived and re-educated feeling for health that Lawrence brings'.

The metaphor of adventure is particularly appropriate for Lawrence. His travels around the globe can be seen as significant in two ways: first, his exile from England and the loss of a clearly defined social role and being — he was often to speak of the frustration of his societal self — generated a sense of alienation which revealed itself in the profound and searching criticism of our materialistic, technological age which he saw impoverishing the quality of human existence. Second, he was a spiritual and mental traveller, concerned to explore and map the unknown places of the human psyche, and to articulate his findings in his art so that they could be understood and become the foundation for renewal both in the individual and in human relationships. The theme of self-exploration and self-responsibility informs nearly all his works. And if his fascination with human psychology sometimes led him into the darker recesses of the human soul, this was part of his search to understand the creative and vital forces in human nature which he felt could reshape and regenerate our world. Of his writings one may indeed say as Coleridge did of Wordsworth: 'No frequency of perusal can deprive them of their freshness. For though they are brought into the full daylight of every reader's comprehension yet are they drawn up from depths which few in any age are privileged to visit, into which few in any age have courage or inclination to descend.'

This volume contains the lectures given at the D.H. Lawrence Centenary International Summer School held at Bristol University in July 1985 with the addition of two commissioned articles from David Ellis and John Turner. By publishing these lectures it is hoped that a wider audience gains the benefit of scholars' insights into those gifts which made Lawrence the artist of genius, the prophet and interpreter of our civilisation on which his centenary reputation deservedly rests.

M.K. 1985

Acknowledgements

I would like to thank Rowena Fowler and the Bristol University Extra-Mural Department for having made the summer school possible; John Betts of Bristol Classical Press for his invaluable encouragement and help in producing this volume; Elizabeth Induni for permission to use her phoenix symbol; and George and Mary Donaldson for their unfailingly generous support and for their help in proof-reading the articles in this volume.

Thanks are also due to the many publishers who have allowed us to quote from their books. Full acknowledgements are given in the footnotes, but we owe special thanks to the following:

Cambridge University Press, for extensive quotation from *The Letters of D.H. Lawrence* and other works;

The Estate of Frieda Lawrence Ravagli and Cambridge University Press, for the extract from the unpublished MS of Lawrence quoted by Worthen (footnote 13);

The Estate of Frieda Lawrence Ravagli and Laurence Pollinger Ltd., for extracts from the works of D.H. Lawrence;

William Heinemann Ltd., for an extract from *Poems* by Arthur Symons;

Michael B. Yeats and Macmillan London Ltd. for extracts from *Essays and Introductions* and *Autobiographies* by W.B. Yeats.

List of Contributors

MICHAEL BLACK is University Publisher (Editorial Director) at Cambridge University Press, and a member of the editorial board of the Cambridge Edition. He has just completed a book-length study of Lawrence's early fiction.

GEORGE DONALDSON is lecturer in English Literature at the University of Bristol. His teaching and research interests include Malcolm Lowry, Blake, Shelley and D.H. Lawrence.

DAVID ELLIS is a Senior Lecturer at the University of Kent, Canterbury. His publications include a translation of Stendhal's *Souvenirs d'Egotisme*, a private press edition of Lawrence's tortoise poems and articles on Jane Austen, Coleridge, Wordsworth, James, Lawrence and Barthes. He is the author of *Wordsworth, Freud and the Spots of Time* (Cambridge, 1985) and has been commissioned by Cambridge University Press to write Volume III (1922–1930) of their proposed biography of Lawrence.

MARA KALNINS is a Senior Lecturer at Bath College of Higher Education. She has written articles on D.H. Lawrence and is an editor for the Cambridge University Press critical edition of his works. She has edited *Apocalypse* (1980) and *Aaron's Rod* (forthcoming 1986) and is currently working on *Sea and Sardinia* for the edition as well as on a critical book-length study of Lawrence's late works.

MARK KINKEAD-WEEKES is Professor of English at the University of Kent, Canterbury, author of several articles on Lawrence, and editor of *Twentieth Century Interpretations of 'The Rainbow'* and of the forthcoming Cambridge Edition of that novel. With David Ellis and John Worthen he will be writing the new Cambridge biography of Lawrence and will be responsible for Volume II

(1912–1922). He has also written books on Samuel Richardson and William Golding, and articles on British, American, African and West Indian writers.

LAURENCE LERNER is Kenan Professor of English at Vanderbilt University, Nashville, Tennessee where he moved after twenty years as Professor of English at Sussex University. He has published three novels and eight poetry collections, edited collections of critical essays, and written several critical books including: *The Truest Poetry* (1959), *The Truthtellers* (1967), *The Uses of Nostalgia* (1972), *An Introduction to English Poetry* (1975), *Love and Marriage: Literature in its Social Context* (1979), *The Literary Imagination* (1982).

CHRISTOPHER POLLNITZ is a Senior Lecturer at the University of Newcastle, Australia. He has written on twentieth-century British and Australian poets as well as on Lawrence and has also edited two volumes of contemporary Australian verse, *Lines from the Horizon* and *Neither Nuked Nor Crucified*.

JOHN TURNER is a lecturer at the University College of Swansea. He is the author of a book on Wordsworth's poetry, *Wordsworth: Play and Politics* (1985), and he is at present completing a collaborative volume on Shakespeare's sense of history. He has also published articles on Lawrence.

JOHN WORTHEN is a Senior Lecturer in English at the University College of Swansea. He has written articles and reviews on Lawrence and edited several volumes of his works: *The Rainbow* (1981) and *The White Peacock* (1982) for Penguin, and *The Lost Girl* (1981) and *The Prussian Officer* (1983) for the Cambridge critical edition. He is the author of *D.H. Lawrence and the Idea of the Novel* (1979) and is currently editing *Women in Love* and *Love Among the Haystacks* for Cambridge University Press. He will be writing Vol. I (1885–1912) for the new Cambridge biography of Lawrence.

Lawrence and Eastwood

JOHN WORTHEN

I

Eastwood 'is a parish and large and improving village, situated on the top and sides of a considerable eminence on the Alfreton Road, Erewash river, Nottingham and Cromford canals, and borders of Derbyshire. It is a mile from Langley Mill station, on the Erewash Valley branch of the Midland railway, half-a-mile from the Eastwood station, on the Great Northern Co.'s line from Nottingham to Pinxton, 8½ miles N.W. from Nottingham, 10½ from Derby, and 135 from London . . . Present estimated population over 5,000.'[1] Thus Wright's *Directory of Nottingham*, 1893. Lawrence is eight years old; he and his family are living in the house in The Breach in Eastwood: their second Eastwood home, the 'Bottoms' of *Sons and Lovers*. And for Wright's *Directory*, Eastwood is 'a large and improving village'. Under a thousand in the late eighteenth century: nearly two thousand in 1861, three and a half thousand in 1881, four and a half thousand in 1886: now, in 1893, says Wright, 'over 5,000'. Let me remind you of Raymond Williams's gloss on the word 'improving': the 'connection between "making something better" and "making a profit out of something" is significant'.[2] Late nineteenth-century Eastwood was a place where profits could be made; a place where men — and sometimes women — could 'get on'.[3]

The expansion of the coal industry in the region was responsible for the Lawrence family being there at all. Lawrence's paternal grandfather, born in Birmingham, had come north to work as a tailor; he had found work at the Barber and Walker pit in Brinsley back in 1841 (when he was 24), right at the start of the expansion, the year after the Midland Railway Company was formed at a meeting in the Sun Inn, Eastwood. John Lawrence's family, growing up in Brinsley, had made the mines their employment. The eldest son, Arthur — Lawrence's father — worked at pits all over the region

1

before finally coming back to work at Brinsley. His brothers —
Lawrence's uncles — were all miners: James Lawrence at
Brinsley until he was killed there in an accident, George
Lawrence at Brinsley, Walter Lawrence first at Brinsley before
moving to Eastwood and then to Ilkeston. The Eastwood
collieries had produced about 150,000 tons of coal a year in the
1850's, but almost ten times that, over a million tons, in the
1890's. By 1910, when Lawrence was twenty-five, there were
over 4,400 men working in all the Eastwood collieries — more
people than the entire population, men, women and children,
had been when he was born in 1885.

That is one way of considering Eastwood. Here is another
way, which begins rather similarly. 'Eastwood, a mining village
of some three thousand souls, about eight miles from Nottingham, and one mile from the small stream, the Erewash, which
divides Nottinghamshire from Derbyshire. It is hilly country,
looking west to Crich and towards Matlock, sixteen miles away,
and east and north east towards Mansfield and the Sherwood
Forest district. To me it seemed, and still seems, an extremely
beautiful countryside, just between the red sandstone and the
oak trees of Nottingham, and the cold limestone, the ash-trees,
the stone fences of Derbyshire. To me, as a child and a young
man, it was still the old England of the forest and the
agricultural past; there were no motor cars, the mines were, in a
sense, an accident in the landscape, and Robin Hood and his
merry men were not very far away.'[4] That, of course, is
Lawrence himself, writing 'Nottingham and the Mining Countryside' late in 1928 or early in 1929, and choosing his title with
care: not 'the Mining Industry' nor 'the Agricultural Countryside', but 'the Mining Countryside'. And Lawrence completes
that paradox by remarking how, 'In this queer jumble of the old
England and the new, I came to consciousness'.[5]

I trust I'm not alone in finding the opening to that essay a
remarkably odd piece of writing. As I chart Lawrence's actual
attachment to Eastwood (and what he made of it, in essay and
fiction) I shall often return to the way in which, at the end of
his life, he created a new version of his — and his country's —
past, calling it 'the old England', and locating it in the Eastwood
and the surrounding countryside of his own boyhood. Let me,
for the moment, simply suggest the oddity of the viewpoint in
'Nottingham and the Mining Countryside'. It is one that looks

out: out and over. After that single mention of what lies behind
— Nottingham, eight miles away — the eye passes out over the
countryside: looking out to Crich (visible from Eastwood only in
clear weather), to Matlock (not visible at all from Eastwood, but
here oddly made the context in which Eastwood exists), and,
beyond that, looking still further north west and north east, to
Mansfield, to Sherwood Forest, to 'the old England of the forest
and the agricultural past'. Contrast the way in which the eye
travels in Wright's *Directory* entry: along Eastwood's links with
its markets, its suppliers and financiers: along the road, the river,
the canals, the two stations, the two railways. We look along the
links that made Eastwood what it was; we look towards Nottingham, and Derby, and beyond them both, to London itself: 8½
miles, 10½ miles, 135 miles. Lawrence's eye passes clean over
the industrial landscape, and the links between that landscape
and its markets; the only 'link' he notes is the river, which he
views as a border, not a waterway. His landscape is empty of
canals and railway lines; it is full of rocks and streams and trees.
Finally, the eye looks back over the ground it has traversed and,
as if for the first time, notices the industry: 'the mines were, in a
sense, an accident in the landscape'. In a sense: the very things
that had made modern Eastwood, its houses, its industry, its
population, its expansion, are seen as accidental, in contrast with
the eye's and the heart's own place: the countryside. As always,
Lawrence *creates* the landscape about which he writes. He is not
a photographic, nor an historical recorder; he is asserting ways in
which he chooses to belong to a place on his own terms. He
makes the place his own; it becomes both the habitation and the
sustenance of his fantasy.

I want to offer one more, very different, account of Lawrence
looking at Eastwood before I start to draw these threads
together: Lawrence paying a visit to Eastwood in the middle
'twenties. William Hopkin, who recorded it, said that they went
for a walk on Lawrence's last visit to Eastwood, which would
make it September 1926. I suspect, however, that it dates from
Lawrence's penultimate visit, in October 1925.

> When we reached Felley Dam [next to Felley Mill Farm], he
> stood still and looked across to the Haggs [the Chambers's farm,
> of course]. I went and sat by the pond. After a few minutes I
> turned and looked at him. He stood as stiffly as a statue, and
> there was an expression of dreadful pain on his face.

After a while he told me to come along. For ten minutes he
never spoke a word, and then he broke out into a lot of brilliant
nonsense.

As we neared his old house [either the Breach house or the
Walker Street house, I think] he never gave it a glance. I asked
when he was coming over again. His reply was 'Never! I hate the
damned place.'[6]

That is something else with which we must reckon, as we gird
ourselves up to celebrate Bert's happy relationship with Eastwood. He was not only nostalgic about it; his relationship with
it was not only that of a man who recreated it as he chose. It
was also a place he deliberately exiled himself from, even if —
in the way of such things — it kept coming back into his life;
was something he could no more depart from than he could (for
example) from the influence of his father and his mother. As he
wrote to his old friend Gertrude Cooper, late in life, about their
youth in Eastwood: 'Sometimes it seems so far off! And
sometimes it is like yesterday'.[7] The eye that passes so
confidently over the beloved landscape of 'Nottingham and the
Mining Countryside' is, in reality, that of an exile whose desire
is not to recover a lost world, but to create one that is, now,
satisfying: one that genuinely fills his imagination: who offers
himself a place to which he is attached simultaneously with
declaring his independence of it. In the end, I suspect that
Eastwood, Nottingham and the Mining Countryside meant more
to Lawrence as places he could turn into symbols of what he
wanted to believe in, than in any other way. But they were also
capable of reminding him of so many roads untaken, so many
loyalties abandoned, that he may have embraced the symbols he
turned them into rather more readily than he could accept the
real places and the actual memories. That confidently moving
eye is that of an exile who both recreates a 'home', and says
that it is lost, irrecoverable. I shall return to this subject at the
end.

II

Some figures and facts. Lawrence was born in Eastwood in
1885, at what is now 8a Victoria Street. I suspect, but cannot
prove, that he never went further than ten miles from Eastwood

market place until he was seventeen years old. He had been to Nottingham High School as a day pupil, and had worked in Nottingham at Haywards Surgical Goods factory. But in 1902, when he was seventeen, he was ill with pneumonia, and was sent to Skegness (where he had an aunt) to convalesce. It was his first time at the sea. He was in the South Midlands during Wakes week, October 1903; there was a summer holiday with the family at Great Yarmouth in 1905; another holiday, with family and friends, at Mablethorpe in Lincolnshire the following year. But all this time he was living at home, with parents, in Eastwood. In September 1906 the daily journeys to Nottingham started again, while he was a student. But, of course, he still lived at home, in Eastwood. Except, perhaps, when he visited his uncle and aunt in Leicester, he only went further than Nottingham on those family summer holidays: Robin Hood's Bay in 1907, Flamborough in 1908. Finally, in September 1908, he was interviewed for a teacher's job on successive days in Stockport (near Manchester) and in Croydon; and got the job in Croydon. That October, he finally left Eastwood. He was just over twenty-three years old.

Summer holidays continued; the Isle of Wight the following year, Blackpool with a friend in 1910. He also travelled from Croydon down to the south coast; to Brighton, to Newhaven, to Dover. Yet the end of the Croydon school term always meant a return to Eastwood; there was no way he could afford to pay for accommodation in Croydon (or anywhere else) when he could live rent-free at home. And, certainly up until the death of Mrs Lawrence in December 1910, he returned to Eastwood *as* his home: though not necessarily happily. After his first Croydon term, we find him writing his Eastwood address 'Lynn Croft', and noting '(How easily I write the old address!)'.[8] But after a paragraph about melting snow and dulling weather, he also remarks 'I am writing in my true Eastwood vein'. Eastwood was a place he obviously linked with unhappiness, though he never quite said why; but I suspect it was because of the peculiar tension of the family home (Jessie Chambers remembered the feeling of it),[9] which never seems to have recovered from the quarrels of the early days and the bitter unfulfilment of Mrs Lawrence all her life. As Lawrence told Louie Burrows when he got engaged to her, 'You will be the first woman to make the earth glad for me: mother, J[essie] — all the rest, have been gates to a very sad world' (i. 195). The darker side of his Eastwood experience — what he called 'the ugly side of the picture', which he deliberately left out of a letter to Blanche Jennings a couple of years earlier (i. 57) — could come back to him even very late in life, as when he told Catherine Carswell, after Eastwood in 1925, how 'the horrors of his childhood had come up over him like a smothering flood'.[10] Away from Eastwood, on summer holiday with his family on the Isle of Wight, he hears the bad news of the illness of his friends and neighbours Mabel Limb and her father (Mabel Limb would die within six months): 'it is very cruel altogether. I begin to hate Eastwood, things happen so cruelly and so perversely there' (i. 133–4). And back in Eastwood in August 1910 — before the illness of his mother had been discovered — we find him writing to Grace Crawford about his home; and he is 'sulking . . . because life seems dreary: it generally does at home' (i. 174). That autumn and winter, of course, sharing the nursing of his mother in her last illness, his feeling of discord and depression at home was confirmed and enhanced a million times. 'I wonder if ever it was true that I was at London. I seem to have died since, and that is an old life, dreamy' (i. 189).

After his mother's death, he wanted even less to go back to Eastwood. That Christmas, his sister Ada and their friend Frankie Cooper both came south, and they went to Hove for the holiday. Lawrence only returned to the Midlands (and not to Eastwood) to Quorn, to see Louie Burrows (to whom he was now engaged: another removal of himself from Eastwood). He didn't return to Eastwood at all until Easter 1911 (and that only after pressure from Ada): 'I *don't* want to come to Eastwood' (i. 229). Finally he relents: 'It would cost a lot for us to go away, and I want to see folk. But I hate Eastwood abominably, and I should be glad if it were puffed off the face of the earth' (i. 233). He was still saying that fourteen years later, when he told Catherine Carswell after his penultimate visit how 'glad he would have been' if Eastwood ' "were puffed off the face of the earth" '.[11] That spring of 1911, too, Ada was planning to move from the Lynn Croft house: 'I am glad you are moving', Lawrence told her (i. 233). Not 'I am glad *we* are moving': he is declaring it no longer home to him.

However, after his pneumonia illness in the winter of 1911, and his convalescence in Bournemouth in January 1912 (where he appeared in the boarding house guest list as 'Mr Lawrence (Croydon)', not 'Mr Lawrence (Eastwood)'), all he could do — without a salary — was go back to Eastwood. He was there from 9 February to 3 May, the longest he had been there for three years, though he interspersed his stay with trips to Nottingham, Shirebrook, Eakring, Staffordshire and London. It was not, after all, as unpleasant as he had feared: 'Everybody in Eastwood is so jolly — I am always out — have scarcely a moment's time for anything' (i. 368). But it is important that it was during these months that he first began to get *Sons and Lovers* into something of the shape in which we now know it; and this was in Eastwood during the coal strike of February–March 1912, with his father (therefore) at home a lot of the time. 'Father, of course, enjoys it' (i. 379) — the strike, that is. They must have seen more of each other than for many years, with Ada at school during the day.

But around 17 March he went to lunch with his Nottingham University Modern Languages Professor (the name appears in his address book: one Prof. Weekley); on 3 May he travelled down to Charing Cross, met Frieda there — and that really was the end of Eastwood as any kind of home, for the rest of his life. Eastwood now meant people who went on living there; Ada and his father, in Queen's Square; Will and Sallie Hopkin, in Devonshire Drive; his old friends May and Will Holbrook, out at Moorgreen. (These were people who knew about Frieda.) And there were the Cooper sisters in Lynn Croft, and Flossie Cullen at the house and shop on the Nottingham Road. There may have been others, but these were the people to whom he addressed letters and postcards which survive, over the next six months. May and Will Holbrook both left the district in the course of the next two years; Flossie Cullen was Ada's friend, rather than his; Ada herself would be marrying and moving to Ripley, six miles away, in August 1913. For Lawrence, Eastwood after his elopement meant the Coopers and the Hopkins, and, in some unexplained way, his father; and after Frankie Cooper's death in 1918 (when Gertrude made her home with Ada), I suspect that the Hopkins remained his only real Eastwood friends. As he told Sallie Hopkin in the summer of 1912, just after he had eloped: 'You know you are one of the very, very few who will take us into your heart, together' (i. 440); that is, him and Frieda together. And it was with the

Hopkins that he stayed when he went back to Eastwood for the first time, to Ada's wedding; though it was obviously impossible for Frieda to go with him, before they too were married. After Sallie Hopkin died in 1923, and his father the following year, there was only Willie Hopkin to draw him back to Eastwood; in the end, therefore, it was necessarily a place of memories rather than of actual friendships and relationships.

III

That might have been the end of the story. To judge by some of Lawrence's outbursts, over the next few years, one would have expected so. Here he is, thinking about Nottingham in 1920: 'Nottingham! Cursed, cursed Nottingham, gutless, spineless, brainless Nottingham, how I hate thee!' (iii. 509–10). Two years earlier, he had remarked about Eastwood that 'I have always hated it' (iii. 250); while back on his penultimate visit, he told Catherine Carswell how weary he was 'of past things — like one's home regions — and don't want to look at them'.[12] (While in the essay 'Getting On', which he wrote after his final visit in 1926: 'I find I can be at home anywhere, except at home . . . The one place where I feel absolutely not at home, is my home place, where I lived for the first twenty-one years of my life.'[13]) With his sister Ada's marriage, anyway, Eastwood was effectively replaced by Ripley as his Midlands base; he must have seen Eastwood more often out of the tram windows, travelling from Nottingham to Ripley, than he actually set foot in it. Appropriately, the first tram through Eastwood ran the afternoon of Ada's wedding . . .

I intend to cover the history of the next twelve years fairly quickly. Lawrence was only in the Midlands briefly in 1914 (though that was his first visit with Frieda); briefly, in 1915; not at all, in 1916; briefly, in the spring of 1917; and then for almost ten months (with interruptions) in 1918 and 1919, in Middleton-by-Wirksworth, at the cottage Ada had rented for him. But Middleton is to the west of Ripley, and Lawrence seems only to have returned to Eastwood for particular reasons, such as to see the Hopkins; when he discovered, rather to his surprise, that 'queer — I can accept it again — no longer have to fight it at all' (iii. 256); 'For the first time in my life I feel quite aimiably towards it' (iii. 250). Now he tells us; he had always had to fight it. Thereafter, it seems that the Hopkins tended to come over to Middleton, rather than the other way round (they came at least twice in the summer of 1918). However, as if to confirm Eastwood's old reputation as the place where things happened 'so cruelly and so perversely' (i. 134), his childhood friend Frankie Cooper fell very ill with TB in the autumn of 1918, and her lingering illness (during which Lawrence visited her in Lynn Croft several times) was followed by her death in December. Lawrence probably went to her funeral on the 22nd; Eastwood was, once again, the place of the death of those he was close to. It was not an accident, and hardly a figure of speech, that he should write in 1925 how 'England just depresses me, like a long funeral'.[14] By then Sallie Hopkin had died, and so had his own father. And in 1926 Frankie's sister Gertrude was also to fall desperately ill with TB, and nearly died; as their childhood friend Mabel Limb had died, back in 1909, and Gertrude's younger sister Ethel way back in 1905.[15] Lawrence himself almost died of influenza and pneumonia in Middleton, in the spring of 1919, less than two months after Frankie Cooper's death in Eastwood. He had good reason to link the place with, in several senses, 'the dead'. As he had written during his 1915 visit to Ripley, his love for his family was something 'which goes back into the past, but not forward into the future', and like 'the love of the dead . . . is very painful' (ii. 487). 'I am fond of my people, but they seem to belong to another life, not to my own life' (ii. 486). There must, therefore, have been some extraordinary moments in Middleton, during those ten months, such as the time when Mountain Cottage held him, his elder sister Emily, his niece Peggy, his nephew Jack, Frieda, *and* his father, with sister Ada only a few miles away and coming over regularly. As Lawrence wrote, 'It is queer — and a bit irritating, to be en famille again' (iii. 245). But the man who described his father, four years later, as having an 'unquenchable fire and relish for living',[16] had actually seen more of him during those months in Middleton than for a very long time; and seen him, too, without the influence of his mother's antagonism. On the other hand, there can be no doubt that the family as a whole was, and remained, oppressive to Lawrence. Not just because he had changed and they (mostly) had not; but also because, in his closest family relationship, with his sister Ada, he could see his mother's hopes for her children most actively realised, in respectability and 'getting on', in ways that must have reminded him very forcibly of her love and ambition for *him*.[17]

He left England in 1919 and was away for four years. But here he is, back in England in December 1923, about to go up to the Midlands to see his family: 'I am due to go to the Midlands to my people, but don't bring myself to set out. I don't want to go. It's all the dead hand of the past, over here, infinitely heavy, and deadly determined to put one down. It won't succeed, but it's like struggling with the stone lid of a tomb'.[18] The metaphor is one he uses continually: he feels 'buried alive', 'dead and dark and buried', feels 'It's like being in the tomb',[19] in London before going up. The metaphor is also implicit in something he had written back in 1908: 'One does feel buried in Eastwood — but the grave is no deeper there than elsewhere' (i. 96). Yet the same sense of oppression had run right through his Midlands letters from Middleton, during 1918 and 1919: it is so 'shut in here' is a continual refrain. There is a link to be made with the literal 'oppression' he suffered, from the effects of damp and smoke on damaged lungs, while in the industrial Midlands; the cause of illness and oppression literally in the air he breathed, making him breathless. He told his sister-in-law Else at the end of his period in Middleton how 'Ich freue mich riesig . . . wieder in einer grösseren Landschaft zu sein — England ist eng, in jeder Beziehung' ['I look forward enormously . . . to being again in a larger landscape — England is narrow, in every sense'] (iii. 345–6). To put it another way, he had to get out, to live.

IV

And yet. There is always an 'and yet'. Lawrence continued to write about Eastwood and the Midlands long after *Sons and Lovers*, which for another writer might well have been a farewell both to youth and to the place of upbringing. The book he planned to write after *Sons and Lovers* was to be called 'Scargill Street', the street crossing Victoria Street in Eastwood, where he was born. What he *did* start was the so-called 'Burns Novel', set in Derbyshire, with village scenes set in the nearby

village of Jacksdale. After giving that up he turned to 'Elsa
Culverwell' and 'The Insurrection of Miss Houghton', the first
certainly, and the second almost certainly, set in a recreated
Eastwood. After that, he turned to 'The Sisters' which, if we
can trust the evidence of its recreation as *The Rainbow* and
Women in Love, would also have drawn upon the setting of
Eastwood. It is an extraordinary record for a man living by the
Lago di Garda, rejoicing at having left Eastwood. The very first
novel he wrote which did not to some degree draw upon the
urban landscape of Eastwood was *Kangaroo*, as late as 1922;
and even that managed to bring in the sensations of the tram
ride between Derby and Ripley in the dark night. Only
Kangaroo and *The Plumed Serpent* (written in Australia and
Mexico) did not draw upon Eastwood, while Lawrence's visits
back to Eastwood and Ripley tended to provoke writing about
them. His first return visit, for Ada's wedding, produced the
plan of 'a bookful of sketches' on Eastwood: 'I am going to do
an article on the Artists of Eastwood. I do the Primitive
Methodist Chapel next' (ii. 57). If he had done those sketches,
they would have made up his first travel book . . . They don't
survive, and perhaps he never did do them; but to help with
them, he asked Hopkin to 'tell me all the things that happen,
and sometimes send me a Rag [the *Eastwood and Kimberley
Advertiser*].' We can assume that letters from Hopkin and his
wife frequently contained just that quality of 'good old crusty
Eastwood gossip' (ii. 122) which Lawrence thanked him for in
December 1913.

Again, his period in Middleton was followed by three novels
which all start in and around a recreated Eastwood: *Aaron's
Rod*, *The Lost Girl*, and *Mr Noon*. All three chart the same
development as was probably the subject of 'The Insurrection of
Miss Houghton': a break out from the confines of the small
English town, the discovery of the new life abroad. But
Eastwood is what they break from.

Finally come those two last visits: 1925, when he hated the
Midlands, and September 1926. Compared with other visits, that
in 1926 was exceptionally brief; only four days in Ripley, only a
passing visit to Eastwood, presumably to see Willie and — now
— Olive Hopkin. But the visit had been prefaced by Lawrence
spending three weeks on the Lincolnshire coast, which he
regarded as being 'up in my own regions', 'my native Midlands',

'where I first knew the sea, so I feel at home'.[20] And it was here that he felt 'a queer, odd sort of potentiality in the people'.[21] Though short, this last visit to the Midlands effectively redirected the course of Lawrence's writing for his last three years; it gave him back England and its fate as a subject for his work.

First, of course, comes *Lady Chatterley's Lover*, its first draft begun within three weeks of his return to the Villa Mirenda in October 1926, and drawing both on present-day and the 'old' Eastwood, as well as on those drives round Derbyshire he had made with Ada in 1925 and 1926. *Lady Chatterley* was a continuing project, up to the summer of 1928. He also wrote some remarkable letters in this period, most notably to Rolf Gardiner in December 1926: 'Go to Walker Street — stand in front of the third house . . . I know that view better than any in the world . . . that's the country of my heart'.[22] There are a number of *Pansies* about home and family, like 'Red-Herring' ('My father was a working man . . .').[23] There is also a sequence of autobiographical writings, started either during or very shortly after his visit to Ripley and Eastwood in 1926, and continuing down to early 1929. As I've written elsewhere about them,[24] I shall confine this mention to a list: the unpublished 'Getting On', a version of '[Return to Bestwood]', drafted in September 1926; the drafts of the 'Autobiographical Sketch' written in 1927 and published in *Assorted Articles*; the autobiographical introduction to the *Collected Poems* of 1928; a draft three-page autobiography written for the publisher Kra in July 1928. There are essays like 'Hymns in a Man's Life', 'Is England Still a Man's Country?' and 'Enslaved by Civilisation', all dating from August–November 1928, and, of course, 'Nottingham and the Mining Countryside', done late in 1928 or early the following year. In a rather different sense, the miniature biography of Mellors's early life and loves in *Lady Chatterley* corresponds closely to Lawrence's own. Oddest of all, there is that piece which Keith Sagar has convincingly entitled 'A Dream of Life',[25] where a perfectly straightforward but richly autobiographical beginning, drawing on recollections of the 1925 and 1926 visits, turns into an extraordinary piece of science fiction, in which the narrator wakes up a thousand years later to find Eastwood regenerated as a kind of Italian hill-top village; agricultural in an old-fashioned English way (truly the 'old

England' reborn), but culturally dependent on Lawrence's knowledge of both ancient Etruscans and contemporary Red Indians. Of all his writing it suggests most fully and (I think) successfully what he meant by 'the old England', as he imaginatively recreates it; and also reveals the narrator's slight but insistent anger with it, as he feels himself alien and dispossessed.

V

What should we make of this sudden outpouring? or, indeed, of the peculiar attraction and counter-attraction which Eastwood obviously had for Lawrence, almost all his life? Hated and rejected and broken free from, yet also written about so much, mythologised, turned into something powerfully symbolic. As Denis Donoghue said so memorably about Yeats, 'He invented a country, calling it Ireland'.[26] I would suggest that in his late writing Lawrence also invents a country, calling it England. It is a country — or a feat of imagination — where he is able to make actual his deepest and most passionate feelings about the way men should live. Here he is in 'Nottingham and the Mining Countryside' re-inventing life in nineteenth-century Eastwood, and in the coal industry, but actually writing about what he thought men had lost. 'The pit did not mechanize men. On the contrary. Under the butty system, the miners worked underground as a sort of intimate community, they knew each other practically naked, and with curious close intimacy, and the darkness and the underground remoteness of the pit "stall", and the continual presence of danger, made the physical, instinctive, and intuitional contact between men very highly developed, a contact almost as close as touch, very real and very powerful'.[27] Lawrence attempted to create exactly that feeling in his 1928 painting 'Accident in a Mine', in which male figures, naked but unheroic, glimmer rather magically out of a brown darkness; and, of course, as the essay notes, Arthur Lawrence too was 'hurt badly, more than once, but he would never stay away'.[28]

When actually back in Eastwood, on his last visit, Lawrence could certainly see nothing of that 'old England'. Eastwood, as he subsequently presented it in essay after essay, was a changed town — because the people had changed. 'Till 1920 there was a strange power of life in them, something wild and urgent, that one could hear in their voices. They were always excited, in the afternoon, to come up above ground: and excited, in the morning, at going down. And they called in the darkness with strong, strangely evocative voices. And at the little local foot-ball matches, on the damp, dusky Sunday afternoons of winter, great, full-throated cries came howling from the foot-ball field, in the zest and the wildness of life.'[29] Lawrence contrasts them with the miners he has seen in 1926: 'now, the miners go by to the foot-ball match in silence like ghosts, and from the field comes a poor, ragged shouting. These are the men of my own generation, who went to the board school with me. And they are almost voiceless.'[30] He had been in Ripley and Eastwood between Monday and Thursday, 13th and 16th September. An uneasy and perhaps inappropriate sense of accuracy makes me want to point out that, if he *did* glimpse a football match in Eastwood while he was there, it would have been a scratch football match, not a proper team game (no Eastwood side played that week, according to the local paper); and it would almost certainly have been played between two teams of men who had been on strike since May, without a proper crowd at all; and a comparison with a real match on the 'damp, dusky Sunday [actually Saturday] afternoons of winter' is no com-parison at all.

Again, a nagging sense of justice makes me want to point out that those colliers had been on strike, without strike-pay, for four and a half months; had been in the vanguard of the General Strike in May; had been left high and dry by its collapse, but were still on strike, with (just to make matters worse) 'something in the nature of a rush back to work at the Eastwood collieries during the past week'[31] — that is, the week Lawrence was there. So that those on strike would naturally have felt their own position more and more hopeless . . . such men might well not have shouted so loud as those boom-town colliers of the 1890's. They had less to shout about.

All this, Lawrence ignores; and so, perhaps, should the reader of '[Return to Bestwood]', because Lawrence is no more writing historically here than he is sociologically in 'Nottingham and the Mining Countryside'. He is writing about loss, and change. He is also presenting himself as a person who has lived through that period of change, and who has — like the rest of us — suffered that same sense of loss. He was born, he tells us in 'Nottingham and the Mining Countryside', in a queer jumble of the old England and the new, his point being that by 1928 the new has finally ousted the old. A more dispassionate historical observer might well comment that, to be born into the Eastwood of the 1880's, into a socially upwardly mobile family like the Lawrences, was to be born very securely into the new England. But, in the late 'twenties, Lawrence is characterising the 'old' for its qualities of masculinity, of wildness, of loneliness: things he once knew, things which his class once knew, things which we all have lost.

On one level, there is a good deal of homage to Arthur Lawrence in all this. In these late essays, the collier — wild, energetic, untamed — is frequently contrasted with his wife (tamed and taming, narrow-minded, money-obsessed); and in 'Nottingham and the Mining Countryside' Lawrence is actually calling the first 'my father', while ignoring his mother completely. She is allowed no place in the analysis; she is subsumed into the mass of the collier wives. Which, when you consider the situation of the real-life Mrs Lawrence — always different, always detached, to her cost and pain — is really quite extraordinary. But, as with the analysis of the place, and the industry, Lawrence's family finds itself doing symbolic rather than literal service in these late essays. He makes it his own, it sustains his fantasy.

And his stress is, anyway, not only on the regeneration of a father figure. In an odd and in some ways perverse manner, Lawrence is asserting once again a sense of *home* in these essays, even if nearly all the time the very idea of 'home' is being denigrated and sympathies are being aroused for the collier who 'roved' over the countryside, escaping when he could from the 'nagging materialism of the woman', while it is the woman who 'idolizes "her own little home" '.[32] This is from '[Return to Bestwood]':

> I feel I hardly know any more the people I come from, the colliers of the Erewash Valley district. They are changed, and I suppose I am changed . . . At the same time they have, I think, an underneath ache and heaviness very like my own. It must be so, because when I see them, I feel it so strongly.
> They are the only people who move me strongly, and with whom I find myself connected in deeper destiny. It is they who

> are, in some peculiar way, "home" to me. I shrink away from
> them, and I have an acute nostalgia for them.
>   And now, this last time, I feel a doom over the country, and a
> shadow of despair over the hearts of the men, which leaves me
> no rest. Because the same doom is over me, wherever I go, and
> the same despair touches my heart.
>   Yet it is madness to despair, while we still have the course of
> destiny open to us.[33]

That has perhaps a finer honesty than the denigration of the
very idea of 'home' we find in 'Nottingham and the Mining
Countryside', written two years later. Its insistence on 'home'
takes us very deeply not only into Lawrence's personal predicament, but into the cultural predicament he understood and
wrote about. 'It is they who are, in some peculiar way, "home"
to me': and yet they are not, because the essay also has to say
that both they and the narrator have changed, and that England
is not what it was, and the sense of loss is part of a pattern of
deprivation.

We get still closer to Lawrence's understanding of this
predicament when we look at his 1927 essay 'Autobiographical
Sketch'.

> I feel, somehow, not much of a human success.
>   By which I mean that I don't feel there is any very cordial or
> fundamental contact between me and society, or me and other
> people. There is a breach.[34]

On the one hand, he feels an acute nostalgia; on the other, he
recognises a gap, a gap that for him literally began in those
houses called 'The Breach'. To some extent, he is interested in
both colliers *and* in their wives because of that deep and original
division in his own early life between working-classness and
middle-classness; between 'tha' and 'you' (to use the terms of
the poem 'Red-Herring'), so that the person you are feels 'in
between'; between pleasure and liberation on the one hand, and
purpose and discipline on the other. To some extent, he had
always imposed this division upon the people and the place of
Eastwood; he had always made them symbols of something he
knew in his bones. But now, in an oddly lonely early middle-
age, they moved him still more strongly; they empowered him
to try and recover '*my* England'[35] out of them, to remake the
England which should have existed as *his* home, all his life, but
which never had.

Why should he start to do this in 1926? I suspect it had something to do with his nearly fatal illness in Mexico, the previous year. He was never in good health again, and must have developed a strong sense of his own mortality. In a strange but characteristic way, in the years before he died he was engaged in *completing* his life, in bringing it to a head; and that involved not only saying what had happened to him, in his upbringing, with his parents, his home, his place, but also saying what kind of sense his life as a whole had made; what it revealed, not only about himself, but about his time, his place. I can find no better way of suggesting how it was that his two relatively brief last visits to Eastwood seemed to have this effect so strongly, while ten months of daily living in the region in 1918 and 1919 had not.

And, too, back in Europe again after his American adventure, and going back 'home' (as 'The Flying Fish' put it) after 'this hurrying away',[36] I think Lawrence was struck even more forcibly by how little he actually belonged to the place whose daily life he still knew so well; how little contact he could make with its people; how hard it was to be a writer *for* the people he cared about. His correspondence with Trigant Burrow in the middle 'twenties was crucial in giving him a new insight into 'the absolute frustration of my primeval societal instinct . . . I think societal instinct much deeper than sex instinct — and societal repression much more devastating'.[37] That line of thinking links, in my mind, with his attempt in all these late autobiographical writings to assert not only what class he, as an individual, belonged to, but what his (and our) society, in England, has been, and now was. And this was genuinely very difficult; because, an exile — *literally* an exile — in the end he really had no class: no society: no 'home'. His homelessness, since 1912, had always been a vaunt: 'I like not to have a home' (iii. 389), he had remarked in 1918. He had made it a proof of his detachment as a writer; no place could claim him, no society could force its demands upon him. He was insistently free. At the end of his life, that stance seemed less important; the kind of human need which it blurred, more important.

So, between 1925 and 1929, partly (I am sure) because of the formulations of Trigant Burrow (but perhaps Burrow only formulated what Lawrence already felt), Lawrence wrote about Eastwood in an attempt to say how — if home were anywhere

— he *did* belong; and, if he *didn't* belong, then why he didn't, and how he then felt. One answer to the problem was to say that 'the place has been transformed'; so that no-one could belong, any more. Another, partial, answer was to say 'my father was right and my mother was wrong'; all that education, that responsibility, that advance, that upward social mobility, that consciousness, had got him nowhere that he wished to be: but the wildness, the roving, the irresponsibility, were his real love, and had been his life; and so, after thirty years, he wanted to assert his real allegiance, and declare his real home, and say how he knew it, for the first time. A more complete answer than either of those, perhaps, was to say — as the final version of the 'Autobiographical Sketch' said — 'I don't feel there is any very cordial or fundamental contact between me and society'[38] — or, as '[Return to Bestwood]' put it, 'I feel I hardly know any more the people I come from'.[39] As he wrote to Burrow, 'I suffer badly from being so cut off . . . it is our being cut off that is our ailment. But what is one to do? . . . At times, one is *forced* to be essentially a hermit. I don't want to be . . . One has no real human relations: that is so devastating'.[40] In his struggles to formulate that, and in the sometimes evasive answers he found, lies a good deal of his significance as a writer. *Lady Chatterley's Lover* addressed itself to an answer; it said that the barriers between the social classes *could* come down; between two individuals, the flame can live, the crocus can flower. But the novel, in its final version, does not confront the question 'how will this couple be able to live in the England of today?' There is a marriage; there is a farm; oddly and remarkably, there will be a child (the first child with which one of Lawrence's major fictions would end: the first future so projected). But what will England be like for such a child? What will its society be? That is not a direction the novel takes, not a question to which in the end it is addressed.

And so, in these last years, we find Lawrence looking again and again at the 'body of his past';[41] sometimes transforming it into an idyll of the 'old England'; sometimes finding himself a stranger within it. Think, when we go round Eastwood to-morrow, that we are not only looking at houses and streets and landscapes that are either still there, or can be transformed in the mind's eye to re-embody their vanished forms. We shall also be looking at a place which was as near 'home' as Lawrence ever had — or perhaps any of us have; but which was not his home, and in the end could only remind him of what he never had and never would possess: a place to which he belonged, and for which he wrote. He could make it a symbol of what it *ought* to have been; that, in its turn, should remind us of what it was not, and never had been.

Notes

1   C.N. Wright, *Directory of Nottingham* (Nottingham, 1893), p. 499.
2   Raymond Williams, *Keywords* (Oxford, 1976), p. 133.
3   See, e.g., the obituary of D.H. Lawrence's elder brother Ernest in the *Eastwood & Kimberley Advertiser*, 13 October 1901: 'London's gaiety could not wrest from him his love for work and his keen desire to get on . . . to fill a high post, to get on and be useful in the world' (p. 2). Cf. Lawrence's essay '[Return to Bestwood]': 'The reward of goodness, in my mother's far-off days, less than twenty years ago [i.e. 1906], was that you should "get on." *Be good, and you'll get on in life.*' *Phoenix II*, ed. W. Roberts & H.T. Moore (1968), p. 260.
4   *Phoenix*, ed. E.D. McDonald (New York, 1936), p. 133.
5   *Phoenix*, p. 135.
6   *D.H. Lawrence: A Composite Biography*, ed. E. Nehls (Madison, 1957–9), iii. 93. Michael Squires has pointed out to me a corresponding moment at the end of the second version of *Lady Chatterley's Lover*, where Connie and Mellors look out to 'the Haggs'.
7   *The Collected Letters of D.H. Lawrence*, ed. H.T. Moore (1962), ii. 963.
8   *The Letters of D.H. Lawrence*, ed. J.T. Boulton (Cambridge, 1979), i. 102. Subsequent references to this edition will appear in the text, in the form (i. 102).
9   E.T. [Jessie Chambers], *D.H. Lawrence: A Personal Record* (1935), p. 35: 'a curious atmosphere such as I had never known before.'
10 *A Composite Biography*, iii. 10.
11 *ibid.*
12 Letter to Catherine Carswell, [17 October 1925].
13 'Getting On', Roberts E144, p. 1, listed in W. Roberts, *A Bibliography of D.H. Lawrence* (Cambridge, 1982), p. 464.
14 *Letters*, ed. Moore, ii. 861.
15 The Midlands in general were notorious for the number of deaths from respiratory diseases: in 1914, for example, in spite of outbreaks of whooping cough, diphtheria and scarlet fever, 25% of those who died in Eastwood were the victims of tuberculosis, pneumonia and bronchitis.
16 *A Composite Biography*, ii. 126.
17 See '[Return to Bestwood]': 'my sister's "getting on" is much more concrete than mine. She is almost on the spot. Within six miles of that end

dwelling in the Breach . . . stands my sister's new house, "a lovely house!"
— and her garden' (*Phoenix II*, p. 261).

18 *Letters*, ed. Moore, ii. 765.
19 Letters to Alfred Stieglitz, 17 December 1923; Thomas Seltzer, 14 December 1923; Idella Stone, 17 December 1923.
20 *Letters*, ed. Moore, ii. 932, 933; *Letters from D.H. Lawrence to Martin Secker* (1970), p. 75.
21 *Letters*, ed. Moore, ii. 933.
22 *Letters*, ed. Moore, ii. 952.
23 'Red-Herring', *The Complete Poems of D.H. Lawrence*, ed. V. de Sola Pinto and W. Roberts (1964), i. 490−1.
24 'D.H. Lawrence's Autobiographies', *The D.H. Lawrence Centenary Volume*, ed. G. Salgado and G.K. Das (1985).
25 Published as 'Autobiographical Sketch' in *Phoenix*, pp. 817−36.
26 Denis Donoghue, *W.B. Yeats* (1971), p. 14.
27 *Phoenix*, pp. 135−6.
28 See *Paintings of D.H. Lawrence*, ed. M. Levy (1964), p. 102; *A Composite Biography*, iii. 227. *Phoenix*, p. 136.
29 '[Return to Bestwood]', *Phoenix II*, pp. 263−4.
30 *Phoenix II*, p. 264.
31 *Eastwood & Kimberley Advertiser*, 17 September 1926, p. 3.
32 *Phoenix*, pp. 138−9.
33 *Phoenix II*, p. 264.
34 *Phoenix II*, pp. 594−5.
35 *Letters*, ed. Moore, ii. 952.
36 *Phoenix*, pp. 783, 788.
37 *Letters*, ed. Moore, ii. 989−90.
38 *Phoenix II*, p. 594.
39 *Phoenix II*, p. 264.
40 *Letters*, ed. Moore, ii. 993.
41 *Letters*, ed. Moore, ii. 859: 'the spirit seems to have flown'.

I am grateful to my friend and colleague Dr John Turner for his extremely helpful commentary on and criticism of this paper.

The Marriage of Opposites in *The Rainbow*

MARK KINKEAD-WEEKES

The opening chapter of *The Rainbow* is, rather pointedly, divided into two: a first section beginning with a timeless world; a second section beginning with a date. This suggests two very different ways of looking at the novel. From one angle, the opening pages show us human life and consciousness in basic forms, against a background untroubled by historical process and social chance. We begin, not with individual personalities, but with archetypal Men and Women, in a timeless Nature. If we then ask what it is that is basic in the life and consciousness of the Brangwens, farming their land on the border of Derbyshire and Nottinghamshire, what is eternally and universally so, we find that Lawrence is developing a language we can use to understand all the individual men and women and all the particular relationships in his three generations. From this point of view we can approach the stories of Tom and Lydia, of Anna and Will, of Ursula and Skrebensky, as though they were undated pictures on the same subject, hung side by side for us to compare and contrast, in order to grasp their underlying significance. But, on the other hand, as soon as we move into the second section of the opening chapter, we are confronted with that date, 1840, and a marked change in the social environment which affects the everyday life of the Brangwens, the building of a canal across their land. From this moment *The Rainbow* begins also to be a social history, seriously concerned to trace major changes in English life from 1840 to 1905. From this angle the structure of the novel looks quite different. Now we must consider a progressive development in time, a gradual movement into history, and ask how each generation of the Brangwens is affected by the gathering pace of social change. We become aware of industrialism and urbanisation; of the spread of education after the 1870 Act; of the gradual emancipation of women; of the growth of rational scepticism

21

and the decline of religious faith. From one point of view the three generations of Brangwens reorchestrate the same basic conflicts in human consciousness and relationships, so that we can understand them better. From the other point of view each generation is in a different position because of the history of their society, and we have to measure the effects of change.

Most accounts of the novel concentrate on the archetypal, a-historical view because that is where Lawrence is most original, and where consequently it has taken longest to learn how to read him, though by following his lead we do discover a basic language which will help to understand and compare the complex individuals and relations that come later. But I want to argue that the historical view is also vitally important — and I'll come back to it.[1]

What we see first, then, is (for Lawrence) true of human beings anywhere and any time. We begin not with individual characters, but with Men and Women in a timeless Nature. There is the flat, rich earth, which the eye moves across, binding it into a unified landscape in which man is at one with nature. There is also however the road, the village, the church tower on the hill, calling the eye up, out, and beyond — what the eighteenth century artist would have called a 'prospect' — a fingerpost pointing to the city, another world of civilisation, intellect and art, the fulfilment of individuality. Between them is the human dwelling, facing both ways. By exploring and opposing the visions of the Men of the Landscape and the Women of the Prospect, we discover two opposite impulses at work below the surface of personality, two kinds of consciousness that we must grasp before we can talk of individual 'character'.

The Brangwen Men do not merely live 'on' the rich earth, they are at one with it, and the charged poetic language tries to realise imaginatively what this involves and means. We are made to experience in these Men what they know in their own emotions, bodies and blood: the variable weather of the skies, the intercourse between the heavens and earth, the seasonal change from Spring to Summer to Autumn to Winter that is the rhythm of the life of all created nature. The life of Man and the life of Nature, seen in this way, are each reflected in the other. It hardly matters from which angle you choose to look; what you see is the same unified existence. In Man, as in Nature, the sap rises, the wave of natural fertility throws the seed forward and leaves the new-born on the earth. The feel of the soil to man at ploughing time and at reaping time is the responsiveness of the lover and the unresponsiveness of the woman awaiting her delivery. We become aware of the earth enacting a human process and of the human being enacting an earthly process. The body and blood of man is both entered by and participates in the lustre of plants and the pulse and energy of animals. His life is at one with the life of the sky, the earth, the beasts of the field, and its vegetation. He uses the world of nature but he is also surcharged with its living, its rhythms of fertility, of harvest, of accumulation and inertia, 'warmth and generating, pain and death'. As our eyes move across the landscape, peopled with human figures, what we see is unity; a together-ness of man with the whole of created nature, done in us as we read, in concrete and rhythmic language.

Such a life is rich and vital — yet the Brangwen Women make us aware of the opposite impulse towards a radically different kind of human consciousness. To them the intercourse of man and nature is blind, dazed with looking 'towards the source of generation'. The key words for the Women of the Prospect are 'outwards', 'towards' that which lies 'beyond'. The front door of the house opens onto the road, up the hill, beyond the village to the City, to Civilisation, the World of Nations. The Women are 'aware of the lips and the mind of the world speaking and giving utterance, they heard the sound in the distance, and they strained to listen'. What is 'beyond' is the life of the mind, of articulate awareness, which not only reflects being but can reflect on it, sharpen it into definition and differentiation, comprehend and utter it in language. What is 'beyond' is also a new freedom and scope for the individual. The women see (even, half-comically in the Vicar, the Squire's Lady, the Local MP) a range of experience, an education of the mind, enabling it to lay hold of the unknown and store up knowledge. Such people have acquired definition as individuals; their children are already marked out from the farm-children, distinctive. And they have a new kind of power and mastery. They do not merely exist in unity with their environment, but are capable of acting on it, shaping and dominating it. Finally this life of mental discovery and individuality can liberate the imagination and become articulate utterance. The voyage of exploration, man's power to traverse the beyond and unknown, can become epic art like the *Odyssey*. Yet we are made aware too, that if this impulse can raise human existence to new freedom, scope and conquest, it is also without the stability of the natural life and can fall below it. (In the village, the Squire is a drunk with a scandalous brother; in the epic, Odysseus has to reckon with Circe and her crew of men degraded below the animals, as well as with the excitements and discoveries of the beyond.)

The impulse of the Women therefore reveals itself as the polar opposite to the impulse of the Men. Where one is a world of being, the other is a world of knowing and acting upon. Where one is a unity with all Nature, the other is a process of separation and distinction. One is a life of the flesh, the other a life of thought and utterance. In one, man is conscious of himself only in togetherness with Nature; in the other he becomes conscious of himself as individual defining and differentiating himself against what is not-him, other. One is permanent and stable; the other holds in change a threat as well as a promise.[2]

There is of course a danger, talking so, that one will make this basic language seem abstract and theoretic, some kind of skeleton key — whereas it is the strength of the novel's opening that it is done so naturally and concretely. And one must not talk too glibly of 'Men' and 'Women'. It very soon becomes clear that we are not meant to think of male and female in any simply differentiated way — we shall soon find both impulses, or forces, operating in everyone of either sex, though in differing proportions. Nor can there be any question of choice or preference: it seems self-evident that life at either extreme would be life impoverished. Rather we are to see all human beings as subject to the opposite pulls of these impulses or kinds of consciousness, below the surface of particular character or deliberate choice. How the conflict is resolved will depend upon differing personalities and relationships and the pressure of different social situations. But by isolating, at first, his basic vision from the complications of individual character and social history, Lawrence seeks to clarify the nature of the opposition in itself. The opening section thus provides a kind of prelude, a pattern of chords announcing major themes, a basic language which we must apply to the novel as a whole.

When we look, then, at the betrothal of Tom Brangwen and Lydia Lensky in the first story, $(76-85)^3$ we are able to see why it is both very matter-of-fact and very strange. When Tom caught sight of the woman in black on the road outside Cossethay, the recognition was instantaneous: 'That's her, he said involuntarily'. Everything else seems to follow as of course: the awareness 'almost without thinking', when the time has come to ask her; the simplicity of ' "What's to do? . . . Bit of courtin', like" '; the straightforward words ' "I came up", he said, speaking curiously matter of fact and level, "to ask if you'd marry me" . . . "No, I don't know" . . . "Yes I want to", she said impersonally . . ." ' But the very simplicity — that is nearly all that is said — pinpoints the strangeness: involuntary, impersonal, without knowledge. They do not respond to each other's personality, about which they know nothing. They are utter strangers, emphasized by the fact that she is a Polish refugee. They seem impelled towards each other by forces well below the level of choice, or even what we would normally understand by sexuality, though that will come. What we seem to be watching is the inevitable, necessary, and therefore matter-of-fact impulse of one 'pole' towards its opposite, because it is opposite; happening at a level which neither the words nor the thoughts of the two people can reach, and that is beyond choice. We have to think in terms of forces impelling men and women to seek the marriage of opposites.

So in the darkness, where storm clouds scud before a great wind and the trees drum and whistle, the black-clad figure confronts the otherworld, lit-up, fire-warmed, beyond the separating glass of the window. Behind him is the unitary world of nature; behind her — the foreign woman, the unintelligible song, the alien child — lie London and Warsaw, politics and revolution, the world beyond the church tower on the hill. But though we are talking of the impersonal attraction of opposites, a kind of natural law, we are now also looking at this man, and that woman, who have individual names and histories. And by this stage we know enough to see that there are conflicts within them, too, which have left them dissatisfied with themselves and their lives, unfulfilled, displaced. So as we watch the scene, we not only see the man from the darkness, the woman in the light; we see also the fragile yellow flowers in his hand, and the darkness in the eyes of the woman and the child. The marriage will have to resolve oppositions within them, as well as between them. And as the opposites meet, the threshold is crossed, the challenge is issued and accepted, we see that for Lawrence the marriage of opposites involves a kind of death of the self, and a kind of rebirth. As Tom and Lydia kiss, there is a self-obliteration, an oblivion, a sinking into darkness. This is painful, a 'blenched agony'; for it is difficult to let go of the self, to commit it to a kind of extinction at the hands of the 'other'. Yet the darkness turns out to be like a womb, and what is born is blazing light, a world freshly created, a whole newness of life. It is only a kiss, but it contains for the Lawrence of 1915 the essence of marriage and of sexual relationship: the committal of opposites to mutual transformation; the loss of the self in order to find it again more fully than before.

Yet this is a continuous process, which is never finished or accomplished. Indeed, to go on talking merely in the terms I have used is not nearly enough, because what authenticates them is the study of a marriage in everyday and concrete realism, and as a process in time: the difficulties of relationship, the tensions over Lydia's child and at the time of her pregnancy, the credible and continuous fluctuation between conflict and harmony. Lawrence's determination to deal with these, in detail and complexity, saves his story from ever becoming merely symbolic or diagrammatic. I only wish I could go into detail [4] — but we can at least notice the conditions for success. Tom and Lydia always respect the otherness of each other, and of little Anna. There is conflict, but no victory or defeat, dominance or subservience, and because of this the conflict is creative. They are able to abandon themselves to each other, but never to merge or absorb; rather they pass through the crucible of self-extinction like phoenixes, 'dying' to their old selves in order to be reborn more fully. In another set of images we approach the novel's title, and its continual biblical reference. The man and the woman, pillars of fire and cloud, are each firmly grounded on their own base, oppposite each other. Each springs both towards and against the other, with its own force. But because neither overbears, the opposite forces pass right through each other, and the result is an arch like a rainbow. They both marry, and fulfil, their separate impulses. But the arch is also a doorway to the unknown and the beyond; the lovers become thresholds for each other, though which each can pass from

exile and the wilderness into the undiscovered beyond themselves, the Promised Land. Moreover the marriage of opposites,
remaining distinct when they have passed through each other,
creates freedom for man, woman, and child, respecting their
continuing otherness. The echoing of the Bible by a writer who
called himself 'a passionately religious man'[5] insists that we see
marriage as a religious mystery: the one way he knows and
trusts in which man and woman can participate in the fundamental creative power which men call 'God'; can experience
Genesis and Exodus, the Promises of new life, the realities of
Death and Resurrection, in their own daily lives; can build, not
in stone or ark but in human relationship, a house for the Lord
to dwell in.

There is also, however, a limiting judgement to be made: an
arch may be like a rainbow, the basic form, but it doesn't marry
the height of heaven with the breadth of earth. In some ways
Tom and Lydia remain personally unfulfilled despite the success
of their marriage; and there are areas of human potential which
stay barricaded away from them, as it were, beyond the canal.
When that canal bursts, Tom is drowned. It is the reverse of the
Flood in the Bible: Noah perishes; yet it is not a wicked world
that is inundated, but a beautiful, if limited one. And Tom has
laid hold of eternity, albeit in a primitive dispensation.

With the second generation, we embark on a process of
comparison, looking on this picture and on that. The scene
corresponding to the betrothal of Tom and Lydia is the coming
together of Anna and Will in the moonlit cornfield, stacking the
sheaves (159–62); and we need to ask both what is like Tom
and Lydia, and what is different. Once again the two human
figures move between a pull toward the darkness and an
opposing pull toward the brilliant defining moon. Again they
seem to obey forces that operate below personality, choice, or
even physical passion. Will out of darkness, Anna drenched in
moonlight, set towards each other, and away, with a deep
natural rhythm, like tides beneath the moon. The stacking of
dewy corn-tresses, hissing together like water, is rich with
associations of fertility, harvest, the creative processes of nature.
The human beings are at one with this, feeling its rhythms,
tidally flowing towards each other. Yet there is also the opposite
and equally natural and tidelike rhythm of separation. But they
meet as two 'others', each with its own motion; and they work

together to make something out of nature beyond themselves. There is a change from being to doing: a weaving, combining, structuring. It is important to notice how Lawrence's style itself taps what is anterior to 'character' and cannot be articulately conscious in the people concerned. The prose can be seen to be working not only in suggestive symbol (in this wordless relationship) but in *rhythms* which themselves mime, and create, the forces at work. Gradually the beat of separate actions approaching and receding, the short sentences, modulate into longer and cumulative swellings and turning, until the meeting is achieved. And as the two 'others' finally come together, we are very much aware of the wonder and mystery of the marriage of opposites both within and between them:

> All the moonlight upon her, all the darkness within her. All the night in his arms, darkness and shine . . . all the mystery to be entered, all the discovery to be made. Trembling with keen triumph, his heart was white as a star as he drove his kisses nearer.

We reach that moment, incandescence within darkness, when the doorway seems about to open into a mysterious dimension beyond, a kind of death and rebirth.

But though the scene re-enacts Tom and Lydia, the comparison alerts us to a sharp sense of anticlimax and loss. Throughout the coming together there has sounded a note of strain, on both sides. There is a tendency in Anna to hold back, resisting the natural movement toward her lover, and its consequences. We have seen this resistance from her earliest childhood — the obverse of the qualities that made her a 'little princess': the assured individuality, self-awareness and wary intelligence, so much greater than her mother's. She is reluctant to meet Will, or give up herself to go through him, beyond; she insists on pulling him out of the kiss into awareness. She short-circuits the process to which Tom and Lydia were able to abandon themselves. And Will's name is also resonant, though this is far removed from allegory. More and more clearly we become aware of 'a low, deep-sounding will in him', vibrating low at first, but beginning, in the prose itself, to drum 'persistently, darkly', till 'it drowned everything else'. When they meet, his voice is 'twanging and insistent'. The conflict of opposites has a new tone, a struggle to withhold the self or dominate the other, which the relationship between Tom and Lydia had not. The corn-stacking, then, prepares us for a developing relationship which will partly fail to achieve the marriage of opposites, and in which the woman eventually conquers.

Yet again, looking at the quality of the long chapter 'Anna Victrix', which traces this process, I must emphasise again that I have only pointed to the basic paradigm of the relation of Anna and Will. What Lawrence then does is to authenticate, and develop, and concretise it in convincing detail, in the process of their honeymoon, their marriage, their parenthood. The time-less essence is interfused with the realistic fluctuation of day-to-day. But we now have, also, to reckon with that other dimension: the historical. We can still use the 'Old Testament' terms to show the 'essential' difference between Tom and Lydia, and Anna and Will. Having conquered, Anna builds a house for herself, rich in possession; but she does not open the door of the promised land for her husband, and cannot enter herself. Because of their vital connection she remains in sight of it, on Mount Pisgah; her house opens under the sign of the rainbow and is filled with the sound of journeying; but Anna and Will do not build the arch or explore the space beyond the threshold as fully as Tom and Lydia had done, despite their limitations. And yet . . . though the achievement is less, the potential strikes one as a great deal more. Anna and Will have wider horizons, and a greater zenith, because they are of the second generation. There are whole new dimensions of life in their story, and new tensions: religion and art, faith and scepticism, education and emancipation, the life of the intellect and the life of the spirit. Perhaps we could say that there is more to marry in Anna and Will, though we would have to say also that the new dimensions of life imply new dimensions of conflict, and make coming together more difficult. This is the point of that great scene in Lincoln Cathedral. To try to imagine Tom and Lydia in such a context is to grasp how much more defined and articulate in consciousness Will and Anna have become; and how much more complex our awareness of what is at stake for them now has to be. The Cathedral, for Will's passionate religious sensibility, is already a union of opposites in which the soul can find consummation. For Anna's rational scepticism, there must be greater multiplicity and separateness, more individualism, greater freedom and space. And the conflict has become more aware, beginning to be articulate, issuing in argument. Still there can be no taking sides for Lawrence. Both lovers have half a truth; but their conflict is not creative, for they do not marry their oppositions and go through, beyond. They seek to impose themselves upon each other, destructively. The greater intensity, the wider scope, the richer potential, not only make the marriage of such opposites more difficult, but offer greater possibilities of damage and partiality. And people are now not only seen as themselves and in their personal relations, but as articulations of the growth of consciousness in history. For Will and Anna inherit a new England born of the industrial revolution and the Education Act of 1870. Will works as a lace-designer in a world of factories, mines and railways. But his inner life, that passion for art and religion, is fuelled by Ruskin and the Gothic revival; and he will go up in the world as the Arts and Crafts movement is taken up by the new Nottingham-shire Education Department. The family move to Beldover is part of the increasing speed of urbanisation. And Anna has had a kind of education and a degree of intellectual emancipation unknown to her mother. As they quarrel in the Cathedral, we are aware of them as people of a new world, as well as variations of an archetypal challenge.

I hope I've suggested something of the kind of reading *The Rainbow* demands. By learning the 'basic' language of the marriage of opposites, one tries to understand Tom and Lydia, and Anna and Will, and to find ways of grasping the nature of their relationships in *essence*. One has also to understand their *personal histories*, as relationships change and settle, through the passage of time. By then bringing to bear the sweep of *social history* into an increasingly complex definition of person-ality, one sees how what Lawrence meant by marriage becomes both richer in potential, and more difficult to achieve. One could then hope to go on to the most complex story of all, the story of Ursula Brangwen, using all we have learnt, and developing it still further both personally, in her affairs with Anton Skrebensky, and also in relation to the greater multitude of possibilities her world offers her.

But this time I'd like to reverse the angles, and begin with the historical dimension, which I have rather neglected. It is surprising how elaborate and careful the novel's chronology turns out to be, how much social detail there is, and how naturally one finds one has taken in, simply by living through them imaginatively, the major changes in the nineteenth century that would affect a middle-class Midlands family like the Brangwens. Beginning with that timeless rural landscape, and ending with Ursula looking out at the hideous new housing that has spread across it, we can focus the results of industrialism and urbanisation. The sprawling ugliness without communal centre shows both the atrophy of the impulse to togetherness, among men and with nature, and the corresponding hypertrophy of the rational intellect. Lawrence is also appalled by the possibility of work-people losing individuality and giving themselves over to mechanical systems, becoming 'instrumental' like John Smith, Loader — or Tom Brangwen Jr., Mine-Manager. But we also, and crucially, see new prosperity and opportunity for the middle-class. The coming of canals and railways has opened new markets for coal and new industrial possibilities. Alfred Brangwen and his son are drawn into the lace factory; but the rapid expansion of Ilkeston [6] makes the farming Brangwens so prosperous that Tom becomes squire-like, and buys an education for his children that puts them almost on the social level of the sons of the Hall. *The Rainbow* has a sharp eye for the mobilities and discriminations of a rapidly changing society; we can see exactly how and why Tom's sons are gentlemen but the young Will is not.

It was of course the spread of education after the great Act of 1870 that allowed Bert Lawrence, miner's son, to become the D.H. Lawrence we know. Tom Brangwen was not really educable, and Will is largely self-educated, but Tom Jr. goes to Nottingham High School, an ancient foundation, and then to what must be the Royal School of Mines which became Imperial College under Thomas Huxley.[7] Lydia had a governess, but Anna becomes one of the first pupils of the Nottingham High School for Girls, only the sixth to be founded by the Girls Public Day School Trust — but unfortunately at such an early stage that it is still like a young ladies' seminary. But in Ursula's time it has become an established girls' grammar school leading to London matriculation, qualification as a teacher, and university entrance. (On the other hand, the seamier side of universal education is also visible in Brinsley Street School, where compulsory attendance up to Standard Five and the raising of the school-leaving age have caused desperate over-crowding — hence those three classes of over fifty each, being taught in the same 'great room' with only glass partitions between.)

The 'widening circles' of the new England reveal greater human potential, the liberation of imagination, art and intellect, and a new personal freedom — especially for women. We see great strides in emancipation and the start of the suffragettes. Yet the new dimension of self-awareness may bring new difficulty in human relations. In a sentence, of Ursula: 'She was aware now . . . And so, it was more difficult to come to him.' Education and emancipation do not seem to bring fulfilment to the 'new women' in the novel; not to Winifred Inger who, for all her liberating influence on Ursula, turns out to be a compromised Diana, only half-formed, settling for a domesticity within a system, both of which she had affected to despise; nor for Maggie Schofield, who has had to divide herself in two in order to succeed in the man's world. Increased self-awareness in Anna, and still more in Ursula, makes them less ready to abandon self in relationship, and fosters a destructive self assertion.

In Ursula's 'liberated' experience, moreover, both school and university are like factories, concerned with system, power, commodity. When knowledge becomes material, it goes dead. In reaction against the scientific materialism of her biology teacher, Ursula glimpses the mystery of living things, the strange organic being of the cell under her microscope. Lawrence is deeply concerned, not by the decay of church religion (which we can watch happening) but by the loss of the religious sense itself, and its replacement by scientific rationalism or anthropological 'comparative religion'. *The Rainbow* at its deepest is indeed a kind of bible, recalling its readers to a religious sense of the world against the current of the nineteenth and early twentieth century. This has nothing to do with creeds or churches of course; as we have seen, human relationship becomes the only true church, and Lawrence rejects Christianity insofar as it has become a religion of death, denial of the body, and aspiration toward a heavenly other world. But he re-interprets the Bible so that the central stories of the Old and the New Testament can be seen to recur in every generation. While portraying the historical decline of religion, *The Rainbow* seeks also to recover a new language for 'God' out of the old scriptures.

So the more we go into these socio-historical perspectives, the clearer it becomes that we cannot talk merely in terms of the effects of industrialism and urbanisation, education and emancipation, rational scepticism and the decline of religion, upon the lives and consciousness of the 'characters' in the novel. For Lawrence, one can understand neither 'history' nor 'character' truly without a much more deep-structural sense of the forces ultimately at work in the universe, and within the human being. History must be seen as sacred, governed by primal energies whose marriage produces Genesis, the Promised Land, Resurrection; and whose disjunction the destructiveness of the Cities of the Plain, the Exile, and the burning fiery furnace. And a true sense of 'character' required a revolution in the novel, a conception of human consciousness quite different from the picture of man-in-society that we get in nineteenth century fiction — which was why *The Rainbow* was so difficult for Lawrence to write, and so little understood by its first readers. After his third attempt, Lawrence wrote to his then publisher Edward Garnett on 5 June 1914: 'You mustn't look in my novel for the old stable ego of the character. There is another ego, according to whose action the individual is unrecognisable, and passes through, as it were, allotropic states which it needs a deeper sense than any we've been used to exercise, to discover are states of the same single radically-unchanged element. (Like as diamond and coal are the same pure single element of carbon. . .)'.[8] There are two kinds of objection here. First, Lawrence is wishing to transcend the old stable *ego* of the nineteenth century novelist (and historian, and philosopher): the view of man as a coherent personality, analysable in terms of his choices. He wants to pierce beyond motivated behaviour, beyond 'thoughts' or even 'feelings' that a man might be aware of, to get to his elemental being — the part of the iceberg that is hidden below the surface. Hence that basic language of the beginning, the opposite impulses that relate man both to the whole physical universe and to his being-in-himself. This is the 'carbon' which is anterior to any particular personality or 'character' and which, in its peculiar state of oppositions, is there in all phases of an individual person. So much has become clear in our experience of the first and second generation: how

Lawrence has gone deeper below the surface than the novel had done before. But with Ursula particularly, one sees that Lawrence is just as opposed to the old *stable* ego; that he wants to capture a sense of the human being as continually fluctuating and changeful because of the oppositions within itself. This will be clearer when we see how many different forms Ursula, the most complex organism of all, throws herself into without ever ceasing to be Ursula. So the iceberg is not a good metaphor — Lawrence wants not only to go deeper under the surface, but also to capture being in a continuous state of transformation, in and out of the crucible of conflict, crystallising in different forms under different conditions, but always elementally the same. Which in turn means that we should not think of Lawrence as merely trying to tap the *un*conscious; for the constant dialectic and change is always between being and knowing in all his people, and that is the ground of creative growth. Moreover it would be false to describe even the Brangwen Men at the beginning as unconscious, if by that one meant 'having no consciousness'. They could not put their experience into words or become articulately aware of it in thought; but they have a richly real and vital sense of themselves and of their life-in-nature, a kind of consciousness opposed to the defining analysing kind. So there are in Lawrence different kinds of consciousness, which antedate 'character' and for which the author must find the language. He must find it, since it involves a kind of penetration, and a kind of flux, only part of which his characters could put into words. Lawrence is of course also an effective dramatist, and uses drama in *The Rainbow* to authenticate and develop what he has discovered, yet drama depends on what people can *say*, and that is not nearly enough. The risk is that he will analyse his people too abstractly, too conceptually, and above all too insistently, telling us what to think — and alas, he does not always avoid it, though I do not think the fault shows in the scenes I've dealt with. For there he seems to have found ways of using language with an intensely exploratory imagination that embodies the impulses of life, and doesn't merely tell us about them. He uses ordinary experience, but makes it richly suggestive; not in the *symboliste* way which makes the art world separate from life, but in a way which can capture a mysterious inner vitality, seeing deeper into concrete experience. And he has learnt to write rhythmically, so that the movements of the prose itself seem to enact in us, as we read, a process-in-time going on in his people. Moreover he came to think of his art, too, as a marriage of opposites: a continuous process of capturing being, which simply is, and trying to make known what had been captured; a systole and diastole between what is palpably there and what is understood; but always in process, always moving on beyond.

Let me finally try to illustrate all this in an outline — necessarily skeletal I fear — of the Ursula story, but leading up to what I think is the most impressive scene of all, gathering the whole book together: the mysterious, disturbing and challenging final episode, where Ursula is terrified by the horses. What we are made to realise about Ursula from the start is that she embodies all the opposites of her family, at peak intensity, and in greater awareness and self-consciousness. She is intensely visionary and intensely sceptical, spiritual and fleshly, arrogant and unfixed, emancipated and primitive, and it is her fate (because of her world) to be aware of herself in all these aspects. Her world also allows her a new freedom and independence that her mother never had, to choose for herself. We watch her continuously trying to resolve her contradictions by pursuing one element of herself to the exclusion of others, but never finding a way of marrying them: 'always the shining doorway was a gate into another ugly yard, dirty and active and dead' (487). She fluctuates, 'allotropically', from possibility to possibility: a female, lesbian relationship with Winifred Inger; the 'male' world of power and dominance in Brinsley Street School: the purely physical life of the five senses with Andrew Schofield; the life of pure mind at Nottingham University. But none can satisfy or fulfil her because all are partial, and reductive of her complex being. In the three crises of her love-affair with Anton Skrebensky — so different in fact, that they are more safely thought of as different relationships — we see further re-orchestrations of the betrothal of her grandparents, and the coming together of her parents in the cornfield. We measure the increasing difficulty of the marriage of opposites, and the increasing destructiveness that results from the assertion of only one part of the self. When the young lovers dance at a wedding, between the fires and lanterns and the dark where cornstacks loom under a brilliant moon, the dance becomes a destructive context for dominance in which Ursula, like her mother, is Victrix, in self-assertion. When Skrebensky returns from Africa in 1905, some years after the South African War, Ursula is reacting against the university and the life of mind. This time they both want, and achieve, a physical fulfilment that is also a superb consummation — of a sort, but it is a meeting in pure darkness, a mating of only the dark sides of themselves. Then, in inevitable reaction again, the terrible scene on the beach shows that she cannot be satisfied while her infinitely aspiring, aware, bright side is denied. Under an incandescent moon, beside brilliant water, she tries to force the polar opposite of the dark consummation, a coming-together in intense awareness, and succeeds only in destroying, like a harpy. Finally she tries to settle for simple domesticity, but that is reducing herself still more. She has tried all the reductive ways. Only the inclusive one, the marriage of opposites remains, and Lawrence faces her with it at the end.

The encounter with the huge horses (538–42) confronts the girl, so ready now to deny the elemental forces in herself, with the powerful presence of those forces and their eternal challenge. The sophisticated, highly educated, self-conscious twentieth century girl of the Prospect and the City, is faced with the unitary landscape of nature: the big wind through which her grandfather walked, the earth with its looming trees, the teeming rain, the power of the animal world that Tom so confidently mastered, the fire from their nostrils. But the summons is not merely to the elemental: it is, as always, to the marriage of opposites. The bird-soul of the aspiring girl comes to the hall of Warriors, attesting the eternity of conflict; but she searches also for a lost stability, beyond conflict and flux. When she looks at the horses she becomes:

> aware of their breasts gripped, clenched narrow in a hold that never relaxed, she was aware of their red nostrils flaming with long endurance, and of their haunches, so rounded, so massive, pressing, pressing, pressing to burst the grip upon their breasts, pressing forever till they went mad, running against the walls of time and never bursting free. Their great haunches were smoothed and darkened with rain. But the darkness and wetness of rain could not put out the hard, urgent, massive fire that was locked within these flanks, never, never.(540)

What the elemental world reveals, again, is the clash of opposites in all created things. The horses are an intensity of conflicting forces that cannot be denied or reduced and must not be, in Ursula. Always the rain tries to put the fire out. Always the fire must remain unquenched, battling against the rain. It is the opposed energies that make the horses what they are, give them their looming archetypal power. But the horses are also gripped, clenched, unfinished. Their oppositions are trying to get free. And if the fire could pass right through the rain and the rain right through the fire there would be . . . a Rainbow. So the horses re-state, both to Ursula and to us, the whole challenge of the marriage of opposites.

But, like all Lawrence's best scenes, the real significance lies not in symbol but in process, in what happens. If we ask, not merely 'what are the horses?' but 'what happens to Ursula?', we see her confronting the challenge, *and failing to meet it.* The challenge, as ever, is to meet the Other and pass through into the beyond. But we know that this must mean a marriage of opposites in oneself that is like a death, and a rebirth. In the first movement of the scene Ursula does succeed in going through, bursting the barrier of the Other; but only by walking with bent head, refusing to look, refusing to think, refusing to know. She merely follows her feet, blindly and instinctively; and she comes through the crucible where her nerves and veins 'ran hot, ran white hot, they must fuse, and she must die'. This is the condition of Tom and Lydia, the old dispensation, unaware. But Ursula is a modern, twentieth century woman, and in the act of bursting through she is forced to know. (The repetition of the words know, and aware, marks the crucial point.) Continually, in Ursula's story, it is her awareness of her intensities that has made her predicament the hardest of all in the novel. So it proves here. As she and the horses pass and re-pass she is forced to know them. As they work themselves up for a climactic confrontation she will have, this time, to go through in full awareness. And she cannot do it. She is terrified. Her limbs turn to water. She climbs a tree and collapses on the other side of the hedge. Instead of going through, she lapses into the element of water alone, becomes unconscious, inert, unchanging, unchangeable, like a stone at the bottom of a stream. This is her 'Flood'. She fails, and failing, she nearly dies literally, as well as inwardly.

On the physical and psychological level this is perfectly explicable. She is pregnant, she has been terrified and in shock, and she miscarries. But on a deeper level Lawrence is suggesting that Ursula has failed, not only because of the inadequacies of Skrebensky, but also because she herself has seemed incapable of the marriage of opposites. As she stumbles along the road and up the hill she is a bitterly ironic commentary on the aspirations of the Brangwen women at the beginning. Yet in her illness she is able to diagnose what has gone wrong. All her efforts to attach herself to life, all her relationships, have been unreal entanglements forced by her will. She has to 'die' to her own self-assertion, to burst all the 'rind' of false relations and unrealities within which her egotism has enclosed her, to trust herself to the elemental forces in life as the naked kernel of a nut does when it bursts its hard covering, before a creative self can be born. The world she is then reborn into, as she recovers, is the mysterious work of divine creation, and she lands on its boundary after crossing chaos. It is an 'undiscovered land', where she recognises only 'a fresh glow of light and inscrutable trees going up from the earth like smoke' — as in the Book of Genesis. She is only on the outmost perimeter, but she is there, on the First Day of her new creation. She must no longer try to manipulate herself, or others, or relationships. She must wait for the coming of a Son of God, from the infinite and eternal to which she now belongs, 'within the scope of that vaster power in which she rested at last.' The Rainbow is not achieved in the novel; the story of how Ursula found her Son of God has to wait for *Women in Love*. But as Ursula sees the sign in the sky at the end it remains covenanted, promised despite tragedy and failure, like the one in the Bible. One may perhaps feel that the promise isn't the logical outcome of the story; that it is Lawrence's own revolutionary optimism breaking through in the language of assertion. But the one in the Bible was gratuitous too, and the promise is no more unconditional here than there. The vision is only seen by the reborn soul that has 'died' to its old self, in the Flood.

Consciousness in time, in flux, in history, must always, for Lawrence, be married to, and transfigured by, consciousness of the timeless, the archetypal and eternal — or man will perish from an inadequate conception of his nature and his world.

Notes

1 It would be quite as justifiable to give a lecture reversing the proportions, so that the historical view was dominant, and I shall be doing so in the Centenary Symposium whose *Proceedings* will be published by Nottingham University Press. There I hope to show the richness of socio-historical insight in *The Rainbow* in much more detail than is possible here.

2 In his 'Study of Thomas Hardy' *The Study of Thomas Hardy and other essays*, ed. B. Steele (Cambridge, 1985) chaps. *vi—viii* Lawrence managed to formulate these opposites and thereby articulate what his three previous attempts at the new novel had been reaching for, imaginatively. As soon as he finished the 'Study' in late November 1914, he took out the typescript of what he had thought the finished novel, then called 'The Wedding Ring', and rewrote it into *The Rainbow*. In the 'Study', the Law of God the Father, the Unifier, is treated as 'female' and the Love of God the Son, the Separator, as 'male'. *The Rainbow's* reversal of this shows that DHL did not wish the emphasis to fall on gender but rather on the marriage of opposites.

3 References will be to the Penguin reprint of the First Edition, ed. J. Worthen (Harmondsworth, 1981).

4 Had I space, I might have chosen the great scene in the barn (112—17), or the argument with Lydia (128—34) — or many another — to try to show in detail how, by dramatising so realistically the tensions of relationship, Lawrence both makes his 'opposites' entirely credible in everyday terms, and also shows convincingly how they can become creative rather than destructive.

5 See *The Letters of D. H. Lawrence*, ed. G. Zytaruk & J.T. Boulton (Cambridge, 1981), ii. 165.

6 By 1881 the four and a half thousand inhabitants of Ilkeston in the 1840s had become 14,000, and by 1891 the population was nearly 20,000.

7 There indeed 'some of the most energetic scientific and mathematical people in London' (283) were to be found.

8 *Letters*, ii. 183.

'Men in Love'?
D.H. Lawrence, Rupert Birkin and Gerald Crich

GEORGE DONALDSON

I must say, at the outset, that I have more questions to ask about *Women in Love* than answers to give; and what answers I do have will be tentative and speculative, hardly more than questions themselves.

While I do think that *Women in Love* is, in F.R. Leavis's words, 'one of the most striking works of creative originality that fiction has to show'[1] — and have been helped most in thinking that by his account of the novel — I do not think, as he does, that *Women in Love*, unlike the novels succeeding it, has what he calls 'the complete and impersonal significance of highly organized works of art' (153). *Women in Love* is a highly organized work of art — no-one can now doubt that — but I am less than sure that its significance is 'complete and impersonal'.

Leavis characterizes the novels succeeding *Women in Love* as novels 'written at great speed in a tentative and self-exploratory spirit' and declares that '*Women in Love*, however, is another matter' (153). Although *Women in Love* was not written speedily, its spirit seems to me no less tentative and self-exploratory than the spirit of the succeeding novels; and, in some things, it is more tentative and self-exploratory. That it is so is the very condition of its being a work of 'creative originality'; but that it is so may also be an aspect of an artistic limitation.

Leavis finds, in *Psychoanalysis and the Unconscious* and *À Propos of Lady Chatterley's Lover* and even the *Fantasia*, 'unmistakably the serenely triumphant reign of intelligence — intelligence that, in creative understanding, transcends the personal plight that feeds it'. The intelligence of these expository and philosophical works is, Leavis goes on to affirm, 'the intelligence of a great creative artist, whose imaginative

41

achievements *are*, at the same time, achievements of intelligence'. But Leavis has a reservation about some of Lawrence's imaginative achievements: 'They are not always, everyone can see, achieved enough to be wholly impersonal works of art, containing within themselves the reason they are so and not otherwise, and leading one, for their significance, not back to the author, but into oneself and out into the world' (153). Leavis is not, in that reservation, thinking about *Women in Love*.

However, *Women in Love* is not, to my mind, a novel in which we have 'unmistakably the serenely triumphant reign of intelligence'. I am not sure that novels can be — or should be — the realm of intelligence's serene triumph, but I am sure that this novel is not. This is not a stricture, pure and simple, since I have no doubts that *Women in Love* is a novel of 'creative understanding', possessed of 'the intelligence of a great creative artist'; what I doubt is that such an intelligence is 'serene' in its triumphs. In my experience of them, the works of even the greatest artists are very seldom, if ever, 'wholly impersonal works of art', transcending the personal plights that feed them; and those that are characterized by their 'creative originality' never do altogether contain within themselves the reason they are so and not otherwise. Of course, if they led one merely back to the author and into oneself, or back to the author alone or only into oneself, there would be no truly creative understanding. The art that is fed by a personal plight need not be — needs not to be — solely personal even though it can never be 'wholly impersonal'.

Lawrence himself wrote, about *Sons and Lovers*, 'But one sheds one's sicknesses in books — repeats and presents again one's emotions, to be master of them'.[2] Mastery cannot be absolutely achieved: 'to be master' of one's emotions is not simply to master them. When Ursula, speaking of Loerke's bronze statuette of a naked girl on horseback, asserts against those who would separate totally the 'world of art' from the 'real world' that ' "The world of art is only the truth about the real world, that's all" ',[3] what she means by 'the truth about the real world' may mean no more, in its immediate context, than that Loerke's ' "stock and stupid and brutal" ' representation of the horse is, as she says, ' "a picture of himself, really" '. The truth of the world of Loerke's art is nothing more than the truth of himself: ' "As for your world of art and your world of reality," she replied, "you have to separate the two, because you can't bear to know what you are" ' (524–6). Lawrence did not have to separate the two, because he could bear to know what he was. Acts of true self-exploration and self-discovery are never merely personal. Of course, Leavis himself did not suppose that the 'world of art' could be separated from the 'real world'; but I wish his valuation of 'impersonality' were less absolute: and that, in formulating his conviction that the world of art should not lead us back to the author but into ourselves and out into the world, he qualified his point of distinction by acknowledging that in the case of all great artists — Lawrence among them — their works do lead us back to them and into ourselves and out into the world, since author and reader and the 'world of art' in which they meet are caught up in the attempt to understand the 'real world'. While we rightly expect great artists to have a greater understanding of themselves and their world than we have of ourselves and of our world — that is, after all, one of the reasons we see them as great — we are fools if we expect them to be all-wise. The sufficiency of art is in 'creative understanding', which if it is really creative can never be 'complete and impersonal'.

However, even the greatest writers may show themselves to be deficient in 'creative understanding'. Henry James found Dickens so in *Our Mutual Friend*:

It were, in our opinion, an offence against humanity to place Mr Dickens among the greatest novelists. For . . . he has created nothing but figure. He has added nothing to our understanding of human character. He is master of but two alternatives: he reconciles us to what is commonplace, and he reconciles us to what is odd . . . But what is the condition of the truly great novelist? For him there are no alternatives, for him there are no oddities, for him there is nothing outside of humanity. He cannot shirk it; it imposes itself upon him . . . Mr Dickens is a great observer . . . but he is nothing of a philosopher. Some people may . . . say, so much the better; we say, so much the worse. For a novelist very soon has need of a little philosophy . . . when he comes to tell the story of a passion . . . he becomes a moralist as well as an artist. He must know *man* as well as *men*, and to know man is to be a philosopher . . . A story based upon those elementary passions in which alone we seek the true and final manifestation of character must be told in a spirit of intellectual superiority to those passions. That is, the author must understand what he is talking about.[4]

James's 'the author must understand what he is talking about' seems to be a more humane expectation than Leavis's requirement for an understanding that transcends the plight that feeds it. But is Lawrence even such an author in *Women in Love*? Is his the condition of a truly great novelist? I think that it is; and not only because he has added to our understanding of human character. He is a great observer, but he is also something of a philosopher who, to quote James again in the same review of *Our Mutual Friend*, 'out of the fulness of his sympathy' is able 'to prosecute those generalizations in which alone consists the real greatness of a work of art' (35). And yet, to be able is not itself an absolute matter, even for the greatest artist. Lawrence, if he is a great artist, must know *man* as well as *men*. When he comes to tell the story of a passion between men, does he tell the story in a spirit of intellectual superiority to that passion? Does he, simply, understand what he is talking about?

I am reassured in my general sense that, in 1985, there are more questions to ask about *Women in Love* than answers to give, by John Worthen's belief, in his book *D.H. Lawrence and the Idea of the Novel*, published in 1979, that the questions Lady Cynthia Asquith asked herself when she read the typescript of the novel in 1918 — ' "what is it all about and *why*?" . . . are still the right questions'.[5] If they were still the right questions in 1979, perhaps they are no less so now, despite the good answers given them by John Worthen himself. I intend, in this paper, to concentrate on only the first of Lady Cynthia Asquith's questions, and to consider it in connection with only one element in the novel: what is it all about, the relationship between Rupert Birkin and Gerald Crich?

It is now time to give specificity to that sense of something unsatisfactory in the novel that has led me to raise the general questions I have. I would like to take up a formulation of John Worthen's about Birkin's 'need' for Gerald. Although I am taking up John Worthen to disagree with him — and fundamentally so — I am glad to be able to say that this is the only point in his account of *Women in Love* where I do fundamentally disagree with him. What he writes is this:

When we find Birkin both as obstinate and as unclear at the end
of the novel about what he wanted from Gerald, as he had been
at the beginning, we don't need to blame a confusion in
Lawrence's own heterosexual and homosexual impulses (as, for
instance, Scott Sanders does); we need to realise that Gerald is a
focus for Birkin of his need for more than a single intimacy, his
need for 'other people', his desire for 'another kind of love'; it is
something the novel has dramatised, not something it has reached
a conclusion about or is offering as a truth. (96)

John Worthen is right to say that we don't need to blame a
confusion in Lawrence's own heterosexual and homosexual
impulses for the fact that Birkin is obstinate and unclear about
what he wanted from Gerald, but only because that doesn't
seem to be where Lawrence's confusion — on the evidence of
Birkin's lack of clarity — lies. But that there is confusion or
uncertainty seems to be incontrovertible.

When John Worthen says 'we need to realise that Gerald is a
focus for Birkin of his need for "other people", his desire for
"another kind of love" ', I find myself dissenting. Firstly,
because the phrase 'another kind of love' is used by Birkin to
describe, not his need for 'other people', but his need for
Gerald: ' "I wanted eternal union with a man, too: another kind
of love," he said'. Although Birkin speaks abstractly, the man in
question — in Ursula's question (' "Did you need Gerald?" she
asked one evening.' (583)) — is Gerald Crich.

However, that is not to meet John Worthen's point with
completeness. There is in the novel, it must be admitted, the
suggestion that Birkin's need for more than a single intimacy is
a need for other people; but that need is not focused in Gerald.
One of the scenes in the novel which might have given rise to
John Worthen's sense of things is the scene that ends Chapter
XXVI, 'A Chair':

'It's one way of getting rid of everything,' she said, 'to get
married.'
'And one way of accepting the whole world,' he added.
'A whole other world, yes,' she said happily.
'Perhaps there's Gerald — and Gudrun —' he said.
'If there is there is, you see,' she said. 'It's no good our
worrying. We can't really alter them, can we?'
'No,' he said. 'One has no right to try — not with the best
intentions in the world.'

'Do you try to force them?' she asked.

'Perhaps,' he said. 'Why should I want him to be free, if it isn't his business?'

She paused for a time.

'We can't *make* him happy, anyhow,' she said. 'He'd have to be it of himself.'

'I know,' he said. 'But we want other people with us, don't we?'

'Why should we?' she asked.

'I don't know,' he said uneasily. 'One has a hankering after a sort of further fellowship.'

'But why?' she insisted. 'Why should you hanker after other people? Why should you need them?'

This hit him right on the quick. His brows knitted.

'Does it end with just our two selves?' he asked, tense.

'Yes — what do you want? If anybody likes to come along, let them. But why must you run after them?'

His face was tense and unsatisfied.

'You see,' he said, 'I always imagine our being really happy with some few other people — a little freedom with people.'

She pondered for a moment.

'Yes, one does want that. But it must *happen*. You can't do anything for it with your will. You always seem to think you can *force* the flowers to come out. People must love us because they love us — you can't *make* them.'

'I know,' he said. 'But must one take no steps at all? Must one just go as if one were alone in the world — the only creature in the world?'

'You've got me,' she said. 'Why should you *need* others? Why must you force people to agree with you? Why can't you be single by yourself, as you are always saying? — You try to bully Gerald — as you tried to bully Hermione. — You must learn to be alone. — And it's so horrid of you. You've got me. And yet you want to force other people to love you as well. You do try to bully them to love you. — And even then, you don't want their love.'

His face was full of real perplexity.

'Don't I?' he said. 'It's the problem I can't solve. I *know* I want a perfect and complete relationship with you: and we've nearly got it — we really have. — But beyond that. *Do* I want a real, ultimate relationship with Gerald? Do I want a final, almost extra-human relationship with him — a relationship in the ultimate of me and him — or don't I?'

She looked at him for a long time, with strange bright eyes, but she did not answer. (451–2)

Does this scene help us to realize that Gerald is a focus for Birkin of his need for other people? Surely, there is no such focus here. What one notices, rather, is Birkin's conflating and confusing two quite distinct things: his need for other people, and his need for Gerald. Birkin's uneasy avowal that ' "one has a hankering after a sort of further fellowship" ' may look like a point of clarification, but 'further fellowship' is a phrase that refuses to focus; in fact, it blurs distinctions. The sort of fellowship found with other people, even 'a few other people' will be different from the fellowship found with a single other person, a single other man. Birkin may have a need for more than a single intimacy, but is it with Gerald *or* with others?

Who might these others be, anyway? ' "Perhaps there's Gerald — and Gudrun —" he said.' That's two people, but only one of them is other than Gerald; and Gudrun falls between dashes, appended to Gerald as a parenthesis or an afterthought. The 'them' of Ursula's questions ' "We can't really alter them, can we?" ' and ' "Do you try to force them?" ' are Gerald — and Gudrun — but, significantly, Birkin, in his reply to that second question speaks only of 'him', Gerald: ' "Why should I want him to be free, if it isn't his business?" ' I say 'significantly', but I am not sure what significance Lawrence intended, and suspect that Birkin's lack of clarity here is his also. Although Birkin goes on to talk about 'other people' and 'some few other people', who they are has no particularity to Birkin; and none in the novel. Ursula says, ' "If anybody likes to come along, let them" ', but there is nobody who might like to come along, other than Gerald and Gudrun.

Where Birkin's 'real perplexity' does focus is in the question he cannot answer and Ursula does not answer for him: ' "*Do* I want a real, ultimate relationship with Gerald? Do I want a final, almost extra-human relationship with him — a relationship in the ultimate of me and him — or don't I?" '

'Other people', 'a few other people', Gudrun, are entirely forgotten by Birkin. What matters to him is his believing that he has nearly achieved a 'perfect and complete' relationship with Ursula, and his desperately wondering whether he does or does not want a similarly 'ultimate' relationship with Gerald. I would suggest that the scene does not work to make us realize that Gerald is a focus for Birkin of his need for other people. If it makes us realize anything, it is that Birkin's need for other people is a lesser thing to him than his need for Gerald or perhaps only a diffuse way of expressing his need for the fellowship of one man. However, if we do realize this we are made to do so by the novel's default: Lawrence seems no clearer than Birkin of his elisions.

Such a judgement may be premature. That Birkin is unsure of what he wants, and whether he wants Gerald or not, is the surety the scene leaves us with. He knows he wants a relationship with Ursula, but he does not yet know if he wants, beyond that, a relationship with Gerald: ' "*Do* I . . . or don't I?" '. Ursula has no answer to the problem that Birkin can't solve, or if her 'strange bright eyes' do suggest she has, it is not an answer they disclose.

At the close of the novel, Birkin does have an answer from her. But he has also decided the question for himself:

> Ursula stayed at the Mill with Birkin for a week or two. They were both very quiet.
> 'Did you need Gerald?' she asked one evening.
> 'Yes,' he said.
> 'Aren't I enough for you?' she asked.
> 'No,' he said. 'You are enough for me, as far as woman is concerned. You are all women to me. But I wanted a man friend, as eternal as you and I are eternal.'
> 'Why aren't I enough?' she said. 'You are enough for me. I don't want anybody else but you. Why isn't it the same with you?'
> 'Having you, I can live all my life without anybody else, any other sheer intimacy. But to make it complete, really happy, I wanted eternal union with a man too: another kind of love,' he said.
> 'I don't believe it,' she said. 'It's an obstinacy, a theory, a perversity.'
> 'Well —' he said.
> 'You can't have two kinds of love. Why should you!'
> 'It seems as if I can't,' he said. 'Yet I wanted it.'
> 'You can't have it, because it's wrong, impossible,' she said.
> 'I don't believe that,' he answered. (583)

Here, at last, Birkin gives simple and direct answers to Ursula's questions. Birkin's need for more than a single intimacy — for more than Ursula — is a need, not for other people, but for another single intimacy — for Gerald. For Gerald to be all men to Birkin is not the same thing as his being for Birkin a focus for his need for other people. If Birkin is as obstinate in his need as he has ever been, he is no longer uncertain about whether he did or did not need Gerald, as he was in his earlier talk with Ursula. But it is too late: Gerald is dead, and the 'unfinished meaning' (351) of their relationship is forever so. If the novel ends inconclusively, it is not only because there can be no outcome for Birkin of his finally certain recognition of his need for Gerald; it is also because Ursula has reached a conclusion about Birkin's need for two kinds of love — ' "I don't believe it," she said. "It's an obstinacy, a theory, a perversity." ' and ' "You can't have it, because it's wrong, impossible." ' — a conclusion that is different from Birkin's own.

Part of the success of Lawrence's depiction of the relationship between Birkin and Ursula is the convincingly independent challenge that Ursula is to Birkin's asserted needs and desires and notions, as here. What, though, is one to make of her disbelief here, at the very end of the novel? Is the novel's inconclusiveness a matter of two irreconcilably contrary views of Birkin's need for Gerald, both equally true of that need as we have seen it in the novel? Or is Ursula's a superior truth to Birkin's, intended by Lawrence to be so or not?

I think this is an issue of some importance, because I can't concur with John Worthen's sense that the novel doesn't offer Birkin's need as a 'truth'. That is how Birkin sees it: he feels his need to be not only his need but the need of all men. It is one of the differences between the Rupert Birkin of the Prologue to *Women in Love* and the Rupert Birkin of *Women in Love* itself that what is felt by the former as a distressing personal plight is apparently not felt as the same plight by the latter. What besets Birkin in the Prologue — the homosexual impulses he cannot deny and will not accept — do not seem to be Birkin's trouble in *Women in Love*. I don't assume that is because Lawrence was trying to hide something from his readers or from himself. The merely 'psychological' truth of the Prologue seems to have been superseded rather than suppressed, the personal problem has been supplanted by something else. As Birkin puts it to Gerald: ' "You've got to admit the unadmitted love of man for man. It makes for a greater freedom for everybody, a greater power of understanding both in men and women" '. Birkin's 'truth' may not be the novel's truth, but is Ursula's? Is the truth of Birkin's need that it isn't a need but 'a theory'; or, as a need, 'a perversity'?

F.R. Leavis, in an essay on Henry James, characterizes the artist's concern for truth:

> The creative writer's concern to render life *is* a concern for significance, a preoccupation with expressing his sense of what most matters. The creative drive in his art *is* a drive to clarify and convey his perception of relative importances. The work that commands the reader's most deeply engaged, the critic's most serious, attention asks at a deep level: 'What, at bottom, do men live *for*?' And in work that strikes us as great art we are aware of a potent normative suggestion: '*These* are the possibilities and inevitablenesses, and, in the face of them, *this* is the valid and the wise (or the sane) attitude.' Lawrence, asked, towards the end, about the creative impulsion in his own work, said: 'One writes out of one's moral sense; for the race, as it were.'[6]

That Leavis should turn to Lawrence is convenient to my concerns, but his paragraph as a whole has relevance since Lawrence, as well as Henry James, informs the whole of it. What Leavis sees as the creative writer's concern is the same as James's sense of the condition of the truly great artist, and there is no question that Lawrence, too, felt he could not shirk it. What, at the end — or by the end — of *Women in Love*, is the 'normative suggestion'? What are the possibilities and inevitabilities, and, in the face of them, what is the valid and the wise (or the sane) attitude? Ursula's or Birkin's? Does the novel unequivocally show? Does Lawrence himself know or not know?

' "It's an obstinacy, a theory, a perversity." ' Is Ursula saying more here than she has already said to Birkin: that he has tried to bully Gerald to love him, but, even then, hasn't wanted his love? Her first two terms seem to suggest that Birkin's supposed need is nothing of the kind — not (to adopt Birkin's thought in another context) 'the interpretation of a profound yearning' but 'only an idea' (329); and what of her third term? Does it merely sum up 'obstinacy' and 'theory', Birkin's perversity being no more than his stubborn adherence to a willed idea? Or does Ursula imply what some readers of the novel have believed about the nature of Birkin's needs?

F.R. Leavis's question, 'What, at bottom, do men live *for*?', has, in this context, an unfortunately apposite phrasing. An early reviewer of *Women in Love* had this to say:

> The main episode of the novel deals with the relations of two men, Gerald and Birkin, and is nothing more or less than a shameful glorification of that state of mind which in practice, as every student of crime is aware, leads to conduct which is condemned by the criminal law. The chapter headed 'Gladiatorial' is sheer filth from beginning to end, and I pay Mr Lawrence the compliment of saying that no other novelist than he could have written it. This is the sort of book which in the hands of a boy in his teens might pave the way to unspeakable moral disaster.[7]

Of course, the reviewer was wrong to say that the main episode of the novel deals with the relations of two men, Gerald and Birkin: the main episode of the novel deals with the relations of a man and a woman, Birkin and Ursula. However, is it the case that the relationship between Gerald and Birkin is a 'shameful glorification' of that state of mind which leads to homosexual acts?

Other more recent critics of the novel have been intent not only on the states of mind that lead to such acts but also on the acts themselves, which they have seen with their own eyes. Among these more recent critics is Jeffrey Meyers who convinced himself that Birkin 'never really moves beyond homosexuality' but 'merely substitutes anal marriage for homosexual love'.[8] J.C.F. Littlewood, reviewing the occasion of Meyers first making public his case, observed of it that there was 'no need to argue that Mr. Meyers's "reading" of *Women in Love* in the interpretive sense of the word is perversely false, his reading in the ordinary sense being so defective'.[9] His judgement in this can speak for mine. In the same review, he also rightly took Stephen Spender to task for his falling below 'the minimum standard of reading and of ability to report faithfully on what has been read'. How far below that standard does Spender come, he asks, when he talks of the Blutbrüderschaft relation as what Birkin wishes to escape from marriage into? In the novel, Littlewood affirms, 'that relation is clearly offered as a necessary *complement* to marriage, not as an alternative', and he further argues that a critic who judged that, nevertheless, Birkin's desire for the relation was, as revealed in the novel, a wish to escape from marriage, 'would not deliver such a judgment as if referring to known fact' (246).

That critical principle is a necessary one, but *Women in Love* confronts it in a particularly problematic way. The question of whether Birkin's desire for a relationship with Gerald is as a complement to or as an alternative to his desire for a relationship with Ursula cannot be altogether settled, because what is offered as fact and what is revealed are both perplexingly unclear. The 'clearly offered' fact of Birkin's relation with Gerald as complementary to his relation with Ursula is perhaps only clearly offered by Birkin himself when he talks about it. If that is one point about which Birkin is clear — in what he says, at least — there are others, crucial to one's understanding of what it is that he wants, that aren't. Meyers suggested that Birkin 'never moves beyond homosexuality' but that begs a question that must have priority: Is it *towards* homosexuality that Birkin is moving?

Is there an answer to that question in the novel? The talk about marriage between Gerald and Birkin near the end of Chapter xxv, 'Marriage or Not' may help towards an answer:

> 'One does have the feeling that marriage is a *pis aller*,' he admitted.
>
> 'Then don't do it,' said Birkin. 'I tell you,' he went on, 'the same as I've said before, marriage in the old sense seems to me repulsive. *Égoïsme à deux* is nothing to it. It's a sort of tacit hunting in couples: the world all in couples, each couple in its own little house, watching its own little interests, and stewing in its own little privacy — it's the most repulsive thing on earth.'
>
> 'I quite agree,' said Gerald. 'There's something inferior about it. But as I say, what's the alternative.'
>
> 'One should avoid this *home* instinct. It's not an instinct, it's a habit of cowardliness. One should never have a *home*.'
>
> 'I agree really,' said Gerald. 'But there's no alternative.'
>
> 'We've got to find one. — I do believe in a permanent union between a man and a woman. Chopping about is merely an exhaustive process. — But a permanent relation between a man and a woman isn't the last word — it certainly isn't.'
>
> 'Quite,' said Gerald.
>
> 'In fact,' said Birkin, 'because the relation between man and woman is made the supreme and exclusive relationship, that's where all the tightness and meanness and insufficiency comes in.'
>
> 'Yes, I believe you,' said Gerald.

'You've got to take down the love-and-marriage ideal from its pedestal. We want something broader. — I believe in the *additional* perfect relationship between man and man — additional to marriage.'

'I can never see how they can be the same,' said Gerald.

'Not the same — but equally important, equally creative, equally sacred, if you like.'

Gerald moved uneasily. — 'You know, I can't feel that,' said he. 'Surely there can never be anything as strong between man and man as sex love is between man and woman. Nature doesn't provide the basis.'

'Well, of course, I think she does. And I don't think we shall ever be happy till we establish ourselves on this basis. You've got to get rid of the *exclusiveness* of married love. And you've got to admit the unadmitted love of man for man. It makes for a greater freedom for everybody, a greater power of individuality both in men and women.'

'I know,' said Gerald, 'you believe something like that. Only I can't *feel* it, you see.' He put his hand on Birkin's arm, with a sort of deprecating affection. And he smiled as if triumphantly. (439−40)

It is 'clearly offered' by the novel, here, that Birkin's conception of a relationship between 'man and man' is of something 'additional to marriage', but what that relationship is to be is quite unclear. What does Birkin mean by a 'perfect' relationship between men here, or, at the close of the novel, by 'sheer intimacy' and 'eternal union'? What does Lawrence mean him to mean? The phrases themselves suggest the possibility of sexuality, but are still perhaps not committed to it even as a possibility. What perfects the relations between a man and a woman, what makes for the sheer intimacy of marriage, what does 'union' speak of? The sexual meanings seem integral; and yet, one remembers, Birkin has been trying to find in his relationship with Ursula a basis and a bond beyond sexual love.

Gerald is apparently mistaken, in thinking that Birkin has suggested that the relation between man and man is to be the same as that between man and woman. But if not the same, how can it be as strong, Gerald wonders: ' "Surely there can never be anything as strong between man and man as sex love is between man and woman" '? His bewilderment springs, inevitably enough, from his observation that ' "Nature doesn't provide the basis." ' Birkin's reply is perplexing in the extreme: ' "Well, of course, I think she does." ' What can he possibly mean? He doesn't say; nor does Lawrence offer a further clarification, either here or elsewhere in the novel. Is the basis provided by nature for the love between men the same basis as the basis for sex love between men and women — a sexual basis? Given that Birkin has just said that the relationship between man and man, as he envisages it, is ' "Not the same" ' as the relationship between man and woman, ' "but equally important, equally creative, equally sacred" ', the logic of his thoughts must be that the basis in nature for the relationship between men is some basis other than sex love, but equal to sex love between men and women in strength and worth. But what that other but equal basis in nature is he doesn't say; and that Lawrence doesn't disclose more of what he means leaves the reader, like Gerald, moving uneasily, but in no particular direction. Readers who have sought to escape what is unsatisfactorily indefinite, by supposing a homosexual implication, have some excuse for their conduct, even though there is no clear justification for it.

Birkin's stated belief that ' "You've got to get rid of the *exclusiveness* of married love" ', and his reasons for believing that necessary, are tenable because intelligible; and his wanting a relationship with a man, additional to marriage, might be a possible solution to his felt need to be free of becoming with Ursula a couple — ' "in its own little house, watching its own little interests, and stewing in its own little privacy" '. I say it might be a possible solution, though I cannot see how it would not merely compound the problem that Birkin wants to be free of: two exclusive relationships instead of one. Be that as it may, Birkin has explained his wish to get rid of the exclusiveness of marriage and proposed his solution. But then, bafflingly, he goes on to give altogether different grounds for his desire for a relationship with a man: ' "And you've got to admit the unadmitted love of man for man. It makes for a greater freedom for everybody, a greater power of individuality both in men and women" '. Birkin offers this as merely additional or supplementary to getting rid of the exclusiveness of married love, but, surely it has priority?

That is certainly how Gerald seems to have understood it, when he reflects a little later on what Birkin has said to him, and there is no suggestion that he has mistaken Birkin's meaning:

> The other way was to accept Rupert's offer of love, to enter into the bond of pure trust and love with the other man, and then subsequently with the woman. If he pledged himself with the man he would later be able to pledge himself with the woman: not merely in legal marriage, but in absolute, mystic marriage. (440)

That Gerald cannot accept Birkin's offer and 'enter into the bond of pure trust and love with the other man' is attributed to his 'numbness' and 'absence of volition', his gladness 'not to be committed'; but there is a very different reason, surely, that ought to be told. The 'bond of pure trust and love' has no substantiality, since Birkin himself is not to be trusted. Birkin's lack of clarity about what he wants is a reason for a reader to mistrust him; but his untrustworthiness is attested to elsewhere by the novel itself: not only earlier in the novel than this late chapter, but later in the novel, in the chapter immediately following, which I have already quoted from, where it is not only observed by Ursula (' "You try to bully Gerald . . . you want to force other people to love you . . . You do try to bully them to love you. — And even then, you don't want their love" '), but can be seen in Birkin's own helpless perplexity (' "*Do* I want a real, ultimate relationship with Gerald . . . or don't I?" '). He says there it's the problem he can't solve.

I have said that Birkin's untrustworthiness is attested to by the novel itself, but that attestation is not complete or consistent. It is usual in the novel for Gerald to be seen as lacking trust or commitment in the scenes with Birkin; and Birkin's final charge against Gerald ('And Gerald! The denier!') seems to be the novel's — and the novelist's — last judgement of him, too. Although Birkin speaks of his uncertainty about whether he does or does not want a relationship with Gerald, he speaks of it only to Ursula. When he talks to Gerald, he talks to him as if he were sure that he wanted a relationship with him, even though the terms of that relationship remain only obscurely articulated. He never sees his own uncertainty and his own unclearness as contributory causes to the failure of his friendship with Gerald, and Lawrence never gives Gerald's doubts and mistrust their due.

'Of course he had been loving Gerald all along, and all along denying it': that is, ostensibly, the moment in which Birkin admits to himself his own unadmitted love for another man. If he has been loving Gerald all along, now, one supposes, he will stop denying it. It is Gerald he accuses, as he stares at the frozen face of his dead friend at the end of the novel, of being 'The denier!'. But Gerald also has a moment when he accuses Birkin, not of being a 'denier', but of being a man who doesn't love him:

> 'I've loved you, as well as Gudrun, don't forget,' said Birkin bitterly. Gerald looked at him strangely, abstractedly.
> 'Have you?' he said, with icy scepticism. 'Or do you think you have?' He was hardly responsible for what he said.
> The sledge came. Gudrun dismounted and they all made their farewells. They wanted to go apart, all of them. Birkin took his place, and the sledge drove away leaving Gudrun and Gerald standing on the snow, waving. Something froze Birkin's heart, seeing them standing there in the isolation of the snow, growing smaller and more isolated. (536−7)

Gerald's questioning of Birkin's bitter reminder of his love for him is not quite a question asked, but a statement of disbelief 'said with icy scepticism'. That identification of Gerald's scepticism as 'icy' is part of the patterning of Gerald's progress towards the place 'surrounded by sheer slopes and precipices' (575), where he finally slips and falls down asleep and dies. But Gerald's disbelief, here, should have another validity besides its being another instance of *his* 'scepticism': after all, his questioning Birkin as he does echoes Birkin's own questions to himself, ' "*Do* I . . . or don't I?" ', and Ursula's unbelieving ' "You try to bully Gerald . . ." '; and is, at the end of the novel, echoed by Ursula in her final affirmation of disbelief — ' "I don't believe it," she said. "It's an obstinacy, a theory . . ." '.

Has Birkin loved Gerald? Or does he think he has? Those questions are not answered. Their being unanswered does not seem to be to be a matter of their being deliberately left open by Lawrence; on the contrary the novel presents an answer that doesn't properly mèet the questions — Gerald, the denier. Gerald is 'the denier' not only at the last, but from the first:

> 'I feel,' Gerald continued, 'that there is always an element of uncertainty about you — perhaps you are uncertain about

yourself. But I'm never sure of you. You can go away and change as easily as if you had no soul.'

He looked at Birkin with penetrating eyes. Birkin was amazed. He thought he had all the soul in the world. He stared in amazement. And Gerald, watching, saw the amazing attractive goodliness of his eyes, a young, spontaneous goodness that attracted the other man infinitely, yet filled him with bitter chagrin, because he mistrusted it so much. He knew Birkin could do without him — could forget, and not suffer. This was always present in Gerald's consciouness, filling him with bitter unbelief: this consciousness of the young, animal-like spontaneity of detachment. It seemed almost like hypocrisy and lying, some-times, oh, often, on Birkin's part, to talk so deeply and importantly.

Quite other things were going through Birkin's mind. Suddenly he saw himself confronted with another problem — the problem of love and eternal conjunction between two men. Of course this was necessary — it had been a necessity inside himself all his life — to love a man purely and fully. Of course he had been loving Gerald all along, and all along denying it.

He lay in the bed and wondered, whilst his friend sat beside him, lost in brooding. Each man was gone in his own thoughts.

'You know how the old German knights used to swear a *Blutbrüderschaft?*' he said to Gerald, with quite a new happy activity in his eyes.

'Make a little wound in their arms, and rub each other's blood into the cut?' said Gerald.

'Yes — and swear to be true to each other, of one blood, all their lives. — That is what we ought to do. No wounds, that is obsolete. — But we ought to swear to love each other, you and I, implicitly, and perfectly, finally, without any possibility of going back on it.'

He looked at Gerald with clear, happy eyes of discovery. Gerald looked down at him, attracted, so deeply bondaged in fascinated attraction, that he was mistrustful, resenting the bondage, hating the attraction.

'We will swear to each other, one day, shall we?' pleaded Birkin. 'We will swear to stand by each other — be true to each other — ultimately — infallibly — given to each other, organically — without possibility of taking back.'

Birkin sought hard to express himself. But Gerald hardly listened. His face shone with a certain luminous pleasure. He was pleased. But he kept his reserve. He held himself back.

'Shall we swear to each other, one day?' said Birkin, putting out his hand towards Gerald.

> Gerald just touched the extended fine, living hand, as if withheld and afraid.
>
> 'We'll leave it till I understand it better,' he said, in a voice of excuse.
>
> Birkin watched him. A little sharp disappointment, perhaps a touch of contempt, came into his heart.
>
> 'Yes,' he said. 'You must tell me what you think, later. You know what I mean? Not sloppy emotionalism. An impersonal union that leaves one free.' (277—278)

The 'element of uncertainty' that Gerald feels about Birkin is, first of all, apparently prompted by a similar element in Birkin — ' "perhaps you are uncertain about yourself" '. But that it is also something in himself is also possibly true of Gerald. In fact, that possibility becomes the exclusive certainty of this encounter: Gerald's mistrust of Birkin is, more and more, seen to be Gerald's self-mistrust. That might be all very well if it were a matter of our discovering it; but we don't discover it, we are told it, and what we are told seems to be different from what we see. We are told that Gerald is 'attracted . . . infinitely' by Birkin's 'spontaneous goodness', but that he also mistrusts it, knowing that 'Birkin could do without him', and that this consciousness of Birkin's 'spontaneity of detachment' fills him 'with bitter unbelief'. A little later we are told that he is 'so deeply bondaged in fascinated attraction, that he was mistrustful'.

Birkin's proposal to Gerald of *Blutbrüderschaft* is seen by Birkin as one of 'their moments of passionate approach'. In what sense is it that? The passionate feelings are put into words, but even before they are put into words spoken to Gerald, they have a rather strange relation to him:

> Quite other things were going through Birkin's mind. Suddenly he saw himself confronted with another problem — the problem of love and eternal conjunction between two men. Of course this was necessary — it had been a necessity inside himself all his life — to love a man purely and fully. Of course he had been loving Gerald all along, and all along denying it.
>
> He lay in the bed and wondered, whilst his friend sat beside him, lost in brooding. Each man was gone in his own thoughts.

Birkin's 'spontaneity of detachment' could acquire a new meaning here as he suddenly sees himself confronted with another problem — 'the problem of love and eternal conjunction between two men'. What is striking is the separateness of the two men, and the nature of Birkin's separateness: his near indifference to the actuality of Gerald. Although Birkin looks at Gerald with 'clear, happy eyes of discovery', the discovery he has made of his love for Gerald has been rather abstractly reached, and the discoveries he goes on to make about him — perhaps 'discoveries' is not the right word since the realizations come to Birkin without surprise — are not of what makes him lovable, or even likeable. The disappointment and contempt he feels at this moment is what his love is brought to by Gerald's reserve. Although Birkin perhaps makes some concession to that reserve in Gerald in his asking if they shall swear to each other, *one day*, he doesn't show any more fully sympathetic understanding of his friend's being unsure of him or of himself. On the contrary:

> They lapsed both into silence. Birkin was looking at Gerald all the time. He seemed now to see, not the physical, animal man, which he usually saw in Gerald, and which usually he liked so much, but the man himself, complete, and as if fated, doomed, limited. This strange sense of fatality in Gerald, as if he were limited to one form of existence, one knowledge, one activity, a sort of fatal halfness, which to himself seemed wholeness, always overcame Birkin after their moments of passionate approach, and filled him with a sort of contempt, or boredom. It was the insistence on the limitation which so bored Birkin in Gerald. Gerald could never fly away from himself, in real indifferent gaiety. He had a clog, a sort of monomania. (278–9)

Birkin is 'always' overcome with contempt or boredom with Gerald, we are told. That prompts a question that is not quite the question Birkin later asks Ursula: does Birkin want a relationship with *Gerald*, or doesn't he?

What does the climactic moment of 'passionate approach' between the two men disclose about their relationship and about Lawrence's depiction of it? The fight between Gerald and Birkin in Chapter xx, 'Gladiatorial', involves them in an approach to each other that is physical: ' "We are mentally, spiritually intimate, therefore we should be more or less physically intimate too — it is more whole" ' is Birkin's justification of their wrestling together, but this is perhaps only his rationalisation since it seems pretty remote from the realities of their mental and spiritual intimacies which have themselves been characterized by mixed feelings, mutual mistrust and hostility as well as affection. And Birkin's way of putting it — ' "therefore we should be more or less physically intimate too — it is more whole" ' — ignores also the immediate fact of what has taken place between them in their physical intimacy. What has taken place is itself not simply a matter of fact.

Have Birkin and Gerald been — to make use of Birkin's phrase — *more* or *less* physically intimate than that earlier reviewer, who found 'Gladiatorial' 'sheer filth from beginning to end', must have believed? He has not been alone in his suspicions: Jeffrey Meyers, of course, finds the fight overtly sexual; and Scott Sanders, among others, shares his reading in the interpretative sense, as well his misreading in the ordinary sense. He believes that 'even without the information provided by the "Prologue", this scene appears explicitly sexual, with the two men "fusing", "penetrating", "joining" '.[10] I think it is questionable to believe that the Prologue provides information that can be applied directly to *Women in Love*; and that it is beyond question that the scene does not appear explicitly sexual. It could be argued that the scene is implicitly sexual, or that the feelings of one or other or both men are, but even that is not incontrovertible. The two men do not 'join' quite as Sanders suggests they do. Although at the climax of their naked set-to they are seen as 'the physical junction of two bodies clinched into oneness' (349), and in their struggle together they have 'seemed to drive their white flesh deeper and deeper against each other, as if they would break into oneness' (348), and although Birkin 'penetrates' and 'inter-penetrates' and 'interfuses' into Gerald's body and being, the significance is not necessarily sexual. At the beginning of their struggle it is not, it has to be said, Birkin's penis but his 'tense fine grip that seemed to penetrate into the very quick of Gerald's being'. As the struggle intensifies, it is still in terms appropriate to the fight that Birkin 'seemed to penetrate into Gerald's more solid, more diffuse bulk, to interfuse his body through the body of the other, as if to bring it subtly into subjection'; 'It was as if Birkin's whole physical intelligence interpenetrated into Gerald's body, as if his fine, sublimated energy entered into the flesh of the fuller man, like some potency, casting a fine net, a prison, through the muscles into the very depths of Gerald's being' (349).

I said, a moment ago, that Birkin 'penetrates' Gerald. It would be truer to say that what the novel says is that he 'seemed to penetrate' Gerald; and what he seems to penetrate Gerald with is his 'physical intelligence' and his 'sublimated energy', not any bodily organ. Sanders assumes that what prevents Lawrence from saying what he means is his 'fear of treating homosexuality directly', a fear which Sanders, considering 'the state of public opinion at the time *Women in Love* was written', judges 'is neither surprising nor dishonourable' (130). Lawrence's contemporary reviewer, you'll remember, thought Lawrence *had* treated homosexuality directly. I think that Lawrence was less fearful than Sanders supposes, and very much more intelligent. 'Behind the notion of *Blutbrüderschaft*', Sanders writes, 'lurks the less mysterious reality of homosexual love which he was unwilling or unable to acknowledge' (126).

' "Is this the Brüderschaft you wanted?" ' Gerald asks Birkin as they talk together after their struggle. Birkin's reply is enigmatically challenging — ' "Perhaps. Do you think this pledges anything?" ' The reality of Brüderschaft has its mysteriousness, though that mysteriousness may turn out to be something that Lawrence as well as Birkin is not wholly clear about. Do we have in the struggle between the two men some indication of what might be 'as strong between man and man as sex love is between man and woman', a physical intimacy that is not sexual, though it is as intense as sexuality and as necessary? If we do, what is involved seems to be as much a matter of Birkin's power over Gerald as his love for him: that's what the novel could be seen to reveal, though it is not clearly offered as fact. Gerald loses the fight with Birkin; his superior physical strength and force are not sufficient to overcome Birkin's differently manifested powers. Yet after the fight Birkin loses interest in him, not on account of his 'fatal halfness' or Birkin's own 'spontaneity of detachment', but because of Ursula:

> He was looking at the handsome figure of the other man, blond and comely in the rich robe, and he was half thinking of the difference between it and himself — so different; as far, perhaps, apart as man from woman, yet in another direction.

> But really it was Ursula, it was the woman who was gaining
> ascendance over Birkin's being, at this moment. Gerald was
> becoming dim again, lapsing out of him. (352−3)

That Birkin is only half thinking his thoughts about the
difference between his and Gerald's bodies — 'so different; as
far, perhaps, apart as man from woman, yet in another
direction' — is something we can as readers be grateful for, if it
allows us to only half think them ourselves. For if we were to
attend to them wholly, we would find ourselves confronted with
another problem. And perhaps we face a problem, anyway: a
problem of Lawrence's art, here, which sets Birkin off in yet
another direction but to no determinable destination; and with
no apparent sense that this new direction is one that, by
introducing the idea of degrees of difference between man and
man as extreme as the sexual difference between man and
woman, re-introduces an uncertainty once again into the
question of what constitutes the basis in nature for a bond
between men as strong as sex love between men and women.

There arises here a question about Birkin's need for what
Ursula says he can't have, the two kinds of love that he has
wanted to be complementary in his life. Is there some
suggestion that they can't be so in the fact that 'But really it was
Ursula, it was the woman who was gaining ascendance over
Birkin's being, at this moment'? For there to be a moment to
moment ascendancy of either Gerald or Ursula does not, of
course, make loving both of them a matter of alternating
between them, or of escaping from one to the other, but nor
can it be a matter of simple addition. If there is such a
suggestion it is barely imagined: 'But really it was Ursula . . .'.
But really? The bald stating of it does not make it, even in the
moment, real.

There is, too, in the immediate aftermath of the fight, a
curious indication of Lawrence's complicity with Birkin in his
seeing Gerald, exclusively, as 'the denier'. Birkin remembers
the moment at the end of the novel, and it is one that has been
anticipated by Gerald's just touching Birkin's hand, 'as if
withheld and afraid', and not pledging himself to the *Blutbrüderschaft* Birkin has proposed:

> 'He should have loved me,' he said. 'I offered him.'
> She, afraid, white, with mute lips answered:

'What difference would it have made!'

'It would!' he said, 'It would.'

He forgot her, and turned to look at Gerald. With head oddly lifted, like a man who draws his head back from an insult, half haughtily, he watched the cold, mute, material face. It had a bluish cast. It sent a shaft like ice through the heart of the living room. Cold, mute, material! Birkin remembered how once Gerald had clutched his hand, with a warm, momentaneous grip of final love. For one second — then let go again, let go forever. If he had kept true to that clasp, death would not have mattered. Those who die, and dying still can love, still believe, do not die. They live still in the beloved. Gerald might still have been living in the spirit with Birkin, even after death. He might have lived with his friend, a further life. (581–2)[11]

Is Birkin, in remembering that clasp, true to it himself? He is, but there is something false about the clasp as it occurs:

He realised that he was leaning with all his weight on the soft body of the other man. It startled him, because he thought he had withdrawn. He recovered himself, and sat up. But he was still vague and unestablished. He put out his hand to steady himself. It touched the hand of Gerald, that was lying out on the floor. And Gerald's hand closed warm and sudden over Birkin's, they remained exhausted and breathless, the one hand clasped closely over the other. It was Birkin whose hand, in swift response, had closed in a strong, warm clasp over the hand of the other. Gerald's clasp had been sudden and momentaneous. (350–1)

Birkin, putting out his hand to steady himself, inadvertently touches Gerald's hand. 'And Gerald's hand', we are told, 'closed warm and sudden over Birkin's'. The two men remain still, exhausted and breathless, 'the one hand clasped closely over the other'. The 'one hand' can only be 'Gerald's hand', syntactically speaking: the hand that 'closed warm and sudden over Birkin's *must* be the same as the hand that is 'clasped closely over the other'. The intervening clause — 'they remained exhausted and breathless' — only indicates the duration of that clasp. Yet apparently that is not so, or rather what appears so is not so, we are told: 'It was Birkin whose hand, in swift response, had closed in a strong, warm clasp over the hand of the other. Gerald's clasp had been sudden and momentaneous'. Perhaps it is enough to say 'it's wrong, impossible'.

In looking at *Women in Love* as I have done, I have been very selective. And, further than that, the line of argument I have been following has been a narrow and rather summary one. I trust that it has been sufficient to demonstrate that, in his representation of the relationship between Birkin and Gerald, Lawrence does not make fully clear what he is talking about. It may be that Lawrence does not fully understand what he wants to say. In case that should seem my presumption, and conclusive evidence of my having fallen below 'the minimum standard of reading and of ability to report faithfully on what has been read', I would like to quote something of Lawrence's that seems to me to corroborate the case I have been trying to make:

> He half wanted to commit himself to this whole affection with a friend, a comrade, a mate. And then, in the last issue, he didn't want it at all. The affection would be deep and genuine enough: that he knew. But — when it came to the point, he didn't want any more affection. All his life he had cherished a beloved ideal of friendship — David and Jonathan. And now, when true and good friends offered, he found he simply could not commit himself, even to simple friendship. The whole trend of this affection, this mingling, this intimacy, this truly beautiful love, he found his soul just set against it. He couldn't go along with it. He didn't want a friend, he didn't want loving affection, he didn't want comradeship. No, his soul trembled when he tried to drive it along the way, trembled and stood still, like Balaam's Ass. It did not want friendship or comradeship, great or small, deep or shallow.
>
> It took . . . [Birkin] . . . some time before he would really admit and accept this new fact. Not till he had striven hard with his soul did he come to see the angel in the way; not till his soul, like Balaam's Ass, had spoken more than once. And then, when forced to admit, it was a revolution in his mind. He had all his life had this craving for an absolute friend, a David to his Jonathan. Pylades to his Orestes: a blood-brother. All his life he had secretly grieved over his friendlessness. And now at last, when it really offered — and it had offered twice before, since he had left Europe — he didn't want it, and he realized that in his innermost soul he had never wanted it.
>
> Yet he wanted *some* living fellowship with other men; as it was he was just isolated. Maybe a living fellowship! — but not

affection, not love, not comradeship. Not mates and equality and mingling. Not blood-brotherhood. None of that.

What else? He didn't know. He only knew he was never destined to be mate or comrade or even friend with any man. Some other living relationship. But what? He did not know. Perhaps the thing that the dark races know: that one can still feel in India: the mystery of lordship. That which white men have struggled so long against, and which is the clue to the life of the Hindu. The mystery of lordship. The mystery of innate, natural, sacred priority.[12]

In the novel in which he appears, the Lawrence character I've called Birkin is actually called Richard Lovat Somers. That novel is *Kangaroo*.

I have not, in this paper, attempted to answer Lady Cynthia Asquith's second question to herself about *Women in Love*. Why *Women in Love* is about what it is about is, of course, a large and difficult question to answer. Even the smaller question — why is the relationship of Birkin and Gerald about what it is about? — is not an easy one to answer. The simple biographical answer that Scott Sanders supposes, won't do; not only because it is simple — though it is that — but because it is merely biographical:

> Lacking an acceptable father-figure, dominated by an aggressive mother, married to an aggressive wife, deeply inhibited in his earliest sexual relations, frail of body — it is not surprising that there should have been a strong homosexual element in Law-rence's make-up. (131)

Lawrence's make-up! I am even less surprised than Scott Sanders that there was a strong homosexual element in Lawrence, but because it was a strength in Lawrence — as his strong heterosexuality was a strength — I am surprised that so weakly made-up a 'biography' will do for a man who claims to understand Lawrence. The reason that I am not surprised that there was a homosexual element in Lawrence is that it is evinced in his writing, even though I do not think it evident in the ways Jeffrey Meyers and Scott Sanders do.

I find myself in something of a critical quandary. Although Lawrence's account of Somers's discovery about himself illuminates some of what is unclear in *Women in Love* — Somers's 'revolution' in his mind being a further stage of

realization of what is not fully realized in *Women in Love* —
I am drawn back to the uncertainties and obduracies of *Women
in Love*. 'Realization' as a quality of artistic representation does
not wholly depend on realization in Somers's sense of the word.
And though *Women in Love* does not seem to me to be fully
realized in either sense — in its depiction of Birkin and Gerald's
relationship at least — it still has a real power. It is the power
of 'creative understanding', searching for new knowledge and
searching for new expression that is convincingly active in
Women in Love even where it is not 'true' in its activities. The
novel is 'tentative and self-exploratory', and though it risks
coherence and even intelligibility for Lawrence to have committed himself as he did to tentative self-exploration in the
novel, it is a commitment I think we should honour even where
our judgement of its effects is a negative one.

T.S. Eliot found both the workmanship and the thought of
Hamlet 'unstable' and judged the play an artistic failure as a
consequence.[13] My account of *Women in Love* has argued that
it, too, is unstable in its workmanship and thought, but I baulk
at the critical judgement. 'Tentative and self-exploratory' does
give some positive value to that instability. How could a work of
art as exploratory in its thought and workmanship as *Women in
Love*, be anything but unstable? The triumph of Lawrence's
intelligence is not serene in *Women in Love* because it is striving
to make known what is not already known, to understand what
is not yet understood.

Notes

1   F.R. Leavis, *D.H. Lawrence: Novelist* (Harmondsworth, 1964), p. 152
    (hereafter, page references in text).
2   Letter to Arthur McLeod, 26 October 1913, *The Letters of D.H.
    Lawrence*, ed. G.J. Zytaruk & J.T. Boulton (Cambridge, 1981), ii. 90.
3   *Women in Love* (Harmondsworth, 1982), p. 526 (hereafter, page references
    in text).
4   Henry James, *Selected Literary Criticism*, ed. Morris Shapira (Harmonds-
    worth, 1968), p. 35 (hereafter, page references in text).
5   John Worthen, *D.H. Lawrence and the Idea of the Novel* (1979), p. 90
    (hereafter, page references in text).

6   F.R. Leavis, 'James as Critic', Preface to Henry James, *Selected Literary Criticism*, ed. M. Shapira, p. 19.

7   W.C. Pilley, *John Bull*, 17 September 1921, in *D.H. Lawrence*, ed. H. Coombes (Harmondsworth, 1973), p. 145.

8   Jeffrey Meyers, 'D.H. Lawrence and Homosexuality', *D.H. Lawrence: Novelist, Poet, Prophet*, ed. S. Spender (1973), p. 146.

9   J.C.F. Littlewood, 'Lawrence', *Essays in Criticism*, vol. xxv, no. 2 (1975), 251.

10 Scott Sanders, *D.H. Lawrence: The World of the Major Novels* (1973), p. 126 (hereafter, page references in text).

11 Where this edition of the Seltzer text reads 'the living room', the Secker text reads 'the living man'.

12 *Kangaroo* (Harmondsworth, 1950), pp. 119–20. In calling this character of Lawrence's by a name that is not the name Lawrence gave him, I am adopting a device used by J.C.F. Littlewood in his article 'Son and Lover', *The Cambridge Quarterly*, vol. 14, no. 4 (1969–70).

13 T.S. Eliot, *Selected Essays* (Glasgow, 1951), p. 144.

Lawrence and the Feminists

LAURENCE LERNER

There is something odd about literary centenaries. Lawrence, born in 1885, would be the grandfather or the great-grandfather of most people present — just possibly the great-great-grandfather of the youngest student, or the father of the most venerable professor. A generation is supposed to react against its father and back to its grandfather, but literary generations move more slowly and in a more complicated way. If I think about what has happened to Lawrence even in my own adult lifetime, the complications are striking. There were dons about when I was a student who doubted whether Lawrence would ever become a classic; then, a generation ago, Lawrence had become our Most Read Writer, with a double role in our literary culture: he was the exciting prophet of the sexual revolution, read by the young in their hundreds of thousands, and he was the apostle of traditional humanism, recommended on a thousand reading lists and lovingly explicated by a hundred lecturers (of whom I was one). It was a fragile alliance, and perhaps it has gone for ever. A good deal has conspired to undermine Lawrence's reputation since Lady Chatterley won her trial in 1960, and nothing more than the rise of feminist criticism.

When I was buying some books for this lecture last month, the girl serving me in Britain's most famous bookshop said, 'Ah, Lawrence. He didn't think much of women, did he?' She turned out not to have read much Lawrence, and though I invited her to the lecture, I don't expect her to travel 100 miles to put her hearsay views to the test. If any one work is responsible for the shift in opinion, it is Kate Millett's *Sexual Politics*, published in 1970. This contains a swingeing attack on Lawrence for his 'transformation of masculine ascendance into a mystical religion'. It sees Lawrence as an admirably astute politician, leading a counter-revolution against all forms of female emancipation. It describes *Sons and Lovers* as the glorification of Paul Morel, the boss (sic!) exploiting his female employees, who is 'in brilliant condition when the novel ends, having extracted every conceivable service from his women, now neatly disposed of, so that he may go on to grander adventures'. *The Rainbow* is filled with 'cynical envy' at Ursula's invasion of the world of daily work, and makes it plain that what she really needs is a husband. Similarly, *Lady Chatterley's Lover* is about how Mellors teaches Connie to relinquish 'self, ego, will, individuality — things woman had but recently developed, to Lawrence's profoundly shocked distaste', by inviting her 'into the hut for a bit of what she really needs'. And so on, all through the novels.[1] There have been plenty of feminist attacks on Lawrence since, though none with quite the brilliant precision of Kate Millett's distortions and omissions, that enable her to give an account of each novel that is almost literally accurate, yet differs profoundly from what most readers read. Our girl in the bookshop may not have read Kate Millett either, nor Faith Pullin, Philippa Tristram or T.E. Apter[2] but that's where she got it from.

And so, stimulated by such critics, I want to try and look at Lawrence's treatment of women with the eyes of 1985. And let's begin by admitting the worst. It isn't difficult to find in Lawrence statements to make even the mildest feminist shudder:

> Down with exalted mothers, and down with the exaltation of motherhood, for it threatens the sanity of our race . . . no creature so perverse as the human mother today. No creature so delights in the traducing of the deepest instincts . . . Remains now for the perverted, idealised mother deliberately to cast off her ideal, self-conscious motherhood . . . Or else man must drag her ideal robes off her, by force.[3]

> We are all fighters. Let us fight . . . Rouse the old male spirit again. The male is always a fighter . . . In fighting to the death he has one great crisis of his being.[4]

> '. . . they look on a man as if he was nothing but an instrument to get and rear children. If you have anything to do with a woman, she thinks it's because you want to get children by her. And I'm damned if it is. I want my own pleasure, or nothing: and children be damned . . . The man's spirit has gone out of the world. Men can't move an inch unless they can grovel humbly at the end of

the journey . . . That's why marriage wants readjusting — or extending — to get men on their own legs once more, and to give them the adventure again. But men won't stick together and fight for it.'⁵

Is this the man whose centenary we are celebrating? Did our literary culture take leave of its senses in its exaltation of Lawrence, and have we needed the women (as so often) to open our eyes? Have I come to bury Lawrence, not to praise him?

It will be a slow process, rehabilitating the author of those passages: I shall need my full hour, and your patience. But it is important to do so, not only for what it tells us about Lawrence, but for what it tells us about literature. There is, first, the simple fact of how Lawrence changed. The passages I have quoted to you come from his later writings, and Lawrence underwent a searing experience during the First War that led to the abandonment of much of what he had previously believed. He was humiliated and ostracised by what he called 'the stay-at-home bullies who governed the country during those years'. His biographers have told us the story very fully. One day in 1915 he went walking on the Downs, the weather was beautiful, and he said 'I seemed to feel all humanity brave and splendid, like the train, and so blind, and so utterly unconscious of where they are going or of what they are doing'.⁶ Paul Delany, who quotes this, adds that it was almost the last time in his life that he showed loving concern towards his fellow men; and even in this remark we can sense a withdrawal, and the seeds of the Nietzschean contempt that he moved towards, the proto-fascism and the male chauvinism — and for once I really mean male *chauvinism*. The biographers usually locate the change in the painful personal humiliations Lawrence endured, but if we want to we can see it as more rational and impersonal — the result, for instance, of reading the pre-Socratics:

I have been wrong, much too Christian, in my philosophy. These early Greeks have clarified my soul . . . You must drop all your democracy . . . There must be an aristocracy of people who have wisdom, and there must be a Ruler: a Kaiser: no Presidents and democracies. I shall write out Herakleitos, on tablets of bronze.⁷

Indeed, the change in Lawrence can equally be seen as a symptom of a change in society as a whole, as Hilary Simpson has so excellently shown, tracing the resemblances between Lawrence's own development, and that of social and political theory from the liberal 1900s to the often proto-fascist 1920s.[8]

In view of all this, our first step is obvious: to defend Lawrence to the feminists, we must begin with an early work. And not to beat about the bush, I'll begin with the greatest of his early works, *Sons and Lovers*, which to non-Lawrentians has always been his finest novel (and they may be right). To do justice to it, we shall need a very full discussion.

No doubt you all know the story, but I want nonetheless to begin with a version of it:

> . . . a woman of character and refinement goes into the lower class, and has no satisfaction in her own life. She has had a passion for her husband, so the children are born of passion, and have heaps of vitality. But as her sons grow up she selects them as lovers — first the eldest, then the second . . . But when they come to manhood, they can't love, because their mother is the strongest power in their lives, and holds them . . . The next [second] son gets a woman who fights for his soul — fights his mother. The son loves the mother — all the sons hate and are jealous of the father. The battle goes on between the mother and the girl, with the son as object. The mother gradually proves stronger, because of the tie of blood.[9]

Clearly that is not just a summary but also an interpretation. Is it a true one? Here is what the mother says about the girl:

> 'She's not like an ordinary woman, who can leave me my share in him. She wants to absorb him. She wants to draw him out and absorb him till there is nothing left of him, even for himself. He will never be a man on his own feet — she will suck him up.' So the mother sat, and battled and brooded bitterly. (Chapter 8)

Is this the concerned, clear-sighted mother, seeing that her son has chosen the wrong girl: or the jealous mother, unable to let go, unable to accept any woman for the son she loves too protectively? As we read, we may find ourselves swinging from one view to the other. Certainly there are moments of such intense Oedipal affection between Paul and his mother, that we feel she would never, never let go:

> He had taken off his collar and tie, and rose, bare-throated to go to bed. As he stooped to kiss his mother, she threw her arms

round his neck, hid her face on his shoulder, and cried, in a whimpering voice, so unlike her own that he writhed in agony:

'I can't bear it. I could let another woman — but not her. She'd leave me no room, not a bit of room — —'

And immediately he hated Miriam bitterly.

'And I've never — you know, Paul — I've never had a husband — not really — —'

He stroked his mother's hair, and his mouth was on her throat.

'And she exults so in taking you from me — she's not like ordinary girls.'

'Well, I don't love her, Mother,' he murmured, bowing his head and hiding his eyes on her shoulder in misery. His mother kissed him a long, fervent kiss.

'My boy!' she said, in a voice trembling with passionate love.

Without knowing, he gently stroked her face. (Chapter 8)

What chance has Miriam against this? It would seem beyond doubt that Paul's chances of healthy sexual love will be strangled by his mother. Yet when Jessie Chambers, the original of Miriam, read the novel, she was bitterly upset, and felt that Lawrence had betrayed her, that the Miriam of the novel was 'reflected in the distorting mirror of Mrs Lawrence's mind'. It must be difficult for anyone to accept a fictional version of him or herself: if we are unfortunate enough to have a novelist for a friend, we run a constant danger of being seen through the distorting mirror of another mind, which will never describe our actions and motives as we do. Why should he? He is creating a fictive world, not doing justice to a real person, and Jessie Chambers' expectation, that Miriam should be a fair representation of her, is unreasonable. An autobiographical novel is still a novel. Jessie Chambers is by no means alone in this: critic after critic has read Lawrence's fiction as a biographical document, and though what they look for may be different, the feminists are no less guilty than the rest on this. The most extreme example I know is Faith Pullin's essay on *Sons and Lovers*, which moves indifferently between Lawrence's behaviour as a man and his activity as a novelist. 'Lawrence's women are allowed their liberty only insofar as they will always, finally, acknowledge him the master'[10] — a meaningful, if tendentious, statement about Lawrence the man, but it is offered as a remark about his novel. Since he *is* the master, being the author, it is hard to extract any literal meaning from such a statement. Kate Millett is doing the same when she disinters the 'cynical envy' that has gone into Lawrence's writing, or describes the plot of *The Rainbow* (Ursula makes a partial success of 'schoolteaching, then gives it up) as follows: 'Lawrence can only sympathise provisionally, *stipulating* that the moment Ursula proves herself she must *consent to* withdraw . . .' (my italics)[11].

These eminent critics have no excuse for their category mistake; Jessie Chambers had, because she had been in love with the author, and cared desperately about the way he saw her. But I have not mentioned her reaction either to condemn or to excuse it, but simply to wonder why she felt it. If it is made clear that the responsibility for the failure of the love affair lies so clearly with the mother, then Jessie has not been seen through that distorting mirror. I think what upset her must have been some of Paul's comments on Miriam, and the discovery that Lawrence was capable of feeling, or at least imagining, them: his constant accusations that she made him 'so damned spiritual', that she was like a nun. And is she? At least as often as these accusations, comes the novel's interpretation of Paul, that he is unfair to her, that 'he hated her bitterly at that moment because he made her suffer', that he may be incapable of loving. Indeed the portrayal of Miriam's sexual hesitation seems to me one of the novel's great triumphs. Lawrence understood very well that there is no simple division of women between the responsive and the unresponsive, that the losing of virginity will entail fear as well as desire, and he shows this in Miriam as he showed it in his brilliant little story, *In Love*. That Miriam is not morbidly spiritual but an intense and perfectly normal young woman who is in love with Paul, seems to be the clearest interpretation of the story, and it is confirmed by Paul's conversation with Clara, the woman who does awaken him sexually, that is placed, for maximum effect, at the end of a chapter:

> 'I know she wants a sort of soul union.'
> 'But how do you know what she wants?'
> 'I've been with her for seven years.'
> 'And you haven't found out the very first thing about her.'
> 'What's that?'
> 'That she doesn't want any of your soul communion. That's your own imagination. She wants you.'

> He pondered over this. Perhaps he was wrong.
> 'But she seems — —' he began.
> 'You've never tried,' she answered. (Chapter 10)

What are we doing when we discuss interpretations of a novel in this way? Interpreting is of course measuring hypotheses against evidence, but in the case of literature it can be problematic what is hypothesis and what is evidence. The obvious answer is that the critic provides the hypothesis, and the text of the novel the evidence. Now the interpretation from which I began, that which told us that the sons can't love because their mother is the strongest power in their lives and holds them, comes neither from critic nor from the text: it is by Lawrence himself, in a letter to Edward Garnett announcing that he has just (the previous day, in fact) sent off the manuscript of the novel. It is written out of the same intensity as the book, and could easily have been put into it (though more easily in the case of a later novel, since it might not have fitted the realistic mode of *Sons and Lovers*). There can be hypotheses, then, that have a status different from those of Millett or Lerner; and there can likewise be parts of the texts that are something like hypotheses. I had no qualms in including, among the quotations that illustrated Lawrence's male chauvinist opinions, an extract from a novel (*Aaron's Rod*), since in that case the context exercises no control over this pure statement of authorial opinion. Explicit hypotheses in *Sons and Lovers* are less glaring, but there is, for instance, Paul's claim that Miriam only wants a soul union, which, as we have seen, is treated with such contempt by Clara. But that was Paul, who doesn't speak for the author. What of the following:

> He courted her now like a lover. Often, when he grew hot, she put his face from her, held it between her hands, and looked in his eyes. He could not meet her gaze. Her dark eyes, full of love, earnest and searching, made him turn away. Not for an instant would she let him forget . . . As if from a swoon of passion she called him back to the littleness, the personal relationship. He could not bear it. 'Leave me alone — leave me alone!' he wanted to cry; but she wanted him to look at her with eyes full of love. His eyes, full of the dark, impersonal fire of desire, did not belong to her. (Chapter 11)

Is this Paul's view of Miriam, or the novel's? The sentences glide in and out of authorial backing. She called him back from his swoon of passion: is that what Paul thinks, or what she did? If it is what happened, is it Paul who calls it 'littleness'? If it is only what he thinks, is the statement that his eyes were full of the dark impersonal fire of desire also what he thinks? As Lawrence moved from the realism of *Sons and Lovers* to the symbolism and modernism of his later fiction, passages like this become more and more common. There is, of course, no uncertainty about what is happening (Lawrence is not that kind of modernist), only about its interpretation. To one school of critics, the difficulty of being sure is a sign of the author's lack of control, his inability to maintain a clear distance from his characters, and will be castigated as shoddy. To another school, it is a sign of the exploratory quality of the writing, the ability to move in and out of one character's perception of another. The argument is perhaps too complex to be settled in general terms, but it is certainly the case that Lawrence is often at his least interesting when the extent of authorial intervention is perfectly clear and identifiable.

Lawrence himself has provided the most famous formulation of the principle I am trying to use: never trust the artist, he wrote, trust the tale. Literary criticism is not possible without some version of this principle, but it is not easy to apply. For the artist may try to damage his tale from outside or from inside his text: as we shall shortly see.

First, however, I must point out that the division of responsibility between Paul and Miriam for the failure of their love is not in any obvious sense a feminist issue, for two reasons. First, that insofar as Paul is held responsible, the responsibility is transferred to his mother, so it's not just a matter of whether it was the man's fault — though we could of course push responsibility beyond the mother to the father, whose brutal treatment drove her into her passionate attachment to her sons. Second, that Paul does not exercise power over Miriam in any way that connects directly with male authority: the opposite would be truer, that her relationship with Paul is a release from the domestic slavery that her family expects of her.

    She was very much dissatisfied with her lot.
    'Don't you like being at home?' Paul asked her, surprised.

'Who would?' she answered, low and intense. 'What is it? I'm all day cleaning what the boys make just as bad in five minutes. I don't *want* to be at home.'

'What do you want, then?'

'I want to do something. I want a chance like anybody else. Why should I, because I'm a girl, be kept at home and not allowed to be anything? What chance *have* I?'

'Chance of what?'

'Of knowing anything — of learning, of doing anything. It's not fair, because I'm a woman.' (Chapter 7)

There is a strikingly similar situation in George Eliot's *Mill on the Floss*, where Tom Tulliver learns Latin, to which he is quite unsuited, because he is the son, and his sister Maggie has to pick it up from his books. Maggie has to contend with the masculine prejudice represented by Mr Stelling, who believes that girls 'can pick up a little of everything. They've a great deal of superficial cleverness; but they couldn't go far into anything. They're quick and shallow.'[12] The response to Miriam's attempts is blunter. 'I'm going to teach Miriam algebra,' says Paul to his mother. ' "Well," replied Mrs Morel, "I hope she'll get fat on it." '

Are we to consider it a coincidence that Maggie, in the novel by a woman, really is cleverer than her brother; and Miriam, in the novel by a man, turns out to be rather slow? Since academic intelligence is presumably equally distributed between the sexes, we should not regard either novelist as more truthful than the other. What they are both showing us is that education matters not only for itself but because it is a sign of power: Mrs Morel is dismissive not only of the usefulness of algebra, but also of Miriam's attempt to overcome the drawback of being a girl.

This issue is more fully treated in the portrait of Clara, who had 'left her husband, and taken up Women's Rights. She was supposed to be clever.' When she first meets Paul, she is cool, even hostile. She knows that she has made herself socially vulnerable:

After tea, when all the men had gone but Paul, Mrs Leivers said to Clara:

'And you find life happier now?'

'Infinitely.'

'And you are satisfied?'

'So long as I can be free and independent.'

> 'And you don't *miss* anything in your life?' asked Mrs Leivers gently.
> 'I've put all that behind me.'
> Paul had been feeling uncomfortable during this discourse. He got up.
> 'You'll find you're always tumbling over the things you've put behind you,' he said. Then he took his departure to the cowsheds. He felt he had been witty, and his manly pride was high. He whistled as he went down the brick track. (Chapter 9)

Mrs Leivers, concerned and friendly, is convinced that something is missing from Clara's life. Clara, on the defensive, refuses to admit this. Paul is more on edge than either, and feels it necessary to be witty at Clara's expense. Now the novel goes on to show that something *was* missing from Clara's life: falling in love with Paul is an enriching experience for her. Yet immediately we must add that this does not invalidate either leaving her husband or taking up Women's Rights, for the view that sexual fulfilment will drive out feminist opinions is itself part of the prejudice that feminism combats.

Later that day they go for a walk, and come across a man leading a great bay horse. They are charmed, and Paul starts his teasing again:

> 'What a treat to be a knight,' he said, 'and to have a pavilion here.'
> 'And to have us shut up safely?' replied Clara.
> 'Yes,' he answered, 'singing with your maids at your broidery. I would carry your banner of white and green and heliotrope. I would have "W.S.P.U." emblazoned on my shield, beneath a woman rampant.'
> 'I have no doubt,' said Clara, 'that you would much rather fight for a woman than let her fight for herself.' (Chapter 9)

Paul really is witty, but he is too pleased with his own wit. Clara really does hold her opinions, and is shrewd, but Paul realised a moment later 'that the upward lifting of her face was misery and not scorn'. This episode is a perfect example of how to handle political arguments in fiction. There are always two dangers: that the people are shoved aside for a piece of undigested politics, or that the political issues are seen merely as a symptom of the personal clash, and Lawrence avoids them both. Taking the politics seriously is not of course a matter that can be judged from this scene alone. In the opening chapters we're shown the marriage of Paul's parents as no marriage had ever before been shown in English fiction: the woman powerless, the husband drunk and bullying:

'The house is filthy with you,' she cried.
'Then get out on it — it's mine. Get out on it!' he shouted. 'It's me as brings th'money whoam, not thee. It's my house, not thine. Then get out on't — get out on't!'
'And I would,' she cried, suddenly shaken into tears of impotence. 'Ah, wouldn't I, wouldn't I have gone long ago, but for those children.' (Chapter 1)

Paul knows scenes like this only too well; when he mocks at Clara's feminism, he makes no connexion with them. It may be that Lawrence didn't intend a connexion, but that doesn't matter — that is only Lawrence's opinions. What he has done is to show the world of the Morels with such fullness and insight that the connexions are there to be made, and we must trust the tale and make them.

Clara is the first sketch of a new woman, and a much fuller version comes in *The Rainbow*, where Ursula Brangwen, in deliberate contrast to her mother and grandmother, is a modern young woman, sexually liberated and setting out to earn her own living:

Ursula would try to insist, in her own home, on the right of women to take equal place with men in the field of action and work.
'Ay,' said the mother, 'there's a good crop of stockings lying ripe for mending. Let that be your field of action.' (Chapter 13)

It is a long struggle for Ursula to get out into the world, first against her parents, only then to find that she has entered a bitter world of struggle. I wish I had the time to discuss Chapter 13 of *The Rainbow* in the kind of detail I have looked at *Sons and Lovers*. Its account of the agony of trying to keep order in a slum school will speak like daggers to any schoolteacher. It has all the wonderful surface realism of *Sons and Lovers*, plus an awareness of a further dimension of experience. School is seen as the breaking of the children's will, the imposing of discipline and the pushing of mechanical knowledge into them. To Ursula, who wants warm human contact with the children, this is unendurable, yet there is no Utopian pretence that it's merely a wicked educational system that stands in the way of success. Conflict is fundamental, and Ursula knows that if she is to survive she must impose her will: which she more or less succeeds in doing, but at a terrible cost: 'Never would she, Ursula Brangwen, the girl she was, the person she was, come into contact with those boys.'

The chapter in which this long struggle is chronicled is called 'The Man's World'. It is not intended as a particularly feminist chapter: Ursula's victory is a hollow one at best. Yet if the career that Ursula fights her way into is not worth having, the reason may be that it is organised on lines that are too exclusively masculine, as a conflict of wills. (Later Lawrence claimed in his polemical writings that the blind imposition of will was feminine rather than masculine, but that is part of his rhetoric for beating at a world he had grown to hate.) *The Rainbow*, Chapter 13, is certainly not reformist in spirit: it implies no programme for improving the quality of schools, and the good teachers are even more contemptible than the bad. But that title — 'The Man's World' — opens up the possibility of a profoundly feminist reading. It gives us a glimpse of an ambiguity that is surely central to feminism: which can either be a programme for allowing women to take on masculine roles, masculine functions and even masculine values, or — and this is what *The Rainbow* might imply — a programme claiming we have too much masculinity in the world, and it would do men no harm to become more like women. The very opposite to the views I began by quoting at you, the views of the Lawrence who wrote *Education of the People* and *Fantasia of the Unconscious*. Once again, we must trust the tale.

If a novel is completely successful in its representation of politics, then it does not matter which side the author is on: what matters is how he perceives — and represents — the total situation. The feminist critic should therefore at least entertain the possibility of reading with sympathy the novels written by the Lawrence whose deplorable views I began by quoting to you: I cannot rest my whole case upon early Lawrence. Let us therefore turn to the other extreme, and look at *The Plumed Serpent*. This is a book it might seem impossible to defend today. It is the story of a neo-Aztec religious revival that plans to take over Mexico, murdering its opponents and its disloyal

followers, and singing interminable uplifting hymns in mono-
tonous free verse. The heroine, Kate Leslie, a lively, intelligent
widow of nearly forty, is drawn into it all, and marries one of
the leaders. It has the ring of a strongly committed political
novel, inviting us to glory in the revitalising neo-Fascist cult of
Quetzalcoatl.

Kate veers between resistance to and acceptance of the cult:

> So, when she thought of him and his soldiers, tales of swift
> cruelty she had heard of him: when she remembered his stabbing
> the three helpless peons, she thought: Why should I judge him?
> He is of the gods. And when he comes to me he lays his pure,
> quick flame to mine, and every time I am a young girl again, and
> every time he takes the flower of my virginity, and I his. It leaves
> me *insouciante* like a young girl. What do I care if he kills
> people? His flame is young and clean. He is Huitzilopochtli and
> I am Malintzi. What do I care, what Cipriano Viedma does or
> doesn't do? Or even what Kate Leslie does or doesn't do!
> (Chapter 24)

There she is, drunk with the rhetoric; here on the other hand
she is standing up for herself:

> 'You treat me as if I had no life of my own,' she said. 'But I
> have.'
>   'A life of your own? Who gave it you? Where did you get it?'
>   'I don't know. But I have got it. And I must live it. I can't be
> just swallowed up.'
>   'Why, Malintzi?' he said, giving her a name. 'Why can't you?'
>   'Be just swallowed up?' she said. 'Well, I just can't.'
>   'I am the living Huitzilopochtli,' he said. 'And I am swallowed
> up. I thought, so could you be, Malintzi.'
>   'No! Not quite!' she said.
>   'Not quite! Not quite! Not now! Not just now! How often you
> say *Not*, to-day! — I must go back to Ramon.'
>   'Yes. Go back to him. You only care about him, and your
> living Quetzalcoatl and your living Huitzilopochtli. — I am only a
> woman.'
>   'No, Malintzi, you are more. You are more than Kate, you are
> Malintzi.'
>   'I am not! I am only Kate, and I am only a woman. I mistrust
> all that other stuff.'
>   'I am more than just a man, Malintzi. — Don't you see that?'
>   'No!' said Kate. 'I don't see it. Why *should* you be more than
> just a man?'

'Because I am the living Huitzilopochtli. Didn't I tell you?
you've got dust in your mouth to-day, Malintzi.' (Chapter 22)

But what good clean dust! Kate Millett doesn't mention this
passage, with its refreshing scepticism about being 'more than a
woman'. There are two ways of comparing it with the previous
passage. One is to listen to them both as if they had a separate
existence from each other, and if we do that how can we fail to
notice the huge difference: the surrender to cloudy abstractions
in the first, the cool resistant voice of the woman puncturing the
rhetoric in the second: ' "Be just swallowed up?" she said.
"Well, I just can't." '

The other is to ask what order they come in. I read you the
sceptical passage second, and so perhaps gave the impression
that Kate was freeing herself from all these natural aristocrats
and their racial myths. But I'm sorry to have to tell you that
they come the other way round in the novel, and that Kate in
the end sinks into acceptance, giving up that sharp, critical and
(I suggest) feminine voice. The action of the book comes down
very firmly behind the cult of Quetzalcoatl.

If *The Plumed Serpent* were a great novel and grew to be
studied like *Paradise Lost* in future generations, there would
arise among its critics a dissident sect who claimed that
Lawrence, being a true poet, was of the woman's party, that he
wrote in fetters when writing of Quetzalcoatl and at fitful liberty
when writing of Kate Leslie, who was the true hero of the book,
and was tragically beaten down. And these dissidents would be
severely rebuked by scholars who pointed out that Lawrence's
intention was to justify the ways of Ramon and Cipriano, who
quoted from his letters his own praise of the book, and who
reminded us that a work of literature can only be appreciated in
the light of the author's intention.

When I claimed that an author's opinions need not concern
us, I should of course have added: unless they invade the tale.
The best we can do for *The Plumed Serpent* is to rescue those
elements in it that Lawrence the male chauvinist went on to
beat down. And now I'm sorry to tell you that Clara and Ursula
do not in the end escape a touch of the same treatment as Kate.

In the case of Clara, the beating down is done through Baxter
Dawes. Though she has left her husband when she first appears
in the novel, she has steadily refused to divorce him, for reasons

she is never fully able to explain. Dawes is a thoroughly nasty piece of work who has beaten her and been unfaithful, who hates Paul out of pure irrational impulse, who picks a fight with him and tries to kill him, and who finally catches typhoid and seems to lose his will to live. The result of all this is to establish a physical bond between him and Paul, and to lead Paul to the belief that Clara has never really ceased to be his wife, and ought to go back to him. He succeeds in imposing this belief on her, and in the end (in what I have to admit is a well-written scene) she does go back to him. I attribute this unlikely renunciation by Clara of all she'd come to believe in to Lawrence's opinions invading and controlling the action, because Baxter Dawes is all too familiar a figure to readers of Lawrence: he is the smouldering, sullen, passionate man who is somehow in touch with the dark gods, whose nastiness is healthier than any loving concern for humanity, and who inhabits every one of Lawrence's later novels, sulking, copulating, preaching: Cicio in *The Lost Girl*, the two grooms in *St Mawr*, the gipsy in *The Virgin and the Gipsy*, and of course Mellors in *Lady Chatterley's Lover*. We can see in Baxter Dawes all too clear a warning of what is to come.

In later years, Lawrence used to say that he thought he had been unjust to his father, and that if he were to write the book again he would be more sympathetic to Morel, and less to the mother. His essay 'Nottingham and the Mining Countryside' sketches for us the view of the mining culture we'd then have had:

> Now the colliers had also an instinct of beauty. The colliers' wives had not. The colliers were deeply alive, instinctively. But they had no daytime ambition, and no daytime intellect . . . The collier fled out of the house as soon as he could, away from the nagging materialism of the woman.[13]

How thankful we can be that Lawrence never did this rewriting. It can't be an accident that Morel, the most successful of Lawrence's surly, sexed and vital men, is the one against whom he bears a grudge: it is that grudge which stiffened Lawrence's treatment of him, and enabled him to see Morel with such ruthless clarity. It is not possible to pass an easy judgement on the rich ambivalence with which Morel is shown to us. On the one hand there is the wiry toughness, the bodily magnetism that attracted Mrs Morel to him in the first place, and which, as Paul realises, enriched her marriage in its early days in a way she will never wholly lose, as well as Morel's handiness, his enjoyment of simple tasks, his pleasure in making toys for the children; on the other hand is his bullying, his selfishness, his exhibitionism, his sometimes unforgiveable treatment of his wife. Lawrence loved Morel for the clear vital flame of his being, and he hated him because Morel was his father: the result is a constantly shifting, always lucid portrait. The rewriting Lawrence wanted to do would have removed the hatred and damaged, because over-simplified, the portrait. It would just have turned Morel into another Baxter Dawes.

The betrayal of Ursula is more subtle, less damaging, than that of Clara. It does not occur in *The Rainbow* itself, but in its sequel, *Women in Love*. She is a grammar school teacher by then, she has passed through her searing sexual initiation with Skrebensky, and she falls in love with Birkin, the school inspector. Everyone knows that the Ursula−Birkin relationship is Lawrence's sketch for the nearest we can come to genuine love in the modern world. They achieve true emotional rapport in the chapter called 'Excurse', after a wonderfully depicted quarrel that, like all the best quarrels, ends by bringing them closer together.

> The tea-pot poured beautifully from a proud slender spout. Her eyes were warm with smiles as she gave him his tea. She had learned at last to be still and perfect.
> 'Everything is ours,' she said to him.
> 'Everything,' he answered.
> She gave a queer little crowing sound of triumph.
> 'I'm so glad!' she cried, with unspeakable relief.
> 'So am I,' he said. 'But I'm thinking we'd better get out of our responsibilities as quick as we can.'
> 'What responsibilities?' she asked, wondering.
> 'We must drop our jobs, like a shot.'
> A new understanding dawned into her face.
> 'Of course,' she said, 'there's that.'
> 'We must get out,' he said. 'There's nothing for it but to get out, quick.'
> She looked at him doubtfully across the table.
> 'But where?' she said.
> 'I don't know,' he said. 'We'll just wander about for a bit.'
> (Chapter 23)

And immediately they sit down and write their letters of resignation.

There is a calm assumption here that perfect love and work are incompatible. It is never discussed or explored, and the scene is one of the most unquestioning and superficial in Lawrence. Birkin's simple cliche — 'We must drop our jobs *like a shot*' — covers the lack of real thought, but Ursula responds to it as if it were a profound insight: 'a new understanding dawned into her face.' Even more extraordinary, there seems no awareness of how completely the decision depends on economic privilege: Birkin has a private income, and does not need to work, and it is not spiritual insight but money that frees him from workaday degradation. The whole episode shows a curious indifference — unusual in Lawrence, virtually unknown in early Lawrence — to the importance of the material basis.

Now this decision of Birkin and Ursula is especially relevant to the present argument, because of its striking resemblance to what the woman is normally supposed to do. Dropping her responsibilities in the outside world 'like a shot' when she marries, even dropping (if she has them) her feminist opinions, she gives up career and radicalism for a good man's love. It is as if Birkin and Ursula were *both* women in their relation to the world of work, both able to withdraw from the struggle and find fulfilment in domestic love.

Yet, once again, if we want a counterstatement, we will find it in the novel itself. A little later, in the chapter called 'A Chair', Birkin and Ursula start arguing about the soullessness of post-industrial England ('mechanism, the very soul of materialism', as Birkin wordily calls it). Critic after critic (including Kate Millett) has told us that Birkin 'is' Lawrence, and here we find him producing a string of Lawrentian commonplaces, about what has happened to 'Jane Austen's England . . . it had something to express even when it made that chair'. I cannot be the only reader of Lawrence who has sighed wearily over his tendency to idealise the past as a stick to beat the present; and Ursula, hearing Birkin, says just that:

> 'It isn't true,' cried Ursula. 'Why must you always praise the past at the expense of the present? *Really*, I don't think much of Jane Austen's England. It was materialistic enough, if you like —.'
> (Chapter 23)

Birkin does not quite say 'You've got dust in your mouth today, Malintzi', since that isn't his vocabulary, but the argument closely parallels that between Kate and Cipriano. And not only does the woman's sensible voice interrogate the masculine rhetoric, but we are given the reminder of economic privilege that was missing from their earlier decision to give up working. For there is a young couple at the jumble market, also looking at furniture, who are getting married because the girl is pregnant, and after Birkin and Ursula have bought the chair, and Birkin has asserted his insistent wish for freedom, for not settling down, they decide to give it to them. Ursula and Birkin argue about the couple. The man is clearly one of Lawrence's sullen sexed smoulderers ('He had a queer, subterranean beauty, repulsive too'), and though Ursula wants to help them, Birkin hates what is happening ('instantly sympathising with the aloof, furtive youth, against the active, procreant female'), and their dispute enacts verbally the struggle between irresponsibility and domesticity that is being enacted in painful action in front of them. And at the same time we are shown the difference between having money and not having it: when Ursula explains that they had bought the chair because they are getting married, and have now decided to live abroad, the girl remarks, first, to her young man: 'It's all right to be some folks.' They take the chair, for they are too sensible not to, but first they need to needle the givers for patronising them:

> 'Cawsts something to chynge your mind,' he said in an incredibly low accent.
> 'Only ten shillings this time,' said Birkin.
> The man looked up at him with a grimace of a smile, furtive, unsure.
> 'Cheap at 'arf a quid, guv'nor,' he said. 'Not like getting divawced.'
> 'We're not married yet,' said Birkin.
> 'No, no more aren't we,' said the young woman loudly. 'But we shall be a Saturday.' (Chapter 26)

Both couples are marrying. Birkin asserts his continuing need for freedom with articulateness and dignity, and can persuade Ursula to accept it, at least in part. The young man has no such ability, and is helpless before the firm possessiveness of the woman. Without losing interest in the emotional dilemma, without dismissing the substance of Birkin's harangues,

Lawrence has shown us that we are seeing a contrast between classes, in a world where money counts.

It is almost always premature to accuse Lawrence's fiction of silences and smug distortions: as we read on, we find that what is missing is, somehow, indirectly present after all. This is the situation diagnosed in the formula, Never trust the artist, trust the tale, and that is why I have used it as a critical principle in this discussion, while at the same time trying to show how difficult it is to apply, since the artist can invade his tale in such varied and damaging ways. In his essay 'The Novel', Lawrence stated his theory as follows:

> It is such a bore that nearly all great novelists have a didactic purpose, otherwise a philosophy, directly opposite to their passional inspiration. In their passional inspiration, they are all phallic worshippers.[14]

So we must trust the tale, for the novelist 'is usually a dribbling liar.' Well, Lawrence was as much of a dribbling liar as any of them, and his lies were mostly about phallic worship. It seems to me a good use of a centenary, to try and rescue his fiction from its didactic purposes.

Notes

1 Kate Millett, *Sexual Politics* (1970), iii. 5.
2 See *Lawrence and Women*, ed. Anne Smith (1978).
3 'Education of the People', *Phoenix*, ed. E.D. Macdonald (1936), p. 622.
4 *ibid.*, p. 658.
5 *Aaron's Rod* (1922), chap. 9.
6 Paul Delany, *D.H. Lawrence's Nightmare* (1978), p. 71.
7 Letter to Bertrand Russell, 7 July 1915. *Collected Letters*, ed. H.T. Moore (1962), p. 352.
8 Hilary Simpson, *D.H. Lawrence and Feminism* (1982).
9 Letter to Edward Garnett, 14 November 1912. *Collected Letters*, p. 160.
10 Faith Pullin, 'Lawrence's Treatment of Women in *Sons and Lovers*', *Lawrence and Women*, ed. Anne Smith (1978).
11 Kate Millett, *op. cit.*
12 George Eliot, *The Mill on the Floss* (1860), Book II, chap. 1.
13 *Phoenix*, p. 136.
14 'The Novel', *Phoenix II*, ed. W. Roberts & H.T. Moore (1968), p. 417.

Lawrence and the Biological Psyche

DAVID ELLIS

By using Freud as a starting-point in both of his so-called
psychology books, Lawrence inevitably involves himself in
problems of terminology. 'We profess no scientific *exactitude*',
he writes, 'particularly in terminology. We merely wish intel-
ligibly to open the way' (234–5).[1] The disclaimer comes towards
the end of *Psychoanalysis and the Unconscious* and is only
decent in a writer who has previously used words like 'unconscious', 'consciousness' and 'pre-conscious' very loosely. In the
third chapter of that book, when Lawrence is discussing the
'strange little cries' of very young children or animals, all three
turn up in the same sentence, but not in a way to make the
distinctions between them very much sharper. 'There speaks the
first consciousness, the audible unconscious, in the squeak of
these infantile things, which is so curiously and indescribably
moving, reacting direct upon the great abdominal centre, the
preconscious mind in man' (219). Here, consciousness, the
unconscious and the preconscious appear to amount to very
much the same thing. They are of course the three crucial terms
in what is known as Freud's first topography of the mind, before
his introduction of the ego, super-ego, and the id. The trouble
with them is that they imply distinctions for which Lawrence has
no use and which threaten to confuse the issue. There is
between him and Freud a radical difference of approach. The
latter's concern to distinguish consciousness very carefully from
the unconscious or the preconscious is related to his preoccupation with what we normally think of as mental life: the
activities associated, in one way or another, with the brain and
central nervous system. As his reference to 'the great abdominal
centre, the preconscious mind in man' suggests, Lawrence
believed that each of the great nerve centres in the body had a
mind of its own: was capable of what it was legitimate to
designate as thought. In one of his dry runs for the view of the
mind he was to elaborate in the psychology books — the essay

on Hawthorne which appeared in the *English Review* in May
1919 — he writes, 'the great nerve-centres of the body are
centres of perfect primary cognition . . . Each great nerve-
centre has its own peculiar consciousness, its own peculiar mind,
its own primary precepts and concepts, its own spontaneous
desires and ideas'; and he goes on to develop his notion of
'physical thought'.[2] For this notion, the Freudian distinctions
between consciousness and its opposite are redundant so it is
not surprising that, in the psychology books, Lawrence does in
fact tend to use the two concepts — and his idea of the
preconscious — indiscriminately. This is only momentarily
disconcerting: it doesn't prevent a reader from seeing what he
means. It is a pity nevertheless that it is only in *Fantasia of the
Unconscious* that Lawrence discovers or first uses a term ('the
biological psyche') which characterises his concerns much more
satisfactorily than 'the unconscious', with its inevitable com-
panions. If his first book had been called *Psychoanalysis and the
Biological Psyche*, it would have raised fewer expectations of
an encounter with Freud with that minimum agreement on
premises any coherent discussion requires.

The surprising thing about Lawrence's biological psyche is
that it is so highly systematic. It is worked out in considerable
detail as if Lawrence had always had ringing in his ears Blake's
'I must Create a System, or be enslav'd by another Man's'. Its
basis is a vertical division down the body which separates the
'sympathetic', soft front from the back (thought of by Lawrence
as 'voluntary'). There is then in addition a series of horizontal
divisions which divide the body into 'planes', starting with the
one around the midriff with its solar plexus at the front and
lumbar ganglion at the back. These planes come into action as
the body develops. The second to function lies above the first
and contains the cardiac plexus and thoracic ganglion. After
which, there are the two centres in the area around the throat
which become active with the onset of puberty (the cervical
plexus and cervical ganglion) and two more in the loins called
the hypogastric plexus and the sacral ganglion. In his meta-
psychology, Freud distinguished three ways of describing the
mind: the topographic, the dynamic and the economic.
Lawrence's topography presents eight great body centres
or 'chakras', as he calls them at one point (234), using an
'old esoteric word' he had probably found in a strange work on

the Book of Revelations.³ But the great difference from Freud's various topographical descriptions is that Lawrence means his to be taken literally. Nothing would have pleased Freud more than to have been able to offer a description of the mind which was biological. But that was something which he felt the state of medical knowledge didn't allow, and he had to be content instead with imagining it as a series of relationships in space. Lawrence, on the other hand, boldly associates particular workings of the mind with what he feels are easily identifiable parts of the body. As he says in the uneasy, bantering tone characteristic of so much of *Fantasia*:

> You've got first and foremost a solar plexus, dear reader; and the solar plexus is a great nerve centre which lies behind your stomach. I can't be accused of impropriety or untruth, because any book of science or medicine which deals with the nerve-system of the human body will show it to you quite plainly. So don't wriggle or try to look spiritual. Because, willy-nilly, you've got a solar plexus, dear reader, among other things. I'm writing a good sound science book, which there's no gainsaying. (278)

Freud thought of his various descriptions of the mind as 'dynamic' because they took into account the energy factor: imagined the difference between the conscious and unconscious, for example, as a conflict of forces. The dynamism of Lawrence's system is conceived by him in terms of constant analogies, implicit and explicit, with magnetism and electricity. He continually presents his body centres as electro-magnetic poles between which there is a complicated play of energy, both within one individual and when the centres of one person are linked with the corresponding centres in another. In *Psychoanalysis and the Unconscious* especially, he implies that it is only when this energy is properly regulated and when there is therefore in the distribution of force a proper balance or equilibrium that, 'The ample, mature, unfolded individual stands perfect, perfect in himself, but also perfect in his harmonious relation to those nearest him and to all the universe' (225). Since it refers not merely to energy but to quantities of energy and how they are diverted or shared out, this ideal of Lawrence's might be regarded as a very rough equivalent of what in Freud is known as the 'economic' point of view. (An example of an economic concept is the 'pleasure principle' which, in its later manifestations, involves imagining that any organism which is assailed by stimuli from either the outside world or its own internal 'energy' will always strive to keep its level of excitation constant or stable.)

As Lawrence fills in the details of his biological psyche, or describes its workings, he writes passages which are bound to strike many of his readers as eccentric. They will wonder how they are meant to respond to so many startling challenges to their commonsense. Freud can have that effect also but there is now a fairly general recognition that, whether he was right or wrong, he is to be 'taken seriously'. And yet, in certain ways, what Lawrence had to say is not any more disconcerting to the non-specialist than much of Freud — not more difficult for the non-specialist to verify (that is) and therefore evaluate satis-factorily. Since this is a suggestion with an important bearing on the general question of how readers can come to terms with Lawrence's psychological writings, it will benefit from illus-tration and a comparison of passages in which Lawrence and Freud are discussing a roughly similar subject. Here first is Lawrence, half-way through *Fantasia*, having firmly established his body-centres and now going on to discuss the 'act of coition':

> We know that in the act of coition the *blood* of the individual man, acutely surcharged with intense vital electricity — we know no word, so say 'electricity', by analogy — rises to a culmination, in a tremendous magnetic urge towards the blood of the female. The whole of the living blood in the two individuals forms a field of intense, polarized magnetic attraction. So, the two poles must be brought into contact. In the act of coition, the two individuals, rocking and surging towards contact, as near as possible, clash into a oneness. A great flash of interchange occurs, like an electrical spark when two currents meet or like lightning out of the densely surcharged clouds. There is a lightning flash which passes through the blood of both individuals, there is a thunder of sensation which rolls in diminishing crashes down the nerves of each — and then the tension passes.
>
> The two individuals are separate again. But are they as they were before? Is the air the same after a thunderstorm as before? No. The air is as it were new, fresh, tingling with newness. So is the blood of man and woman after successful coition. After a false coition, like prostitution, there is not newness but a certain disintegration.
>
> But after coition, the actual chemical constitution of the blood

is so changed that usually sleep intervenes, to allow time for chemical, biological readjustment through the whole system.

So, the blood is changed and renewed, refreshed, almost re-created, like the atmosphere after thunder. Out of the newness of the living blood pass the new strange waves which beat upon the great dynamic centres of the nerves: primarily upon the hypogastric plexus and the sacral ganglion. From these centres rise new impulses, new vision, new being, rising like Aphrodite from the foam of the new tide of blood. And so individual life goes on. (106–7)

The simplest approach to this passage, as to so much in both psychology books, is via the attitude it displays to 'science'. A reason for choosing it is that Lawrence here makes it much clearer and more explicit than he usually does that he is looking to certain areas of scientific enquiry for metaphors or similes. Electricity is the obvious example, and it is through electricity that he can then combine his scientific images with others of a more traditionally Romantic character in order to produce an appeal to individual experience, the equivalent of 'Is it not like, does it not feel like this?' The combination seems at first most striking in 'a thunder of sensation which rolls in diminishing crashes down the nerves'. Yet it is very doubtful whether in this phrase Lawrence meant his reference to the nerves to be other than literal; and the doubt acts as a reminder that, insofar as science comprises in this passage anatomy or bio-chemistry, it is not *only* present as a convenient provider of imagery. When Lawrence says that 'the actual chemical constitution of the blood' is altered after coition he is no more speaking metaphorically than when he refers to the hypogastric plexus and the sacral ganglion, both of which, he would have claimed, can be found in 'any book of science or medicine which deals with the nerve system of the human body.' On those occasions the emphasis for the reader is changed, rather disconcertingly it seems to me, from 'Is it not like this?' to 'This is how it is'.

The comparison with Freud should seem fairer and have more point if it is taken from what he called his metapsychological writings since it is in those that — as the term implies — he chooses not to stand on his medical dignity and speculates in areas where he is sometimes no better qualified than rival specialists from different disciplines (philosophers, for example), or even the occasional gifted amateur. *Beyond the Pleasure*

Principle is as good an example as any of Freud's meta-psychology and that it was first published in 1920, just a year before the appearance of *Psychoanalysis and the Unconscious*, adds to its relevance here.

> Let us, however, return to the self-preservative sexual instincts. The experiments upon protista have already shown us that conjugation — that is, the coalescence of two individuals which separate soon afterwards without any subsequent cell-division occurring — has a strengthening and rejuvenating effect upon both of them. In later generations they show no signs of degenerating and seem able to put up a longer resistance to the injurious effects of their own metabolism. This single observation may, I think, be taken as typical of the effect produced by sexual union as well. But how is it that the coalescence of two only slightly different cells can bring about this renewal of life? The experiment which replaces the conjugation of protozoa by the application of chemical or even mechanical stimuli (cf. Lipschütz, 1914) enables us to give what is no doubt a conclusive reply to this question. The result is brought about by the influx of fresh amounts of stimulus. This tallies well with the hypothesis that the life process of the individual leads for internal reasons to an abolition of chemical tensions, that is to say, to death, whereas union with the living substance of a different individual increases those tensions, introducing what may be described as fresh 'vital differences' which must then be lived off. As regards this dissimilarity there must of course be one or more optima. The dominating tendency of mental life, and perhaps of nervous life in general, is the effort to reduce, to keep constant or to remove internal tension due to stimuli (the 'Nirvana principle', to borrow a term from Barbara Low [1920, 73]) — a tendency which finds expression in the pleasure principle; and our recognition of that fact is one of our strongest reasons for believing in the existence of death instincts.[4]

The most obvious, immediate difference from Lawrence is that Freud makes no apparent effort here to evoke in the reader feelings appropriate to the subject. He is much less self-evidently 'literary'. In his work as a whole, Freud would be by no means averse to talking of new vision 'rising like Aphrodite from the foam of the new tide of blood'; but he uses allusions like this sparingly and not at all in the passage above. With the attention to rhythmic pattern or the use of rhetorical questions and repetition, they are part of Lawrence's stock-in-trade.

As the reader becomes conscious of a less literary manner, he is also made aware of a different and much more demanding notion of 'science'. Freud has a note at the end of the second sentence ('both of them') which refers back to his own detailed and technical account of 'experiments upon protista' a few pages before. What he had described were the efforts biologists had quite recently been making to test the hypothesis that 'all living substance is bound to die from internal causes' (44). Prominent in the description is the American who observed the repro- duction by binary fission of the 'slipper animalcule' (*Para- mecium*) until the 3029th generation, without being aware of any degeneration in the stock. This was because — other experiments seemed to show — he isolated 'one of the part- products' and placed it in 'fresh nutrient fluid' whenever fission occurred. If that wasn't done, then the animalculae would show 'signs of senescence' which could only be halted by 'conjugation' — an exchange of substances with rejuvenating rather than reproductive effects for the two individuals concerned (47–9). Reading about these things is very different from turning over the pages of Lawrence's psychology books; yet, as I have suggested, there are certain ways in which the effect is similar. The difficulty with Lawrence lies in adjusting to his use of science as both metaphor and fact. His appeal as to whether or not these are our impressions often tends to be compromised by an intermittent insistence that they must be (because science says so). On the surface at least, science is only ever one thing for Freud, and in the passage above his procedure also appears to distinguish itself completely from Lawrence's by being properly 'scientific': moving from small facts to large conclusions in an easy inductive sequence. Yet the truth is surely that non- specialists can only ever have an illusion of following him. Who but the specialist is able to estimate the validity of experimental work in biology at the turn of this century: to say quite how or in what respects conjugation in *Paramecium* is indeed 'the forerunner of the sexual reproduction of higher creatures', as Freud assumes it is; or to decide whether Lipschütz's account of the 'celebrated experiment' in which Loeb induced segmentation in sea-urchins' eggs by the application of 'certain chemical stimuli' can bear so much weight (48). The consequence is that most readers are completely in Freud's hands and not very well prepared therefore to resist the enormous leap — partly faciliated by 'individuals' (*individuums*), which has the same breadth of meaning in German as it does in English — from unicellular organisms to human life. Freud appears to lessen the distance travelled with characteristic rhetorical, or one might just as well say literary skill. A harmless filler — 'As regards this dissimilarity there must of course be one or more optima' — prepares the way for the shift from the protozoa to 'mental life'. (What kind of mental life — *Seelenleben* — could one reasonably attribute to the slipper animalcule?) And by restating in this context his pleasure principle, Freud implies that it has some necessary relation to the experimental material he has discussed, or even that this material serves to confirm it.

Freud's aim in *Beyond the Pleasure Principle* is to establish that, in addition to the sexual instincts, which are at the origin of not only self-preservation but also all change or development, there are instincts whose activity consists in urging every organism back to its previous state. It is the attempt to show that these regressive 'death instincts' have at least equal priority with whatever urges life forward which leads him from an apparent contradiction of the pleasure principle in human behaviour — the 'compulsion to repeat' or periodically re-create in the mind unpleasurable material — to experimental work on the Protozoa. As long as it could be claimed that, in their capacity to divide in two indefinitely, unicellular organisms like the Protozoa enjoyed a species of immortality, then death could be viewed as a 'late acquisition' and there could be 'no question of there having been death instincts from the very beginning of life on this earth' (47). Freud never pretends that in his treatment of these issues he is being anything other than speculative but the closeness of his reasoning, and the ingenious twists and turns of his argument, make it an extraordinary intellectual adventure. Readers can take from it any number of suggestive thoughts about their own mental life and very useful categories for describing mental life in general. But what is not available to them, in the passage above but also I think in the book as a whole, is any properly established, causal relation between biology on the one hand and human psychology on the other. The constantly implied reminder that we all belong to the same evolutionary chain, no matter how many thousands of links there may be between ourselves and *Paramecium*, is not therefore sufficient to prevent Freud's details of biological experiments finally assuming the character of figures of speech. The organisms he describes are too primitive, and our knowledge of life-processes too imperfect, for their behaviour to provide anything more than implicit similes for his impressions of mental life. It only appears in this and other passages as if these impressions depend and grow out of science, whereas in fact it is the prestige of science which is being used to persuade, or intimidate, readers into accepting them.

There is a similar variety of persuasion in Lawrence (and hence a similarity of effect), but it does him less good because his science is so recognizably less expert. When he talks of a change in 'the actual chemical constitution of the blood', it is reasonably certain that he would have had much less to say than Freud if challenged for the formula. He hadn't, like Freud, spent several years in the research laboratories of a Medical Faculty. But against Lawrence also in this context is a fundamental ambiguity in his attitude to science. On the one hand, thanks largely to Aldous Huxley in his otherwise excellent introduction to the first edition of the letters, Lawrence is well-known as the irrational opponent of all things scientific. That impression is one which Huxley appears to have gathered from his contacts with Lawrence in the last two or three years of his life; but some support (of a dubious kind) could of course have been found for it earlier. In *Psychoanalysis and the Unconscious*, for example, Lawrence insists that the mystery of new life can never be explained by the 'scientific' laws of cause-and-effect, and he denies that the nature of any new creature derives from the nature of its parents. 'This causeless created nature of the individual being is the same as the old mystery of the divine nature of the soul. Religion was right and science is wrong' (214). Only when scientists have the 'super-scientific grace' to admit this 'first new item of knowledge', he says, can there be a new science of the unconscious, more complete in knowledge (216). This appears to be the kind of science which he is speculating about in the 'Foreword' to *Fantasia*, 'a vast and perhaps perfect science of its own, a science in terms of life' which existed before the Flood and was taught by priests 'esoterically in all countries of the globe, Asia, Polynesia, America, Atlantis and Europe' (12). Despite all of which, and despite all the many other occasions when Lawrence attacks conventional science for being arrogant, mechanistic and unimaginative, he is remarkably anxious to refer to its supposedly demonstrable facts when defending his biological psyche.

> But the unconscious is never an abstraction, *never to be abstracted*. It is never an ideal entity. It is always concrete. In the very first instance, it is the glinting nucleus of the ovule. And proceeding from this, it is the chain or constellation of nuclei which derive directly from this first spark. And further still it is the great nerve-centres of the human body, in which the primal and pristine nuclei still act direct. The nuclei are centres of spontaneous consciousness. It seems as if their bright grain were germ-consciousness, consciousness germinating for ever. If that is a mystery, it is not my fault. Certainly it is not mysticism. It is obvious, demonstrable scientific fact, to be verified under the microscope and within the human psyche, subjectively and objectively, both. (242−3)

In *Beyond the Pleasure Principle*, Freud makes a good deal of Weismann's distinction between the mortal 'soma', or body in the narrower sense, and the potentially immortal germ-cells (*Das Kleimplasma*), seeing in it a 'dynamic corollary' of his own division between sexual and death instincts. (It was partly because Weismann thought that the distinction did not extend to unicellular organisms that Freud was so interested in work on the Protozoa.) Weismann's work on the germ-cells was well known in England.[5] If the faint echoes of it here ('germ-consciousness, consciousness germinating for ever') do nothing else, they reinforce the general impression of someone who intends on this occasion to be properly scientific ('objective'). The difficulty is that in *Psychoanalysis of the Unconscious* and more obviously in *Fantasia*, subjective and objective verification do not always coincide and that Lawrence's appeal in some places to the latter (conventional science) is compromised by his attacks on it in others. Appeal he often does nevertheless. Where in the developed foetus, he asks, shall we look for the 'creative-productive quick', 'the quick both of consciousness and of organic development'? 'Surely our own subjective wisdom tells us, what science can verify, that it lies beneath the navel of the folded foetus' (218). The distinction between the voluntary and sympathetic is first established, he claims, by a division in the original nucleus formed at conception and this 'as science knows, is a division of recoil' (35). When he comes to make his case against bi-sexuality, it is largely in objective terms. 'Every single living cell,' he says, enunciating what he clearly feels is a well-known scientific truth, 'is either male or female' (96). And as a previous quotation about the solar plexus shows, Lawrence feels that the importance he attributes to the body-centres must be all the more convincing because any text-book on anatomy will show the reader they exist.

★   ★   ★

We know from the letters that when Lawrence was pondering his biological psyche he asked Edith Eder if she could send him a book 'which describes the human nervous system, and gives a sort of map of the nerves of the human body? . . . Ask Jones or somebody'. She responded with some pages from a medical text-book which Lawrence found 'repulsive with diagnoses, and not very plain for me. — I wanted a book of physiology rather than medicine. But it managed'.[6] It can't have managed as well as Lawrence hoped when a commentator who is on the whole sympathetic to him, James C. Cowan, is able to describe the results of these researches as 'anatomical nonsense'. There are, Professor Cowan points out, two broad divisions in the nervous system: the central and peripheral. The peripheral system can be further divided into a voluntary part, mediating voluntary functions, and a part now called autonomic (sympathetic in Lawrence's day) which mediates those functions which are involuntary. 'Only two of Lawrence's dynamic centers, the solar or celiac plexus and the cardiac plexus can be located ana-tomically. There are no such single structures as *the* lumbar ganglion and *the* thoracic ganglion. The group structures, which are designated collectively as lumbar ganglia and thoracic ganglia, rather than assuming opposite functions from the plexuses, send their processes through these plexuses and have the same purpose of regulating functions of abdominal and thoracic viscera. All four of the structures which Lawrence proposes as primary affective centers are divisions of the autonomic nervous system'. It is therefore wrong, Professor Cowan says, to attribute to them the ability to originate impulses, consciousness or any of the 'more complex functions of personality' associated with the central nervous system (in the brain and spinal cord); and he concludes, 'In reifying his metaphor into literal fact, Lawrence burdens his four dynamic centers with more than these peripheral circuits can actually bear'.[7]

It is not surprising to discover that Lawrence was misinformed; as he says himself, he was after all 'an amateur of amateurs' (11). On many occasions moreover, there was no possibility of either him — or indeed Freud — getting the 'facts' completely right. The matters which concerned them both, the transmission of sense stimuli (for example) or the relation of the reception of those stimuli to mental consciousness, were, and still are, relatively obscure. Lawrence's awareness that this awkwardness could be used to his advantage is indirectly apparent in one of his many allusions in *Fantasia* to how Einstein's Theory of Relativity had altered people's thinking about the cosmos.

> The universe is once more in the mental melting-pot. And you can melt it down as long as you like, and mutter all the jargon and abracadabra, *aldeboronti fosco fornio* of science that mental monkey-tricks can teach you, you won't get anything in the end but a formula and a lie. The atom? Why, the moment you discover the atom it will explode under your nose. The moment you get down to the real basis of anything, it will dissolve into a thousand problematic constituents. And the more problems you solve, the more will spring up with their fingers at their nose, making a fool of you. (149−50)

No-one did more than Einstein, the philosophers and historians of science tell us, to undermine 19th century certitudes and prepare for a world in which, amongst many other changes, physical laws once regarded as immutable were discovered not to hold once the scale became very large or very small. Long before Thomas Kuhn, there were scientists who would have thought it naive to talk of 'the real basis' of things. But that this basis is so often illusory hardly absolves the serious enquirer from the effort to be as accurate as possible (problems are worth solving *precisely because* their solution leads to others); not does it abolish the distinctions between a professional and amateur acquaintance with the science of one's day — working on the frontiers and in the backyard. Freud knew most of what there was to know in his time about the nervous system. Like

Lawrence, he was nevertheless moving in a general area of enquiry where knowledge was quite peculiarly and self-evidently provisional so that, in his metapsychology, the trustworthiness of anatomical or biological data is in the end likely to be a less reliable criterion of value than inner coherence. We care less that the information conveyed to us in *Beyond the Pleasure Principle* should be correct than that the theory of instincts offered in that book should be coherent enough to serve as a useful model.

Because Lawrence was far less knowledgable than Freud, this is even more the case with *Psychoanalysis and the Unconscious* and *Fantasia*. That is to say that if Lawrence's readers decide that they often have to treat the biological psyche as a manner of speaking, then at least they must feel it makes good sense in its own terms and can therefore serve effectively as a metaphor for how the mind works. The particular circumstances in which they make that decision will of course vary a good deal but what is important, it seems to me, is that it should never be easy, *a priori* or automatic (not all the scientific information Lawrence offers is wrong). Professor Cowan does Lawrence a dubious kindness when he accuses him of 'reifying his metaphor into literal fact'. The truth is rather that Lawrence meant his body centres to be taken literally and it is his readers who, when they discover (or immediately recognize) that the facts concerned are wrong, transform them into metaphors: it is they who, in this or that particular instance, choose no longer to attend to the difficult and often confusing distinction he either makes or (more usually) implies between science as metaphor and verifiable truth. That attention is vital for anyone with a concern for either Lawrence's intentions or an accurate characterization of the psychology books. But at a second stage of response, there is the realization that Lawrence had no alternative but to be wrong, more or less (the degree and kind of error matters very much to those not content to lean back and mutter condescendingly, 'What can you expect?'); and that it is finally less damaging to show that his plexuses and ganglia do not conform to what we know of the human nervous system, or even to what was known in his day, than it would be to demonstrate he can be self-contradictory or confusing on matters which are important.

Considering its intricacy, there is a remarkably high degree of consistency in Lawrence's system. The divisions on each side of his vertical line are clear. If difficulties arise, it is likely to be with the horizontal divisions, and especially with the distinctions Lawrence tries to draw between the first 'plane' and the second. This is partly because he chooses to call these planes areas of subjective and objective knowledge respectively. The result is both coherent and thought-provoking when he is dealing with the two body-centres in the lower and upper back (the lumbar and thoracic ganglia). When a child asserts its independence from the lumbar ganglion, Lawrence says, it has a subjective awareness of self but no realisation of what that self is distinguished from. 'It has no objective consciousness of that from which it reacts, the mother principally. It is like a swimmer endlessly kicking the water away behind him, with strong legs vividly active from the spinal ganglia' (226). In assertion from the thoracic ganglia, on the other hand, awareness of self is accompanied or indeed established by contradistinction with what in the world is other.

> Curious indeed is the look on the face of the Holy Child, in Leonardo's pictures, in Botticelli's, even in the beautiful Filippo Lippi. It is the Mother who crosses her hands on her breast, in supreme acquiescence, recipient; it is the Child who gazes, with a kind of *objective*, strangely discerning, deep apprehension of her, startling to northern eyes. It is a gaze by no means of innocence, but of profound, pre-visual discerning. So plainly is the child looking across the gulf, and *fixing* the gulf by very intentness of pre-visual apprehension, that instinctively the ordinary northerner finds him antipathetic. It seems almost a cruel objectivity. (238)

A good many of Lawrence's illustrations in the psychology books are taken from art. Like this one, they show how intently he looked at pictures and how stimulatingly original his responses could be. The activity he ascribes to the child here is recognizable as one he elsewhere associates with artists themselves — artists of a certain kind. One thinks of Winifred Crich drawing her dog or Gudrun observing the wedding guests at the opening of *Women in Love* — settling them for ever as they pass before her along the path to the church. The two examples confirm that for Lawrence objective knowing from the thoracic ganglion is a source of power, and also therefore of potential cruelty. Which is partly why he insists in *Psychoanalysis and the*

Unconscious that 'there must be the twofold passional circuit of separatist realization, the lower, vital self-realization and the upper, intense realization of the other, a realization which includes a recognition of abysmal *otherness*. To stress any one mode, any one interchange, is to hinder all, and to cause corruption in the end' (240–1). This is the ideal of balance, equilibrium or harmony which dominates the earlier book.

The differences Lawrence establishes between subjective and objective knowledge in the voluntary mode are thought-provoking enough for the fact that the thoracic ganglia do not function as he thinks they do to seem relatively unimportant. His anatomy, or perhaps more strictly, physiology may be mistaken but it helps to make clear and memorable a valuable psychological distinction. On the 'sympathetic' side (or rather front) things are more problematic. On the whole, Lawrence sees the function of the solar plexus as assimilative: drawing in the outside world so that the child's subjective knowledge of that world becomes indistinguishable from knowledge of itself. From the cardiac plexus, there is in contrast a going-out towards discovery of the other. 'From the cardiac plexus the child goes forth in bliss. It seeks the revelation of the unknown. It wonderingly seeks the mother. It opens its small hands and spreads its small fingers to touch her. And bliss, bliss, bliss, it meets the wonder in mid-air and in mid-space it finds the loveliness of the mother's face' (39). It is not only children in pictures that Lawrence had looked at intently. The sentences are from *Fantasia*, but in both the psychology books he sees the eventual aim of the child's efforts here as leading to union with the mother, being 'added on to her' (40). In the earlier work, he describes the activity of the cardiac plexus in terms of 'a streaming forth of the self in blissful departure', a 'perfect surpassing of all sense of division between the self and the beloved', or 'the sheer and unspeakable bliss of the sense of union, communion, at oneness with the beloved' (237–9). He recognizes that if the cardiac plexus were alone active, the self would lose its integrity — 'it would pass out and merge with the beloved' — and that therefore this centre needs to be held in balance by the thoracic ganglion. But it is not at all clear how this balancing act is to be achieved, nor why Lawrence should persist in calling the cardiac plexus a centre of knowledge when it continually involves the search for self-forgetfulness.

The terms he uses suggest rather that its activity is a complement to the assimilative functions of the solar plexus: losing
oneself in the world rather than incorporating the world in
oneself; and that the consequent striving for oblivion could have
nothing to do with knowledge, of the 'objective' kind at least.

Both the psychology books challenge their readers to distinguish the metaphorical from what is meant to be taken literally.
Fairness to Lawrence's meaning makes this distinction important, as does the need to resist the illegitimate persuasive power
generated by its absence (without it, the prestige of science
supports what are no more than speculations). On the many
occasions when Lawrence's intention to present scientific facts
can be identified clearly, they often prove to be wrong. I have
suggested that in recognizing this, readers should also acknowledge that there was frequently no alternative to error, and that
accuracy of information is consequently a less reasonable
expectation of a system like Lawrence's than self-consistency.
The example I have just offered of that expectation being
disappointed is more an exception than the rule and needs, in
any case, to be considered in relation to the extraordinary
ambition of Lawrence's aims in the psychology books. To an
extent the significance of which has never perhaps been wholly
appreciated, Lawrence was, if not completely incapable of
remaining content with half knowledge and being in uncertainties, then at least very far indeed from the Keatsean ideal of
negative capability. Believing, in the formulation he attributes
to Birkin, that it all hangs together 'in the deepest sense', he
had an unusually strong inclination to discover quite how
everything was connected. The all-inclusiveness of his aim in
Fantasia is bound to produce inconsistencies, although their
occasional presence in that book, and its predecessor, cannot
always be explained by ambition. At times, there are other,
more significant factors at work. If one of these deserves
whatever special emphasis one can hope attaches itself to
concluding remarks, it is because its relevance extends well
beyond the psychology books to the whole of Lawrence's work.

The commonest observation made about Lawrence's thinking
is that he is an inveterate dualist whose strongest instinct is to
pit one term or quality against another. The truth of this has led
many critics to talk of Lawrence's 'dialectic' when it is
everywhere evident how difficult he found it to initiate a

movement of thought which deserves that name. His 'syntheses' are frequently weak, unconvincing or simply non-existent. This can be illustrated in an impressive passage in the third chapter of *Psychoanalysis and the Unconscious* where Lawrence is attempting to describe the experience of the baby at the breast.

> The powerful, active psychic centre in a new child is the great solar plexus of the sympathetic system. From this centre the child is drawn to the mother again, crying, to heal the new wound, to re-establish the old oneness. This centre directs the little mouth which, blind and anticipatory, seeks the breast. How could it find the breast, blind and mindless little mouth? But it needs no eyes nor mind. From the great first mind of the abdomen it moves direct, with an anterior knowledge almost like magnetic propulsion, as if the little mouth were drawn or propelled to the maternal breast by vital magnetism, whose centre of directive control lies in the solar plexus.
>
> In a measure, this taking of the breast reinstates the old connection with the parent body. It is a strange sinking back to the old unison, the old organic continuum — a recovery of the pre-natal state. But at the same time it is a deep, avid gratification in drinking-in the sustenance of a new individuality. It is a deep gratification in the exertion of a new voluntary power. The child acts now separately from its own individual centre and exerts still a control over the adjacent universe, the parent body. (220)

The solar plexus, Professor Cowan reminds us, does not have any of the attributes of what would ordinarily be called consciousness; but by evoking so vividly the new-born baby's ability to take the breast (the effect of which is to make observers feel that, from the start, it 'knows what it's doing') Lawrence makes it very clear what, in this instance, he could mean by the 'first mind of the abdomen'. The first of its activities he describes is not at all assimilative but rather the basis or primitive forerunner of the 'streaming forth of self' he associates with the cardiac plexus. In Freudian terms, it is the most obvious form of 'regression' and the feelings supposedly derived from it are known as 'Oceanic'. One might have expected Lawrence to contrast this first activity with the solar plexus in its assimilative function but the reference to 'the exertion of a new voluntary power' suggests instead what is in this context a slightly premature intrusion of the lumbar ganglion.

More important here than this minor inconsistency is the difficulty raised by the phrase 'But at the same time' in the second paragraph. How can the two activities described in the passage as a whole go on simultaneously? For all his quarrels with Freud, Lawrence is often very close to him and particularly in his assumption that what happens between mother and child has a determining effect on the child's later contacts with others. This makes it legitimate to take the use of 'at the same time' as an involuntary indication of what — the fiction shows — is the chief dilemma of human relations for Lawrence: the problem which preoccupies his characters more often and more persistently than any other. The nature of the dilemma becomes clearer as he expands on the role of the solar plexus shortly after the passage I have quoted.

> The flux between mother and child is not all sweet unison. There is as well the continually widening gap. A wonderful rich communion, and at the same time a continually increasing cleavage. If only we could realize that all through life these are the two synchronizing activities of love, of creativity. For the end, the goal, is the perfecting of each single individuality, unique in itself — which cannot take place without a perfected harmony between the beloved, a harmony which depends on the at-last-clarified singleness of each being, a singleness equilibrized, polarized in one by the counter-posing singleness of the other. (221–2)

The problem of 'at the same time' is now dramatised by a hint of logical inconsequence in the last sentence. The aim of life is perfect individuality but that can only be achieved through love relationships whose harmony depends on each partner having an 'at-last-clarified singleness'. Emphasis on the difference between singleness and individuality will save this sentence from absurdity, but in context it nevertheless carries the strong implication that individuality is achieved through relationships in which the participants are already individuals. If that is so, it will seem no wonder that Birkin should find life so hard; and that his other 'way of freedom', whereby the soul 'never forfeits its own proud individual singleness, even while it loves and yields',[8] should so often appear to manifest itself in a restless alternation between wanting to associate with a woman and striving to retain his independence. He is of course by no means the only male character in Lawrence who is anxious to square this particular circle.

> 'I don't care', said Lilly. 'I'm learning to possess my soul in patience and in peace, and I know it. And it isn't a negative Nirvana either. And if Tanny possesses her own soul in patience and peace as well — and if in this we understand each other at last — then there we are, together and apart at the same time, and free of each other, and eternally inseparable. I have my Nirvana — and I have it all to myself. But more than that. It coincides with her Nirvana.'
>
> 'Ah yes,' said Aaron, 'But I don't understand all that word-splitting.'
>
> 'I do though. You learn to be quite alone, and possess your own soul in isolation — and at the same time, to be perfectly *with* someone else — that's all I ask.'
>
> 'Sort of sit on a mountain top, back to back with somebody else, like a couple of idols.'
>
> 'No — because it isn't a case of sitting — or a case of back to back. It's what you get to after a lot of fighting and a lot of sensual fulfilment. And it never does away with the fighting and the sensual passion. It flowers on top of them, and it would never flower save on top of them.'
>
> 'What wouldn't?'
>
> 'The possessing one's own soul — and the being together with someone else in silence, beyond speech.'
>
> 'And you've got them?' [9]

The encouragement to trace back to childhood this effort to conceive being, 'together and apart at the same time', comes from Lawrence rather than Freud. As *Aaron's Rod* develops, it is not Lilly but Aaron himself who is shown trying to discover what the effort means in practice. The consequences justify the scepticism of his last question ('And you've got them?'), just as Ursula's scepticism about Birkin's 'other way of freedom' might be said to be largely justified by what happens to him. But in both cases the novel form makes for a complex effect. Novelists are not committed to making the same kind of 'sense' as the authors of discursive works and, at the very least, dramatization allows one in this instance to appreciate as an agonizing human dilemma what tends to be present in the psychology books as little more than logical contradiction. Their evident purpose is to present a 'system', but the coherence of that system momentarily breaks down when two contradictory processes are described as operating simultaneously. The result is a temporary obstacle to the recognition that what may not be scientifically valid can nevertheless serve as a valuable description of experience, for how can what remains obscure be properly measured against one's own sense of life and feeling for probabilities? This is a more significant matter than errors of fact, partly because Lawrence's authority derives far less from what he knows than from what he has observed, felt and understood; but it is also a reminder that his dualism can sometimes lead nowhere. Like Blake or like the Heraclitus he first discovered in Burnet's *Early Greek Philosophy*, Lawrence was fond of insisting on the truth that there is no life without conflict; but there are occasions when some reconciling factor or synthesis is essential to prevent conflict becoming sterile: to escape a continual and frustrating restatement in different terms of the same two, irreconcilable opposites.

Any close attentive look at the various models of the mind's workings which Freud elaborated during his career will suggest that the inconsistencies in Lawrence's biological psyche are par for the course. But Freud was too well-informed for his elaborations to include information in obvious conflict with contemporary scientific knowledge, or even many details destined to be contradicted by future research. He also knew too much to claim (explicitly at least) that what he was offering were anything other than 'models'. Unlike Lawrence, he was aware of quite why the happy day when general descriptions of biological and psychological phenomena would perfectly coincide was such a long way off. Although there are many others, these differences would alone be sufficient to explain how it is that one is so much more likely to hear of someone that his ego needs reinforcement than that he is suffering from . . . an under-stimulated lumbar ganglion. These expressions are of course only very vaguely equivalent. The terms and models which Freud so successfully made current have a specificity which, at the very lowest level of interpretation, derives from their being the product of a specific intellectual ethos and a very particular, highly rationalistic temperament. That is one of their strengths but it also means that they may fail to comprehend all that one might want to mean by 'mind' and need to be complemented or challenged by the terms and models of men whose training, experience and gifts were different. If I have failed to be convincing about any other, here is at least one immediately clear reason why it would be just as much an error to make the patent scientific inaccuracies in the biological psyche an excuse for dismissing it out of hand as it would be to suppose that Lawrence's genius in fiction provides him with a guarantee of infallibility in psychology.

Notes

1   The page references, here and throughout my text, are to the edition of *Fantasia of the Unconscious* and *Psychoanalysis and the Unconscious* published by Penguin (Harmondsworth, 1971). I use this edition reluctantly and because it is the only one widely available in the UK. An article at least as long as this present one could be written on its inadequacies. Many of these were no doubt unavoidable but it was perverse to add to them by printing Lawrence's earlier and shorter text (*Psychoanalysis and the Unconscious*) after and as a kind of addendum or postscript to *Fantasia*.
2   See *The Symbolic Meaning*, ed. A. Arnold (Arundel, 1961), p. 135.
3   See James M. Pryse, *The Apocalypse Unsealed* (1910). This curiosity includes on p. 17 a cross-section of the human torso with its seven principal ganglia or 'chakras'. It may well be therefore that Lawrence first got the idea of his body-centres from Pryse but, if so, it is worth noting that his own are very different (he made a considerable effort to ensure that they were properly scientific).
4   See the Standard Edition of Freud's *Complete Psychological Works*, vol. XVIII (1964), pp. 55–6. The page references following my subsequent quotations from *Beyond the Pleasure Principle* are to this edition. The reference in this quotation to the English analyst Barbara Low, who was a close friend of Lawrence and the probable source of much of what he knew about Freud, is accidental.
5   See Peter Morton, *The Vital Science. Biology and the Literary Imagination* (1984).
6   See *The Letters of D.H. Lawrence*, ed. J.T. Boulton & A. Robertson (Cambridge, 1984), iii 243; 245. The Jones Lawrence refers to here is the future biographer of Freud.
7   See the section on the psychology books in James Cowan's *D.H. Lawrence's American Journey* (Cleveland, 1970), p. 20.
8   *Women in Love* (Harmondsworth, 1982), pp. 331–2.
9   *Aaron's Rod* (Harmondsworth, 1968), p. 128.

'Raptus Virginis':
The Dark God in the Poetry of D.H. Lawrence

CHRISTOPHER POLLNITZ

*The subject requires that I should narrate
the rape of the Virgin.*[1]

In Aphorism 51 of *The Joyful Wisdom* Nietzsche declared against the search for ultimate truth and in favour of 'truthfulness' or experiment in his philosophy:

> I favour any *skepsis* to which I may reply: 'Let us try it!' But I no longer wish to hear anything of all those things and questions that do not permit any experiment.[2]

For five years from 1913 to 1917 Lawrence made repeated efforts to write his 'philosophy' in its 'final form' (BL III, 163).[3] But in the twenties he abandoned writing 'philosophies' and created instead an organizing myth, the myth of an unknown or dark god. I shall argue in this paper that the myth partly originated in Lawrence's reading of Nietzsche; and more contentiously I shall argue that the shift from his 'philosophy' to his myth was a shift in Lawrence's thinking towards Nietzschean scepticism and relativism.

Lawrence himself, as well as Lawrence scholars who have been, in previous decades, more eager than most to find moral imperatives in literature, has furnished reasons for finding his myth more simply affirmative than it is. In *Studies in Classic American Literature*, for instance, Lawrence sets out his myth as so many items of a personal faith:

'That my soul is a dark forest.'
'That my known self will never be more than a little clearing in the forest.'

111

'That gods, strange gods, come forth from the forest into the clearing of my known self, and then go back.'

There is my creed. (*SCAL* 22)

This is not an unusual tone in Lawrence's prose, a tone of moral urgency in which there is no scepticism to detect. But the passive creed of the *Studies* makes way in *Mornings in Mexico* for a ritual reaching out to cosmic energies, and becomes in *Etruscan Places* a myth of descent and revitalization. The myth of the dark god itself undergoes deaths and resurrections. I shall dispense in this paper with a definition of myth and of literary myth, partly because my aim is description rather than theory, and partly because Lawrence's myth, which draws on classical mythology, unifies disparate experiences by reference to a quasi-divine narrative and is enunciated for the most part as a matter of mystic apprehension, is immediately recognizable as a literary myth. But it should be said that his myth of the dark god is unlike at least some forms of traditional myth in Lawrence's continuous recreation of it. Lawrence's scepticism reveals itself in his ceaseless revisions of the myth. Any one version has the same status as any one aphorism of Nietzsche's: it is 'a preliminary standpoint for experiment, or a regulative fiction' (*JW* Sect. 344).

My paper is concerned to identify some of the materials Lawrence used in his bricolage. Nietzsche provided some of these, as has been mentioned, but the extent of Lawrence's reading of Nietzsche is unclear. Lawrence spoke to Jessie Chambers about the Will to Power in 1908;[4] he referred Koteliansky to one of Nietzsche's parables from *Thus Spake Zarathustra* (*BL* II, 546); and writing to Bertrand Russell in 1915, he gave the current title of his philosophy as *Le Gai Savaire*, a pun on Nietzsche's *Die Fröhliche Wissenschaft* (*BL* II, 295, 300). But punning on the book's title is hardly evidence that Lawrence had mastered this, the central volume of Nietzsche's oeuvre;[5] and in the case of other works like *Metamorphoses*, to which there may be an allusion in *Birds, Beasts and Flowers*, there is even less evidence of familiarity with the author. Lawrence may have called his second volume of poetry *Amores*, but his only other reference to Ovid is a commonplace, to the Thracian exile (*BL* III, 242; *LG* 314). My approach to possible sources in this paper is experimental.

In proposing them I shall ask only the indulgence Nietzsche
allowed to his questions: I shall ask, 'Let us try them!' But my
conviction, having tried *The Joyful Wisdom*, is that the work is
one of a handful, like Pryse's *The Apocalypse Unsealed* and
Burnet's *Early Greek Philosophy*, which exerted a permanent
influence on Lawrence's creative thinking.

★   ★   ★

Tom Marshall's observation on Lawrence's 'Pomegranate' (*CP*
278), that it begins with a gesture of Whitmanesque self-
assertion by the poet, and Sandra Gilbert's comment, that it
continues as a Browningesque dramatic monologue, are the two
best insights available on the poem.[6] There has been little
discussion of its twenty-nine lines as an introduction to the
themes and symbolic patterns of *Birds, Beasts and Flowers*.
Monologues create the character of an auditor as well as
speaker, and, particularly in conjunction with 'Peach', the
auditor of 'Pomegranate' makes an impression of being female.
The truculent opening lines of 'Pomegranate' therefore introduce *ab ovo* the theme of sexual antagonism. Monologues also
teach scepticism towards their speakers. This speaker's
Whitmanesque assurance, that 'what I assume you shall
assume,'[7] is called in question by the hypothesis of a listener
who is actively assuming the contrary. By mid-poem the
dogmatic speaker of the first lines has dwindled, it seems, to a
player in a social comedy who is arguing about his itinerary,
about where and when on his Italian tour he has seen
pomegranates. But in the last ten lines the speaker's questioning
of his auditor's preconceptions leads to sudden symbolic
dilations which restore the speaker's claims to significant
knowledge. In the arcane poem within 'Pomegranate' the
speaker lays claim to an ancient knowledge, the knowledge of
an initiate. Yet having been placed in a sceptical posture we, as
readers, are asked to try this claim before accepting it.

The knowledge the speaker claims not to be wrong about is a
knowledge of natural process, of the pomegranate's flowering,
the setting of the fruit and the fruit's maturation. The
knowledge extends by association to historical process, since
each phase of this fruition is linked to a site and period, to

ancient Greek Syracuse, to medieval Venice and to the countryside around Renaissance Florence. This neat historical progression is upset, if the Etruscan past of this last area is given its due weight; but the associations of regal maleness, able to confer life, remain. To trace this line of royal largesse, it is best to begin where 'Pomegranate' begins, in Sicily 'When Athens' army fell at Syracuse.'[8] The line, 'In Syracuse, rock left bare by the viciousness of Greek women,' is a key to the poem's arcane meanings.

Lawrence visited Syracuse twice, in April and May of 1920, and gave some account of his visits in the 'Introduction to *Memoirs of the Foreign Legion*' (*PII* 328, 343–46). A postcard to his sister Ada describes the latomies or stone-quarries of the Syracusan mainland as 'a wonderful place,' 'in which the Athenian youths died so horribly' (*BL* III, 509). Lawrence had read Thucydides with enthusiasm in 1916 (*BL* II, 592). The climax of Thucydides' *History* comes in Book VII, with the internment of the Athenian prisoners-of-war in a latomy. Crowded 'in a deep and narrow place' and 'afflicted by hunger and thirst,' they suffered not only their own wounds but the stench of their dead who 'lay heaped one upon another.' 'Of all the Hellenic actions which took place in this war,' Thucydides grimly concludes, 'this was the greatest.'[9] The card Lawrence sent his sister was of the *Latomia de' Cappuccini*, which George Dennis considered the latomy most likely to have served as the Athenians' dungeon, being 'the largest and most picturesque.' It was 'planted with oranges, pomegranates and cypresses.'[10] Lawrence must have been struck with the pomegranate-trees in the latomy ('Oh so red, and such a lot of them') and have seen in their red flowers an image for the prisoners' maimed bodies, for in *The Lost Girl* he reverts to the scene in order to evoke the overcivilized, heavy look of the pregnant Mrs Tuke. Her head is 'like a head on one of the lovely Syracusan coins' and her eyes have

> the dangerous Greek look of the Syracusan women of the past: the dangerous, heavily-civilized women of old Sicily: those who laughed above the latomia. (*LG* 274)

Although Syracusan coins, a new issue of which celebrated the victory over Athens,[11] explain Lawrence's sense of the beauty and sophistication of the women of Syracuse, it is hard to account for this tale of their malicious pleasure in conquest. The story is not in Thucydides; possibly it is a local tradition. What can be ascertained, as presiding over this initiation of the cycle of natural and historical process, is some form of sexual antagonism. The line unlocks an image of female triumph over a male humiliation and wounding, as if, lurking among the pomegranate-trees of Syracuse, the speaker had caught a glimpse of the Magna Mater.

In 'America, Listen to Your Own' Lawrence takes Venice to epitomize the decadence of modern Europe, though he also hearkens back to a time when, 'wedded [to] the Adriatic,' the city-state had had the potency to outrank every other Mediterranean power (*P* 91). Lawrence's historiography is akin to Ruskin's, for whom Venice rose under the rule of the doges and fell as they were displaced:

> For six hundred years, during which the power of Venice was continually on the increase, her government was an elective monarchy, her King or doge possessing, in early times at least, as much independent authority as any other European sovereign, but an authority gradually subjected to limitation, and shortened almost daily of its prerogatives, while it increased in a spectral and incapable magnificence. The final government of the nobles, under the image of a king, lasted for five hundred years, during which Venice reaped the fruits of her former energies, consumed them, — and expired.[12]

Although Ruskin describes an effigy of Doge Tomaso Mocenigo, whose 'pure and lordly' features are 'gathered in sharp folds,'[13] it is unclear what visual representation lies behind Lawrence's characterization of the doges' 'ancient eyes.' What is clearer is that their eyes were wrinkled with some hard-won secret of power a youthful Venice once knew. What the Etruscan past of Florence meant to Lawrence in 1920 will be discussed at greater length in an analysis of 'Cypresses.' It will become more apparent then why Lawrence thought of the Tuscan countryside as the cradle of a peculiarly powerful male civilization, able to bring forth in its later Renaissance days supreme expressions of maleness like Michelangelo's David. This 'kingly, generous' fruition need not refer only to political dominance, but may include that 'self-sufficiency which has superabundance, and imparts to all men and things' (*JW* Sect. 55), which Nietzsche thought of as indispensable to great art.

There is an outstanding difficulty in the key line. The triumph of the Syracusan women over the Athenian captives is evidence of their viciousness, but how did it make a 'rock left bare' of Syracuse? Let us take George Dennis's *Handbook for Travellers in Sicily* with us and cross the mole from Syracuse to Ortygia. There, on the west side of the port, we shall light upon a brackish pool 'lined with masonry' and 'encircled with papyrus.'[14] This pool, the fountain of Arethusa, is Syracuse's link with the world of Greek mythology; for Artemis transformed the nymph Arethusa, as she fled from the river-god Alpheus in Achaea, into a stream of water that flowed underground and undersea, till it broke surface again as a freshwater spring in Ortygia. Ovid has the best telling of the myth in his *Metamorphoses*. Book v of the *Metamorphoses* is a comedy of the sexual manners and duels of the classical hierarchy, a comedy only resolved by Jove's decision that Pluto's rape of Proserpine did no real harm. In the present context the importance of Ovid's retelling is that he intertwines the rape of Arethusa with the rape of Proserpine. Arethusa has seen Proserpine being carried off to the underworld, and has reported the abduction to Ceres. Ceres revenges herself on Sicily, which has permitted the rape, by blighting its fields:

> she reproached all lands, calling them ungrateful and unworthy of the gift of corn; but Sicily above all other lands, where she had found traces of her loss. So there with angry hand she broke in pieces the plows that turn the glebe, and in her rage she gave to destruction farmers and cattle alike, and bade the plowed fields to betray their trust, and blighted the seed. The fertility of this land, famous throughout the world, lay false to its good name . . .[15]

'The viciousness of Greek women,' which reduced Sicily to infertility and Syracuse to a bare rock, may therefore have been their withholding of themelves from the fertilizing passion of the dark god. Just as the auditor of 'Pomegranate' denies the speaker his knowledge of process, the reluctance of Greek women (Proserpine, Arethusa and Ceres) has robbed the male principle of its prerogative and turned the heart into a stone.

Even if it were certain the auditor of 'Pomegranate' is female, the speaker's quarrel with her would not be entirely sexist. We have all, the speaker's questions admit, a virginal reluctance to give ourselves up to that self-loss and renewal which might be called 'raptus virginis,' possession by the dark god. Yet only by giving ourselves to becoming, as the pomegranate and the setting sun do, can we realize our potential. Lawrence's symbolism and syntax echo Nietzsche's in *The Joyful Wisdom*:

> Why has nature been so niggardly towards humanity that she has not let human beings shine . . . according to their inner abundance of light? Why have not great men such a fine visibility in their rising and setting as the sun? (*JW* Sect. 336)

Nietzsche goes on to prophesy a new breed of solar aristocrat, one who will possess a historical sense that will enable him 'to regard the history of man in its entirety as *his own history*.' Despite doubt and suffering he will enter the battle of existence greeting 'the dawn and his happiness.' He will be capable of a happiness 'which, like the sun in the evening, continually gives of its inexhaustible riches' (*JW* Sect. 337). To a degree this type of humanity is being realized in the speaker of 'Pomegranate'. He sees the death of the Athenians and the cunning of the doges as part of his affective processes. He gives himself to a petty quarrel aware of its part in a larger, arcane pattern. He lies down in the heart, conscious that even this small shake-up might show something new in its dawn-kaleidoscope.

Pluto was permitted to keep Proserpine part of the year because of the pomegranate-seeds cunningly fed her by Ascalaphus. This is one of a number of mythological allusions which haunt about the shape of Lawrence's 'Pomegranate'. The description of the fruit's 'gold-filmed skin' as 'ruptured' may recall that the pomegranate was sacred to Dionysus, a fact Lawrence would have gleaned from *The Golden Bough*.[16] His image therefore refers to Dionysus' dismemberment at the hands of the Titans. Robert Graves believes the fruit was connected with Dionysus because of the wound-like appearance of the red seeds in the fissure.[17] Removed from their historical context, the wounded Athenian youths also become types of the dying god, giving their lives to the triumphant Magna Mater in order to ensure continuance of the life-cycle. If the focus is widened to take in all of *Birds, Beasts and Flowers*, it will be seen that 'Pomegranate' introduces a mythic cycle similar to Graves's 'one story' of the White Goddess.[18] Other parts of the cycle are delineated by other poems in the volume. The male principle, which does combat with the Goddess, is hypostasized as the dark god. Rape and dismemberment are, at least in a psychic sense, needed to ensure the cycle. The combat between god and goddess is more even-handed than in Graves's myth: if anything, the male principle is superior to the female.

Lawrence's cycle begins with the wounding and breaking up of the old identity. There may follow a period of descent through stages of dissolution towards oblivion, but out of the descent a new identity emerges and matures through various phases, each of which may also involve some self-loss and restoration. So fulfilled, the male self is confident in its sexual dominance, but it may also harden in this role and lose the capacity for change. A reversal of sex roles is possible: the stony ego which cannot be torn open by the female principle may be cloven by the male. The sequence of events is most fully articulated in *Tortoises*, but no poem in *Birds, Beasts and Flowers* exhibits all its phases. A similar apocalyptic cycle is worked out by the major characters in *The Rainbow*, Ursula Brangwen even coming to understand something of the stages her experience passes through. But it is a mark of Lawrence's avoidance of 'final forms' in the twenties that he leaves the mythic cycle of *Birds, Beasts and Flowers* to be reconstructed in full by the reader.

It is the recurrent imagery of the volume that brings the fragments of the cycle into brilliant focus. This is especially notable in that phase of the cycle, often abridged to omit dissolution, when 'The end cracks open with the beginning.' It is then that the iron boughs of the almond tree yield, as if crucified, their 'dawn-hearted' 'sore-hearted-looking' blossoms; then that the baby tortoise's 'little mountain front' gapes open to reveal its 'soft red tongue' and mouth, the mouth that will cry in its maturity; then that the earth itself breaks open to reveal a new being, the 'Brilliant, intolerable lava . . . Walking like a royal snake down the mountain towards the sea' (*CP* 304–6, 353, 293). The birth of the new form is often volcanic, serpentine or phallic, as when the fig-tree puts forth a Dionysian branch 'issued sideways from the thigh of his predecessor' (*CP* 299). There are new selves like the cyclamens with 'their rosy muzzles' or the 'tiny, fragile, half-animate bean' of the tortoise; tired egos longing to burst free, like the figs or like the bull in 'St Luke'; and in 'Peach' there is the self as billiard-ball, totally rational and unrenewable (*CP* 311, 352, 279). The dark god who presides over and suffers through the cycle is named as Pluto, Dionysus, Ulysses, Osiris, Christ; but despite his protean forms, we often glimpse him in the same setting, among the uprights of trees. He is in the 'flickering men of Etruria' in their cypress-groves; is an American *genius loci*, slipping through an 'industrial thicket' 'of many-stemmed machines and chimneys that smoke like pine-trees'; is blind Samson moving among those pillars of Western technological civilization which he will bring tumbling about him before he dies (*CP* 297, 293, 287−89). To resist change when it comes to the self, to a civilization or to the earth, is to make that change the more destructive: to restrain this volcanic cycle is like trying to plug a volcano. The god will break forth, as the stranger imprisoned in Pentheus' house broke forth, in a form the more violently eruptive for being suppressed.[19]

★   ★   ★

The principal contributions to defining Lawrence's myth of the dark god have been George Ford's chapter in *Double Measure* on 'The "S" Curve: Persephone to Pluto' and Patricia Merivale's chapter on Lawrence in *Pan the Goat-God*.[20] Ford's coal-darkened, subterranean rapist, who steals his virgin from the upper world, has provided an enduring insight into Lawrence's internal biography. Merivale's book, which shows Lawrence's modernist Pan developing out of and reacting against Victorian and Edwardian versions, has been the forerunner of other studies placing Lawrence's fiction in relation to these periods. But neither of these critical approaches has allowed Lawrence's myth its metaphysical scope, its capacity, particularly in Lawrence's poetry, to consider in a single symbolic phrase a multiplicity of experience. Again, although Lawrence's dark god is sometimes a haunter of the underground, sometimes of the woods, sometimes he is both, and needs as well the attributes of a dying god. Periodically Lawrence himself grew averse to naming, as gods, the shifting pluralities of religious experience. His knowledge of classical mythology was enriched by what he came to learn of other primitive religions like that of the Aztecs. But his dark god never lost a European outline, and the

Greek god whose characteristics best meet those required by Lawrence's myth is Dionysus.

Dionysus is not a rapist, but this hiatus in his myth is more than made up for by his rites, the *orgia*. And there is something peculiarly modern about the adoption of Dionysus as a god of the sexual libido: Dionysian characters who are destructive but in some degree liberating rapists are not confined to Lawrence's fiction in the twenties. In Katharine Susannah Prichard's novel of north-western Australia, *Coonardoo*, 'Dionysus' is no more than the name for a St. Mawr-like horse. The villain of the novel, Sam Geary, is a man who, like Jack Grant in *The Boy in the Bush*, models his sexual behaviour on the Old Testament patriarchs, though Geary offers his favours to the gins on his own and his neighbours' stations. But in Prichard's dramatization of *Coonardoo*, *Brumby Innes*, Sam Geary is transformed utterly into an almost admirable, sexually amoral protagonist. Innes's exploits among black women make him a Dionysus to the whites and a *narloo* to the aborigines, *narloos* being evil spirits whose barbed penes could 'stretch for miles underground to reach and hold unsuspecting women.'[21] Behind Lawrence and Prichard's dark rapists lurks a more recent manifestation of Dionysus than the Greeks or the Romans knew. Although Nietzsche has little to teach us about sex, there is no doubt that Dionysus reborn in his work is a god of sexual energy. Nietzsche beats a puritanical present with a pagan antiquity in *Twilight of the Idols*:

> To the Greeks, the symbol of sex was the most venerated of symbols, the really deep significance of all the piety of antiquity. All the details of the act of procreation, pregnancy and birth gave rise to the loftiest and most solemn feelings . . . All this is what the word Dionysus signifies . . . (*TI* 119)[22]

Nietzsche's Dionysus is the principal antecedent of Lawrence's dark god. This is not the Dionysus paired with Apollo in *The Birth of Tragedy* to make up a dialectical theory of tragic art, but the Dionysus who, from *The Joyful Wisdom* on, moves to centre stage as Nietzsche's tutelary deity of becoming and of life-affirmation:

> The word '*Dionysian*' expresses . . . an ecstatic saying of yea to the collective character of existence, as that which remains the same, and equally mighty and blissful throughout all change; the

great pantheistic sympathy with pleasure and pain, which declares
even the most terrible and questionable qualities of existence
good, and sanctifies them; the eternal will to procreation, to
fruitfulness, and to recurrence; the feeling of unity in regard to
the necessity of creating and annihilating. (*WP* Sect. 1050)[23]

Both Lawrence's and Nietzsche's Dionysus stand for acceptance
of the senses and sensuality, for the power of instinct and
the unconscious. Both are opposed to Western idealism and 'the
Crucified'; Nietzsche's attacks anticipate Lawrence's rhetoric in
his late essays: 'only Christianity . . . flung *filth* at the very
basis, the very first condition of our life' (*TI* 119). In a period of
social decay both see their god as embodying 'a desire for
destruction, for change, for Becoming' (*WP* Sect. 846). Old
patterns of belief must be swept away to make room for a new
humanity, and the creative power that fertilizes this development is also Dionysian:

> The being richest in overflowing vitality, the Dionysian God and
> man, may not only allow himself the spectacle of the horrible and
> questionable, but even the fearful deed itself, and all the luxury
> of destruction, disorganization and negation. With him evil,
> senselessness and ugliness seem as it were licensed, in conse-
> quence of the overflowing plenitude of procreative, fructifying
> power, which can convert every desert into a luxuriant orchard.
> (*JW* Sect. 370)

Dionysus is not only a power of social renovation. In *Beyond
Good and Evil* he is invoked as the 'genius of the heart' who
remakes affective selves, 'whose voice can descend into the
nether-world of every soul.' He is a genius

> from contact with which every one goes away . . . richer in
> himself, newer than before, broken up, blown upon, and sounded
> by a thawing wind; more uncertain perhaps, more delicate, more
> fragile, more bruised, but full of hopes which as yet lack
> names . . . [24]

Later translators, Hollingdale and Kaufmann, render the
German here not as 'broken up' but 'broken open' so that the
symbolism of the passage anticipates the cracking hearts and
worlds of Lawrence's cycle.

Differences should also be observed. Nietzsche's emphasis on
the need to affirm suffering is, on balance, greater than
Lawrence's. Sceptical about Greek pantheism and disgusted by

animism, Nietzsche allows nothing of the *genius loci* into his Dionysus. Correspondingly little of Nietzsche's proto-existentialism passes into Lawrence, who would seem to have been deaf to those passages which speak of the imposition of value:

> Whatever has *value* in the present world, has not it in itself, by its nature, — nature is always worthless: — but a value was once given to it, bestowed upon it and it was *we* who gave and bestowed! We only have created the world *which is of any account to man*! (*JW* Sect. 301)

Set this beside essays in which Lawrence speaks against anthropomorphism and in favour of equilibration by 'a new act of attention' with another living thing (*PII* 431–35; P 259), and it becomes evident that Lawrence's metaphysics remained more Romantic and epistemological than Nietzsche's. And more religious: Nietzsche, reducing his Dionysus to a philosophical term, could claim that he did 'not deify the unknown' (*WP* Sect. 1011); Lawrence wanted passionately to do precisely that, to remythologize an all too mechanistic universe. Accordingly, there is no eternal recurrence to confront in Lawrence's cycle:

> Nietzsche talks about the *Ewige Wiederkehr* . . . But each cycle is different. There is no real recurrence. (*P* 461)

Neither, it might be remarked, is there any of Nietzsche's stringency and élan in Lawrence's philosophical writing.

★   ★   ★

Further adumbrations of Lawrence's dark god can, happily, be found where Lawrence is demonstrating his élan, in *Birds, Beasts and Flowers*. 'Cypresses' (*CP* 296–98) shows how the dark god might inform a society, with the hints it gives about the 'great secret,' or lost religion, of the Etruscans. In 1921 Lawrence wrote to Catherine Carswell particularly asking '*what* . . . was the secret of the Etruscans, which you saw written so plainly in the place you went to?' (*ML* 669) But a year earlier he would seem to have solved the puzzle in 'Cypresses,' a poem whose procedures are themselves, however, of the nature of a puzzle. The hints and riddles of 'Cypresses,' while they cannot match the riddle of the Etruscans themselves, do require some deciphering.

In *Etruscan Places* Lawrence decided that one of the conundrums his poem had posed — 'Were they then vicious, the slender, tender-footed Long-nosed men of Etruria?' — could be dismissed as the propaganda of a rival city-state with imperial ambitions (*EP* 98, 111). But in 'Cypresses' the question can only be answered by asking what were the unmentioned vices, and who laid the charge. In 1926, when he began work on *Etruscan Places*, Lawrence confessed that all he had read was 'that old work,' George Dennis's *Cities and Cemeteries of Ancient Etruria*.[25] It appears Lawrence had read Dennis earlier, indeed before he wrote 'Cypresses' in September 1920,[26] because his information about the Roman and Greek aversion to the 'vicious' Etruscans derives from Dennis's guide. Lamenting that they have not been allowed to testify on their own behalf, Dennis lists the vices laid at the Etruscans' door:

> had it not been for their tombs, we should have known them only through the representations of the Greeks and Romans, which would give us a false and most unfavourable impression. For the Greeks describe them as pirates and robbers, or as effeminate debauchees; the Romans brand them as sluggards, gluttons and voluptuaries. Yet the former acknowledged their power at sea, their commercial importance, and their artistic skill; and the latter were forced to confess that to Etruria they owed most of their institutions and arts: still neither have paid that tribute to her civilization which we have now learned to be due . . .[27]

The Romans' opinion of the Etruscans is summed up in a passage from Virgil:

> slow ye are not to hear the call of love, or when the wry-necked fife gives the word for the Bacchic dance: ay, there is your passion, there your delight, till the favouring seer announce the sacrificial feast, and the fat victim invite you to the tall trees of the grove.[28]

The hint of rites among 'tall trees' is developed in 'Cypresses.' Living on his Taos ranch, Lawrence wrote of how he had 'become a degree more like unto the [pine-]tree' growing by his door, and how, because of his 'act of attention,' the pine had grown a shade more like him (*P* 25). The Etruscans' uncanny resemblance to the 'supple, brooding, softly-swaying pillars' of their groves has been brought about by a similar communion.

Moreover, because they once received the trees into their blood-consciousness, the secret of their blood-being has been 'wrapt inviolable in soft cypress-trees.' Though 'inviolable' the secret is accessible to any who approach the trees with something like the 'old thought' of the Etruscans. Foster-children 'of silence and slow time,' the 'darkly monumental' trees are Lawrence's Grecian urn, teasing us out of thought into connection with the lost civilization and the living universe. They are also, as we shall find, 'a friend to man.'

Another puzzle is the comparison of the Etruscans' mysticism with 'Africa's imperturbable sang-froid' and with the pre-conquest Mexico of Montezuma. Lawrence characterized Montezuma as 'a priest, a decadent and sensitive character . . . filled with mystic apprehension' and deeply attuned to the spirit of the American continent (*SM* 23–24). Behind the comparison lies Lawrence's conviction at this time — an item in a statement of faith Lawrence elected to call a *Fantasia* — that

> the great pagan world of which Egypt and Greece were the last living terms . . . had a vast and perhaps perfect science of its own, a science in terms of life. (*FU* 12)

The science was universal until, at the close of the last Ice Age, the land bridges sank and separated Aztec priest from Etruscan *lucomo*. Lying behind Lawrence's theory is the Theosophists' 'universal Wisdom-Religion' as propounded by Blavatsky in *Isis Unveiled*.[29] In 1920 the Etruscans mattered to Lawrence less in themselves than as representatives of what he took to be a universal antediluvian vitalism. The second piece in the puzzle is supplied by Leo Frobenius' *Voice of Africa*, an unscholarly memoir by a rogue German anthropologist whose 'fantasies' Rawdon Lilly enjoys reading in *Aaron's Rod* (134). As Daniel Schneider has shown, Frobenius was another believer in a 'high-toned philosophy, which once girdled the world, at its earliest dawn' but was dispersed with the sinking of Atlantis. The 'Yoruban philosophy' of West Africa was one remnant of this ancient tradition and 'must . . . have been coeval with the condition of ancient Etruscan civilization.' Yoruban social organization is centered around the Oro, 'a community of men' of whom Frobenius notes that they 'are much more strongly predisposed toward communion with their own sex, that is to say, the formation of the state, than women.'[30] It is a little hard to see the Oro for the trees in 'Cypresses,' but this is, no doubt, the social organization of the dark figures in the grove.

The hero of *Aaron's Rod* is also granted intimations of the Etruscan past by the cypresses outside Florence. After Rawdon Lilly has explained to him that Florence is a place where 'men for a moment were themselves' (*AR* 277), Aaron Sisson begins to comprehend the epiphanies of maleness he has received in Florence, from the Tuscan farmers, from the David and, above all, from the cypresses:

> He lay and watched tall cypresses breathing and communicating, faintly moving and as it were walking in the small wind. And his soul seemed to leave him and to go far away, far back, perhaps, to . . . lost races, lost language, lost human ways of feeling and of knowing . . . In the afternoon, Aaron felt the cypresses rising dark about him, like so many high visitants from an old, lost, lost subtle world, where men had the wonder of demons about them . . . (*AR* 309–10).

But what rites were practised by these demonish 'lost races'? How homosexual were their 'abominations'? The earlier, periodical version of 'Cypresses' included, between lines 55 and 56, a verse-paragraph missing from the English edition of *Birds, Beasts and Flowers*. The speaker asks what he would not do to bring back the 'Evil-yclept Etruscan':

> Among the cypresses
> To sit with pure, slim, long-nosed,
> Evil-called, sensitive Etruscans, naked except for their boots;
> To be able to smile back at them
> And exchange the lost kiss
> And come to dark connection. [31]

I do not know that this passage was bowdlerised by Lawrence's publisher, but I suspect it. Yet 'the lost kiss' the speaker longs for has the quality of a ritual gesture. Let us reconsider the notion that the 'act of attention' brings out likenesses in subject and object. The 'wavering' Etruscans and the swaying pillars of the cypresses are like each other, but each is even more like a third thing, the phallus. The 'marrow-thought' of the Etruscan religion would therefore have been a meditation focused not on the trees alone but on the male creative principle. What the Etruscan Oro practises is a kind of higher homosexuality through which the men gain power and pride, not necessarily from sexual contact with each other, but from identification with the male principle. Lawrence's poetic evocation of this community may be contrasted to his depiction of social relationships in the leadership novels, where the central idea seems always obscured and encumbered by the need to create more or less plausible personal and political arrangements. The historical fantasy of 'Cypresses' allows him to project his hypothesis in its pure form. But it is pure fantasy. What Roman historians and satirists found objectionable about the Etruscans was not at all their feeling for their fellow man but their unbridled uxoriousness: they dined with their wives.[32] By the time Lawrence came to write *Etruscan Places* it suited him to praise the Etruscans for this, their heterosexuality, instead: it was this affronted the Romans' imperial dignity and provoked them to call the smiling Etruscans vicious (*EP* 140).

If 'Cypresses' is one of Lawrence's most evasive poems, 'Medlars and Sorb-Apples' (*CP* 280−81) is one of his most elusive. 'The right virtue of a medlar' is 'to be rotten ere you be half ripe.'[33] Medlars are left on the tree through the first frosts of October and November; then, after picking, they are allowed to decay still further, or 'bletted.' Mulling over his Italian epithet for the fruit's texture, *morbido*, or 'soft, tender,' Lawrence's speaker is probably considering the flavours of *morboso*, 'sensitive,' and *morbo*, 'disease,' in the word. As in 'Pomegranate' the speaker lies down in the heart's process. The ripening and more particularly the rotting of the fruit becomes a symbol or an arcane correspondence for different forms of decadence, social, sexual and physical. The social dimension is only sketched in, in the reference to the 'pussyfoot West['s]' denial of the pleasures of fermenting fruit sugars. In 'Grape' the reference to American prohibition is more explicit. Though decadent, the West has not the strength to enjoy the pleasures and refinements of its decay, and refuses Dionysian intoxication out of fear:

> Our pale day is sinking into twilight,
> And if we sip the wine, we find dreams coming upon us
> Out of the imminent night. (*CP* 286)

For Nietzsche and Lawrence the solution to the decline of the West is to 'go forward, — that is to say step by step further and further into decadence' (*TI* 101). So the Lawrentian soul continues, 'naked-footed,' 'falling through the stages of decay' as it passes 'down the strange lanes of hell' to be 'distilled in separation.' For Nietzsche too this is the vindication of *décadence*, that it produces, not materials for a social structure, but individuals. In an aphorism from *The Joyful Wisdom* entitled 'The Characteristics of Corruption' he commends the decay of moral traditions as an autumnal process that matures, first tyrants, then individuals:

> Yet a little while, and this fruit of fruits hangs ripe and yellow on the tree of a people, — and only for the sake of such fruit did this tree exist! (*JW* Sect. 23)

'Cypresses' speaks of a 'lost kiss,' 'Medlars and Sorb-Apples' of a kiss of loss, 'a spasm of farewell, a moment's orgasm of rupture.' These oxymora give notice that the sexual level of the poem is the most elusive. It helps to remember two things. Firstly, the Dionysus invoked in 'Medlars and Sorb-Apples' is the sophisticated Orphic Dionysus, a psychopomp and a guide to the mysteries of the separation of the spirit from the body. Secondly, in the month before composing this poem, Lawrence had bidden a temporary farewell to Frieda, who had journeyed north to her family in Bavaria.[34] But the poem also speaks of 'a new partner, a new parting, a new unfusing into twain.' It is doubtful there was a new partner for Lawrence in Fiesole, but an article by Peter Fuchow has shed light on a constellation of possible partners who gathered around Lawrence in London in the autumn of 1917. The most important of the entanglements that developed was an abortive affair between Lawrence and Hilda Aldington. By reference to some six novels, notably H.D.'s *Bid Me to Live*, Fuchow is able to recapture at least one side of Lawrence's failed affair with the Imagist poet.[35] The other side is preserved in a letter of Lawrence's to Cecil Gray, in which he answers Gray's accusation that he, Lawrence, had become a Christ or Dionysus to a regiment of Magdalens or maenads:

> As for me and my 'women', I know what they are and aren't, and though there is a certain messiness, there is a further reality . . . my 'women', Esther Andrews, Hilda Aldington etc, represent, in an impure and unproud, subservient, cringing, bad fashion, I admit, — but represent none the less the threshold of a new world, or underworld, of knowledge and being . . . The old

> world must burst, the underworld must be open and whole, new
> world. — You want an emotional sensuous underworld . . . my
> 'women' want an ecstatic subtly-intellectual underworld, like the
> Greeks — Orphicism — like Magdalen at her feet-washing . . .
> (*BL* III 179–80)

To keep his female disciples, but keep them at a distance,
Lawrence seems to have offered them an Orphic, disembodied
sexual relationship like that Count Dionys offers Lady Daphne
(*CSN* 270, 274).

Lawrence's own disquiet at the arrangement or at its
repercussions was expressed in 'Phantasmagoria' (later retitled
'Late at Night') from *New Poems*:

> Tall black Bacchae of midnight, why then, why
> Do you rush to assail me?
> . . .
> Is there some great Iacchos of these slopes
> Suburban dismal?
> Have I profaned some female mystery, orgies
> Black and phantasmal? (*NP* 31)

H.D. felt at first encouraged by Lawrence, then rejected, and
on the whole perhaps 'profaned.' She reshaped her bitterness
into one of her finest treatments of Greek myth, 'Eurydice':

> So you have swept me back,
> I who could have walked with the live souls
> above the earth,
> I who could have slept among the live flowers
> at last;
>
> so for your arrogance
> and your ruthlessness
> I am swept back
> where dead lichens drip
> dead cinders upon moss of ash;
>
> so for your arrogance
> I am broken at last,
> I who had lived unconscious,
> who was almost forgot;
>
> if you had let me wait
> I had grown from listlessness
> into peace,
> if you had let me rest with the dead,

I had forgot you
and the past.

Yet, H.D.'s Eurydice confesses, the suffering of being awa-
kened to life, then left in hell, has intensified her sense of self:

> At least I have the flowers of myself,
> and my thoughts, no god
> can take that;
> I have the fervour of myself for a presence
> and my own spirit for light;
>
> and my spirit with its loss
> knows this;
> though small against the black,
> small against the formless rocks,
> hell must break before I am lost;
>
> before I am lost,
> hell must open like a red rose
> for the dead to pass.[36]

Lawrence's 'Medlars and Sorb-Apples' is, in part, a companion
to H.D.'s 'Eurydice,' showing how Orpheus also suffers yet is
'distilled' by the lovers' 'unfusing into twain':

> Each soul departing with its own isolation,
> Strangest of all strange companions,
> And best.

Reading 'Medlars and Sorb-Apples' as a sequal to H.D.'s
'Eurydice' is also an aid to understanding the Virgilian allusion,
Iamque vale, for it is Eurydice who speaks these words as she is
swept back into the encircling night of hell.[37] By transposing her
cry to Orpheus, Lawrence indicates that he too has his hell to
harrow, his heart torn apart by the pains of leave-taking while
his soul's joy deepens at its ever more tenuous grasp of physical
existence. At this stage we may be overtaken by a pang of
sympathy for Ursula Brangwen and her fury about Rupert
Birkin's 'spiritual brides' (*WIL* 345). The 'exquisite' sensations
and all but disembodied relationships of 'Medlars and Sorb-
Apples' are irreconcilable with Lawrence's official sexual ethic.
But then, there are more Lawrences than we have discovered in
the first hundred years.

The descent in 'Medlars and Sorb-Apples,' 'naked-footed'
over 'frost-cold leaves' down the 'leaf-clogged, silent lanes of

hell' is like the descent of Fancy towards death in Keats's 'Ode
to a Nightingale': some senses are sharpened, some anaes-
thetized, but the end would be loss of all sensation. The process
of self-refinement does not stop, for Lawrence, with the
achievement of isolation, nor are we ever tolled back to the self.
Other Keatsian and autumnal processes of the body — intoxication, illness, perhaps death — continue the experiment of soul-
making. 'Medlars and Sorb-Apples' anticipates the descents of
Last Poems, but goes beyond even them in its rejoicing at a
potential escape from the body and the female principle. The
farewells of the atactic last lines come close to asking Blake's,
and of course Christ's, question of the Mother, 'what have I to
do with thee?'[38] In his 'philosophies' Lawrence deals at length
with the spirits of destruction and corruption:

> The spirit of destruction is divine, when it breaks the ego and
> opens the soul to the wide heavens. In corruption there is
> divinity. Aphrodite is, on one side, the great goddess of
> destruction in sex, Dionysus in the spirit . . . It is the activity of
> departure. And departure is the opposite equivalent of coming
> together; decay, corruption, destruction, breaking down is the
> opposite equivalent of creation. (*PII* 402)

The paragraph helps identify the poem's 'white gods,' gods of
'autumnal excrementa,' with the Magna Mater. The dark god
and his white antagonist preside over the process of dissolution
in 'Medlars and Sorb-Apples,' with the soul itself in the role of
virgin or initiate. Though there are oppositions in the poem, it
goes beyond the vitalist dialectics of the 'philosophies' and their
'opposite equivalents,' beyond Lawrence's customary emphasis
on the body and beyond the gods created by the body.
Ultimately the soul is itself, and creates from itself, the poem
suggests; yet its concluding cry, of *sono io*, is one of praise to
the gods. It is the Dionysian life-force that has carried the
initiate of Lawrence's imagination to the margins of life and
perhaps beyond. From this extreme pitch of existence he looks
back and, not knowing if his way is forward or back, gives his
cry of assent. 'Medlars and Sorb-Apples' will not be accom-
modated within the 'final form' of Lawrence's 'philosophies.' It
is too exploratory, too experimental — the most experimental of
all Lawrence's poems in *Birds, Beasts and Flowers*.

★   ★   ★

In his compact monograph on myth K.K. Ruthven asks us to pity the poet who chooses to spin his own myths out of his own bowels:

> Mythopoesis is the growth-point of mythology, but hazardous to those who cultivate it . . . the strain of manufacturing a Schlegelian mythology out of the deepest depths of the spirit is enormous, for you end up with Gottfried Benn papering the walls with your own skin, while psychoanalytic critics stand around discussing your obsessive imagery . . . and mulling over Freud's remark that mythopoeic impulses manifest themselves nowadays in the form of neuroses . . . [39]

The three poems analysed might be used to outline a regression from a fantasy of resolved heterosexual conflict to a dream of a homosexual Arcadia and finally to a vision of narcissistic latency. They seem openly to invite psychobiography, but it is an invitation I wish to decline. The abuses of the method are obvious in the case of a writer as imaginatively experimental with his sexual polymorphism as was Lawrence. But while I wish to disclaim the ambitions of the psychoanalytic critic, I should like briefly to trace the ancestry of Lawrence's dark god in his poetry, and note how often manifestations of the god associate sexuality with violence.

A figure like the dark god's first makes his appearance in 'Discord in Childhood,' a poem copied into Lawrence's second college note-book in 1909 but probably composed earlier.[40] In the notebook the poem is part of a sequence, 'A Life History: In Harmonies and Discords,' of which it makes up the third 'Discord.' The dark father, though we only recognize him as such by analogy with *Sons and Lovers* (77–78), undertakes his nocturnal violence ('the dreadful sound Of a male thong booming and bruising') to the accompaniment of a storm-racked ash-tree ('the lash of the tree Shrieked and slashed the wind'). The conflict seems to be resolved in the male's favour, and both conflict and resolution are sanctioned by the overarching Norse world-tree. In 'Discipline,' another poem whose first draft dates from 1909, the young schoolmaster-poet finds himself, as he supervises his class, re-enacting his father's role. He weaves over the class 'a dark net of . . . discipline' which he has plaited from the 'thongs' or 'roots' of his soul.[41] The net, mesh or web in Lawrence's early poetry is a symbol for the necessary interrelatedness of the natural and the human. In 'Cruelty and Love' (later retitled 'Love on the Farm') there is the young farmer returning to his nervous, dreamy wife after displaying his mastery over the farm. Reluctantly at first, then gratefully, she becomes his creature. She abandons her preconceptions of love for the sake of a darkness in him, which threatens violence but also promises the destruction of her old self: 'I drown Within him, die, and find death good' (*LP* 7). The evidence of the poetry bears out George Ford's psychobiographical tracing of Lawrence's dark heroes to the personal archetype of his collier father.

Lawrence's delineation of the life-force as a dark god whose sexuality is that of the rapist, associated with violence or the threat of violence, owes as much to the peculiarities of his early home-life as to his later study of Nietzsche. The delineation is, in varying degrees, sexist. In the Dionysian flux of self-creation and destruction the woman's role is to suffer psychological and, at times, physical trauma; and the man's role is to suffer too, chiefly from having to inflict this trauma. There is more to sex in Lawrence, but it is in this psychic process the chief significance of sex lies for him. While destruction remains a psychic process, Lawrence writes of it maturely and confidently, but once physical suffering intrudes an ambivalence enters his tone, an urgency of exhortation as if he needs to convince himself as well as his reader.

Similar doubts arise in Lawrence's writing about the Dionysian process in civilizations, about the level of revolutionary violence acceptable for the creation of a new heaven and earth. The problem is a Blakean and Shelleyan one of course, but Lawrence handles it less firmly than his Romantic predecessors: witness the strange atmospherics of the deaths and executions in *The Plumed Serpent*. For most of his life Lawrence studiously avoided social and political positions so that his time as a teacher, when some of the duties of leadership did devolve upon him, holds a special interest. There is a revealing letter to Blanche Jennings in which he speaks of his difficulties maintaining discipline. 'I can be cruel, but not stern,' he confesses. 'So I struggle with my nature and with my class, till I feel all frayed into rags' (*BL* I, 85). The notion that a true man and a true leader should be able to inflict pain remains a tentative and nervous hypothesis throughout Lawrence's work. It seldom is the same thing as Nietzsche's 'Let us try it'; for Lawrence never stops trying it. It is not a hypothesis he is testing but an obsession he cannot be rid of. What, we might wonder, would Lawrence have said to the book from Livy's *History* in which the Roman historian describes the viciousness of an actual Dionysian cult in the year 186 BC:

> A nameless Greek came first to Etruria . . . a priest of secret rites performed by night. There were initiatory rites which at first were imparted to a few, then began to be generally known among men and women. To the religious element in them were added the delights of wine and feasts, that the minds of a larger number might be attracted. When wine had inflamed their minds, and night and the mingling of males with females, youth with age, had destroyed every sentiment of modesty, all varieties of corruption first began to be practised, since each one had at hand the pleasure answering to that to which his nature was more inclined. There was not one form of vice alone, the promiscuous matings of free men and women, but perjured witnesses, forged seals and wills and evidence, all issued from this same workshop: likewise poisonings and secret murders, so that at times not even the bodies were found for burial. Much was ventured by craft, more by violence. This violence was concealed because amid the howlings and the crash of drums and cymbals no cry could be heard as the debauchery and murders proceeded.[42]

(The violence had political as well as sexual overtones; Livy considered this outbreak of the cult was a threat to the *civis Romanorum.*) The conduct of this cult would not have persuaded Lawrence to repudiate *his* Dionysus. But to what extent might rites like these, in the service of the irrational, have served as a temptation to Lawrence?

Profound things can be found in Lawrence's 'philosophies,' in those parts which deal with aesthetics. The insight that 'a work of art . . . must contain the essential criticism on the morality to which it adheres' (*P* 476) could hardly be bettered, unless by adding that it may be the essential criticism on the myth to which it adheres. In *Birds Beasts and Flowers* 'the essential criticism' of the Dionysian myth comes in the poems written from America. These poems do more than test whether the American spirit of place corresponds to the Dionysian *homo sylvestris* envisaged in 'The Evening Land.' While confirming that the spirit of place is a dark god, the American poems ask

what kind of humanity is created in response to this unknown.
So the Lawrentian speaker in 'The Red Wolf,' though he knows
himself rejected by the 'dark old demon' of the desert, decides

> to sit down on my tail right here
> And wait for him to come back with a new story. (*CP* 405)

Yet in the next poem, 'Men in New Mexico,' the speaker finds
to his dismay (and the mockery to which this dismay is
subjected is evident in the Nietzschean allusion of 'twilight') that
the men here are no more capable of a social rebirth than the
men elsewhere. The ancient gods have fallen asleep in them as
they have in the desert mountains:

> They camped and went to sleep
> In the last twilight
> Of Indian gods;
> And they can't wake. (*CP* 407)

The poems that close *Birds, Beasts and Flowers* group themselves into contradictory pairs. In the last poem of the volume,
for instance, 'The American Eagle,' the speaker attempts to
convince himself that a reversion to the savage gods of the
continent might create a new race of American *Übermenschen*,
'full of power of life.' Americans should emulate the

> Eagle of the Rockies, bird of men that are masters,
> Lifting the rabbit-blood of the myriads up into something
> splendid,
> Leaving a few bones
> . . .
> Drinking a little blood, and loosing another royalty unto the
> world. (*CP* 414)

But earlier, in 'Eagle in New Mexico,' he had just as firmly
rejected the offer of power in exchange for blood-sacrifice as
against his instincts:

> I don't yield to you, big, jowl-faced eagle.
> Nor you nor your blood-thirsty sun
> That sucks up blood
> Leaving a nervous people.
> . . .
> Even the sun in heaven can be curbed and chastened at last
> By the life in the hearts of men.
> And you, great bird, sun-starer, heavy black beak
> Can be put out of office as sacrifice bringer. (*CP* 374)

Birds, Beasts and Flowers begins with a gesture of self-assertion, and ends with a queue of self-doubting questions. It begins in the 'dawn-place' of the Mediterranean (*PII* 328), and ends in descending night in the Taos desert, an ashen night of self-questioning. The desert and the deracinating sense of the collapse of the West, religiously at least, suggest likenesses to the ending of T.S. Eliot's *The Waste Land*; and indeed, I hope my study of Lawrence's sources and allusions has shown the poetry of *Birds, Beasts and Flowers* very much belongs to the modernist mainstream. But there is an expectancy about Lawrence's volume unlike the ennui and exhaustion which mark the close of Eliot's modernist classic. With their loosely juxtaposed, contradictory shifts in response and opinion, the poems which conclude *Birds, Beasts and Flowers* are closer in spirit to Nietzsche's aphoristic structures than to Eliot's carefully arranged fragments. They refuse solutions and despair, system and closure. It has often been remarked how Lawrence's making an experiment of his own life imbued much of his writing with the hectoring tone of the proselytizer; too little remarked how the freshness in his writing originates in the same commitment. His poems do not wait and see; they try and see.

And his poems are more satisfying in their handling of the myth of the dark god than his leadership novels of the same period. Lawrence introduces into *Kangaroo* and *The Plumed Serpent* the sceptical points of view of his wait-and-see protagonists, Richard Lovat Somers and Kate Leslie, but what he cannot annul in these fictions is the sense that the political violence of the novels is a *dromenon* attendant upon the *mythos*, a rite which had to happen and therefore, for the Nietzschean, should happen. Freed from social realism, the poems can be pure 'thought-adventures' (*K* 312) — freer in their speculation, more agile in their scepticism — in a way the novels, dragging after them the moral horror of what happened to happen, cannot. In this way *Birds, Beasts and Flowers* anticipates Lawrence's fictional successes in the later twenties, when he turned from the tyranny of social realism to the sceptical freedom of legend and fairytale, romance and parable.

136   *D.H. Lawrence: Centenary Essays*

Notes

1   Ovid, *Fasti* IV, 417: 'Exigit ipse locus, raptus ut virginis edam', trans. J.G. Frazer.
2   Friedrich Nietzsche, *The Gay Science*, trans. Walter Kaufmann (New York, 1974), p. 115. Lawrence would probably have read the translation in Oscar Levy's *Collected Works: The Joyful Wisdom*, trans. Thomas Common (New York, 1964; first published 1909–11), p. 87. References in the body of the text hereafter will be to the Common translation. They will use the abbreviation JW, and show the aphorism or section number, for ease of comparison to other editions.
3   References to Lawrence's works in the body of the text use the following abbreviations:

AR   *Aaron's Rod* (Harmondsworth, 1950)
BL   *The Letters of D.H. Lawrence*, ed. J.T. Boulton *et al.* (Cambridge, 1979–84), i–iii.
CP   *The Complete Poems of D.H. Lawrence*, ed. V. de Sola Pinto and W. Roberts (1972).
CSN   *The Complete Short Novels* (Harmondsworth, 1982).
EP   *Mornings in Mexico and Etruscan Places* (Harmondsworth, 1960).
FU   *Fantasia of the Unconscious; Psychoanalysis and the Unconscious* (Harmondsworth, 1971).
K   *Kangaroo* (Harmondsworth, 1950).
LG   *The Lost Girl*, ed. John Worthen (Cambridge, 1981).
LP   *Love Poems and Others* (1913).
ML   *The Collected Letters of D.H. Lawrence*, ed. H.T. Moore (1962)
NP   *New Poems* (1918).
P   *Phoenix* (1936).
PII   *Phoenix II* (1968).
SCAL   *Studies in Classic American Literature* (Harmondsworth, 1971).
SL   *Sons and Lovers* (Harmondsworth, 1948).
SM   *The Symbolic Meaning*, ed. A. Arnold (Arundel, 1962).
SS   *Sea and Sardinia* (Harmondsworth, 1944).
WIL   *Women in Love* (Harmondsworth, 1960).

4   Jessie Chambers, *D.H. Lawrence: A Personal Record* (Cambridge, 1980; first published 1935), p. 120.
5   Subsequently Lawrence thought of *Morgenrot* for a title, either in imitation of Nietzsche's *Morgenröte* or because, in wartime, he wanted a German title (*BL* II 315, 317).
6   Tom Marshall, *The Psychic Mariner* (New York, 1970), p. 117; Sandra Gilbert, *Acts of Attention* (Ithaca, 1972), p. 133.
7   Whitman, 'Song of Myself,' 1.
8   Byron, *Childe Harold's Pilgrimage* IV, xvi. Byron also links the defeat of the Athenians at Syracuse to the fall of the Venetian doges.
9   *Thucydides*, trans. Benjamin Jowett (Oxford, 1900), II, 87.
10 George Dennis, *A Handbook for Travellers in Sicily* (1864), p. 342.
11 Margaret Guido, *Syracuse: A Handbook to Its History and Principal Monuments* (1963), p. 18.

12   John Ruskin, *The Stones of Venice* (1907), I, 2–3.

13   *ibid.*, I, 24. See also Lawrence on Hiero I of Syracuse (*BL* III, 518).

14   Dennis, *Handbook*, p. 330.

15   Ovid, *Metamorphoses*, trans. Frank Justus Miller (1916), V, 474–82. For a demythologizing, eheumerist account of why Sicily is stony ground, see *SS* 33–34.

16   J.G. Frazer, *The Golden Bough* (1925), V, 14.

17   Robert Graves, *The Greek Myths* (Harmondsworth, 1960), I, 110.

18   See Graves, *Poems Selected by Himself* (Harmondsworth, 1972), p. 104; and *The White Goddess* (1961).

19   See Euripides, *The Bacchae*, trans. Gilbert Murray (1904), p. 35. When Dionysus is imprisoned by Pentheus, 'the fire that sleeps' awakens and 'an earthquake suddenly shakes the pillars of the Castle.'

20   George H. Ford, *Double Measure* (New York, 1969), pp. 26–60; and Patricia Merivale, *Pan the Goat-God* (Cambridge, Mass., 1969), pp. 194–219.

21   Katharine Susannah Prichard, *Coonardoo* (Sydney, 1973; first published 1929); *Brumby Innes and Bid Me to Live* (Sydney, 1974), p. 102.

22   *Twilight of the Idols*, trans. Anthony M. Ludovici (New York, 1964; first published 1909–11), p. 119. References hereafter use the abbreviation *TI* and the page number.

23   *The Will to Power*, trans. Anthony M. Ludovici (New York, 1964; first published 1909–11), Sect. 1050. References hereafter use the abbreviation *WP* and the section number.

24   *Beyond Good and Evil*, trans. Helen Zimmern (New York, 1964; first published 1909–11), Sect. 295.

25   Letter, 4 April 1926, *Letters from D.H. Lawrence to Martin Secker, 1911–1930*, ed. Martin Secker (1970), p. 72.

26   Keith Sagar, *D.H. Lawrence: A Calendar of His Works* (Manchester, 1979), p. 105.

27   George Dennis, *Cities and Cemeteries of Ancient Etruria* (1907), I, 70–71.

28   *Aeneid*, trans. John Conington (New York, 1910), p. 271; XI, 736–40.

29   H.P. Blavatsky, *Isis Unveiled* (Pasadena, 1960; first published 1877), I, vii.

30   Daniel J. Schneider, ' "Strange Wisdom": Leo Frobenius and D.H. Lawrence,' *D.H. Lawrence Review* XVI (1983), 183–93. Quotations from Frobenius, *The Voice of Africa* (New York, 1968), pp. 263, 322, 168, 161, are taken from Schneider.

31   *The Adelphi*, I (1923), 369–70.

32   See Dennis, *Ancient Etruria*, p. 40.

33   *As You Like It* III, ii, 119–20.

34   Sagar, *Calendar*, p. 104.

35   Peter E. Fuchow, 'Rino and Julia: The Hilda Doolittle — D.H. Lawrence Affair Reconsidered,' *Journal of Modern Literature*, VII (1980), 51–76.

36   H.D., *Collected Poems, 1912–1944*, ed. Louis L. Martz (New York, 1983), pp. 51–55. Fuchow quotes *Bid Me to Live* to the effect that Julia (H.D.) wrote an 'Orpheus sequence' about Rico (Lawrence). See also Martz's introduction, p. xx.

37   Virgil, *Georgics* IV, 497–98.

38   'To Tirzah,' *Songs of Innocence and of Experience*.

39   K.K. Ruthven, *Myth* (1976), p. 70.
40   The notebook is Ferrier, MS 5: see Carole Ferrier, 'D.H. Lawrence's Pre-1920 Poetry: A Descriptive Bibliography of Manuscripts, Typescripts and Proofs,' *D.H. Lawrence Review* VI (1973), 333—59.
41   Ferrier, MS 1 and MS 5. See *CP* 943 for a text substantially that of MS 5.
42   *Livy*, trans. Evan T. Sage (1949), XI, 241—43.

Purity and Danger in D.H. Lawrence's *The Virgin and the Gipsy*

JOHN TURNER

1. Introduction: An Image of the Wild

> What care I for my house and my land?
> What care I for my money, O?
> What care I for my new-wedded lord?
> I'm off with the wraggle taggle gipsies, O!
>
> ('The Wraggle Taggle Gipsies')[1]

What Wordsworth saw in the 'wild eyes' of his sister, in that 'wild secluded scene' a few miles above Tintern Abbey, was an imagery of hope. Her 'wild ecstasies' articulated for him the rebelliousness of his own desires and delights, and yet sustained them within the holding environment of a discipline of love. The moment seems to have been an important one in his life: it shows him still in creative touch with his own rebelliousness, his 'purer mind' unsubdued by the impurity which he felt had gained upon him during the previous years of city life. The defensive organizations of the false self, we might say today, had not suppressed the true; and as the poem moves towards its conclusion, the wild and the tame become free to play together, each enriching the other.

The moment that Wordsworth describes, however, is of more than personal importance; it has an emblematic significance too. It crystallizes out certain developments of consciousness that had been occurring during the previous fifty years and that now seem to characterize much twentieth-century culture. For the first time a major writer has committed himself to an imagery of wildness in his search for authenticity in a civilization which he felt to be stifling. Wordsworth, together with the other Romantic poets, stands at the head of a libertarian tradition in

139

Britain which enabled Donald Winnicott in the 1960s to write of what he called the anti-social tendency: 'The child knows in his bones that it is *hope* that is locked up in the wicked behaviour, and that *despair* is linked with compliance and false social-ization.'[2] Wildness, even wickedness, express the true self: the child needs to embody his desires in action (acting-out), the writer needs to embody them in imagery — they each must reaffirm their crucial and perhaps precarious hold upon those inner energies in which their sense of creativity, authenticity and hope is felt to reside. For Wordsworth, as we have seen, the wild and the tame could play together, but for post-Romantic writers the wild was to become increasingly marginalized and, in consequence, increasingly difficult to integrate into a spirit of love. Increasingly it was to be associated with the anti-social, the wicked, even the taboo.

The image of the gipsy has played an interesting part in this history, and Lawrence's tale *The Virgin and the Gipsy* estab-lishes its meaning by reference to a long oral and literary tradition in which the dominant culture and gipsy counterculture have been brought into opposition — a tradition newly alive in the nineteenth century although dating from long before it. For in real life, of course, there has always been mutual antagonism between the two cultures, each projecting upon the other those desires and habits destructive of its own order. Each believes the other dirty, licentious and animal-like; and despite a measure of economic interplay between them, each society has always maintained its own ethnic purity and independence by a system of taboos and pollution beliefs. Here is Judith Okely's account of the matter from the start of her fascinating anthropological study of gipsy life, *The Traveller-Gypsies*:

> The state has attempted to control and exercise force against Gypsies, partly because they avoid wage-labour, are of no fixed abode, and because they seek intermittent access to land. Those who confront the prevailing order, be it in small ways, those who demonstrate alternative possibilities in economic spheres, in ways of being and thinking, those who appear as powerful symbols, must, it seems, be contained and controlled. Although in fact the Gypsies' threat is trivial, their presence exposes profound dissatisfactions in the dominant system.
>   Folklore and exotic literature often convey the ideological and symbolic disorder which the Gypsies appear to represent.[3]

It is a literature of elopement and abduction, a literature that entertains the danger of wildness and thus might bring the dominant community to confront the deep ambivalences that underlie its own taboos. Yet all too often, especially in the lyric poetry of the nineteenth century, this is precisely what does not happen. The image of the gipsy does not *explore* ambivalence; it does no more than articulate a fugitive desire to escape.

At its simplest, therefore, the lure of what Masefield called in *Sea Fever* 'the vagrant gipsy life' is little more than a glamorized *Wanderlust*: thus vagrant and gipsy can seem to be synonyms. Kipling gives voice to this desire in its most typical lyrical vein:

> Out of the dark of the gorgio camp,
>   Out of the grime and the grey
> (Morning waits at the end of the world),
>   Gipsy, come away![4]

The parenthesis here is revealing, for the desire to escape seems itself no more than parenthetical within the life that feels it. It has the cadence of nostalgia which belongs, as Winnicott says, to 'the precarious hold that a person may have on the inner representation of a lost object'.[5] The image of the gipsy, that is, tells us of something that is almost gone, both from the individual imagination and the social culture. Within the very different tones of Keats' *Meg Merrilies* and Arnold's *The Scholar-Gipsy* we can hear the same harmonic note: a nostalgia for more natural connexions between man and man, men and nature, a longing for a vitality and delight that seem almost wholly subdued by the demands of adulthood in an industrial civilisation. Such nostalgia, articulating a desire which the author can neither integrate nor abandon, was particularly common (and particularly a preoccupation of poetry) when Lawrence was growing up. Here, for instance, is Arthur Symons:

> The gipsy tents are on the down,
> The gipsy girls are here;
> And it's O to be off and away from the town
> With a gipsy for my dear![6]

There is no attempt here to engage seriously with the realities of an alternative culture; the poet, although seemingly entertaining danger, is in fact content to remain at home in the safety of his verses. The poetry keeps alive his desire to escape but only by isolating it within the society of his mind.

The prose writers, however, partly because of the traditions of their genre, were more searching; and novels like *The Mill on the Floss* and *Jane Eyre* succeed in capturing something of the dangerous ambivalence that had gathered around the image of the gipsy. A serious interest in gipsy life, as opposed to a concern for its picturesque possibilities, had perhaps begun in Britain during the decade after the French Revolution, in the wake of Schiller's *Die Räuber*. Wordsworth, for instance, in his *Adventures on Salisbury Plain* shows a political interest in the limits that a dominant culture and a gipsy counterculture impose on one another; and he traces the difficulties of psychological integration in his vagrant heroine to the restrictive pressure of hostility between different social groups and classes. His vagrant, attracted to both cultures, can find her home in neither — a self-division that only a truly egalitarian society can heal. But such radical theorizing was short-lived in literature and, during the course of the nineteenth century, gipsy life was used chiefly (as by George Eliot and Charlotte Brontë) for expressive reasons — for the excitement of the ambivalent feelings aroused by its alien culture.

There was one prose writer, however, known to Lawrence and perhaps recalled when he came to write *The Virgin and the Gipsy*, for whom the fantasies of gipsy life were more than literary imaginings and for whom the ambivalence that surrounded gipsy life was lived out in acute personal anguish. That writer, of course, was George Borrow, the author of *Wild Wales*; and in his two books *Lavengro* and *The Romany Rye*, as a delighted Lawrence once observed to Jessie Chambers, he 'so skilfully blended autobiography and fiction that no one could tell where one left off and the other began.'[7] This blending is in fact the result of Borrow's anguish, of his inner division between two cultures. On the one hand is his hostility towards 'that mad puppy they calls gentility'[8] and his yearning after the wild beauty of gipsy life — particularly, it seems to me, after images of male beauty, of 'a very tall man with a countenance heroically beautiful, but wild, wild, wild.'[9] On the other hand are the facts of his upbringing, his religion and his talents for literature and scholarship — facts that fated him always to be an observer of the wild life after which he hankered. Perhaps the saddest moment in either book occurs in *The Romany Rye* when the narrator, after fancying himself a scholar-gipsy three hundred years ago, suddenly turns upon himself and asks: 'Supposing I had accomplished all this, what would have been the profit of it; and in what would all this wild gypsy dream have terminated?'[10] The books are tumultuous with contradiction, authoritarian prejudice and an associated depression; they are the works of a baffled imagination, unable to find the images that might bring integration and yet determined never to yield the field to the hated gentility of the Victorian middle classes.

This seems to me the point from which to approach Lawrence's *The Virgin and the Gipsy*, a tale similarly dedicated to an imagery of gipsy life in order to attack the gentility of British society. Lawrence, however, was a much more self-conscious, intelligent writer than Borrow, as well as a much more gifted one: he understood the inevitable incompleteness in which his own attack would involve him — and still he would not yield. He has built his story out of the implacable antagonism between two peoples, studied objectively in their economic and social relations and subjectively in the competing loyalties they exert within the divided imagination of his young heroine. The insight of the writers of the revolutionary decade — Blake, Wordsworth, Godwin — has been recovered, though without their radical panacea: classes and cultures in conflict reproduce that conflict in the minds of their individual members.

On first reading, however, there seems a moment in *The Virgin and the Gipsy* when Lawrence is about to evade the challenge of this conflict; and this is the moment of entrancement when we see the gipsy at the top of the stairs of his caravan and Yvette at the bottom. At this point the tale seems set to follow the traditional pattern of ballads like 'The Wraggle Taggle Gipsies', in which a woman throws over all the advantages of class, education and wealth in order to roam the wildness of nature with her chosen gipsy. But Yvette and the gipsy are interrupted by the arrival of the 'Eastwoods': now it will be her place rather than his, the rectory rather than the caravan . . . and by this simple change of story-line Lawrence fundamentally alters the tradition in which he is working. Gone is the nostalgic dream of escape — in its place, a gathered hostility, a determination to bring the familiar dream home to the family where it originated, to make the opposed worlds of gipsydom and gentility interact and to draw out the contradictions of ambivalence in despite of all the anguish of self-division. Lawrence's tale is an assault upon the taboos of his society and its false religious consciousness, and it derives its force from the insights into primitive religion that he had found in the anthropological writings of Frazer and his followers. *The Virgin and the Gipsy* aims, as we shall see, to complement the historical process described by Jessie Weston in her book *From Ritual to Romance*; it aims, that is, to reclaim for romance the powers of its ancient ritual origins — and it sets out to do so in the first place by its assault upon taboos that have outlived their usefulness.

2. The Rectory

> The greatest of all lies in the modern world is the lie of purity and the dirty little secret.
> (D. H. Lawrence: 'Pornography and Obscenity')[11]

The story begins with a scandal — the reported defection of She-who-was-Cynthia. We begin at once, that is, in the realm of taboo, of those codes and conventions that bind groups of people together by rigorous distinction between desirable and undesirable behaviour. What shows that we are dealing with taboo rather than with simple prohibition is the peculiarly electric response, the rawness of the touched nerve, when the mind confronts the unthinkable, the unnameable. She-who-was-Cynthia deserts her husband and 'the scandal knew no bounds' (5):[12] we are in the presence of those unconscious desires that for Freud lay at the heart of all taboos — for, as he observes, 'these prohibitions must have concerned activities towards which there was a strong inclination'.[13] Lawrence too in *The Virgin and the Gipsy*, like Freud in *Totem and Taboo*, is writing at least as much out of his knowledge of anthropology as of psychology. His interest is in the strategies by which a society preserves itself against the threat of change, and consequently in the strategies which the writer may adopt to compel it to change. Some words from Mary Douglas' *Purity and Danger* are relevant here:

The idea of society is a powerful image. It is potent in its own right to control or to stir men to action. This image has form; it has external boundaries, margins, internal structure. Its outlines contain power to reward conformity and repulse attack. There is energy in its margins and unstructured areas.[14]

Lawrence sees how gossip, scandal and taboo serve to breed compliance and preserve the purity of upper-middle-class culture against the danger of rebellion; and he shows too how members of that class respond both protectively and self-protectively to the figure of the wounded vicar by consoling him with a rectory tucked safely far away in the distant north. But he also sees the energies that lie at the margins of that society — energies only furtively and uncreatively tapped when the *bounds* dissolve in the vicarious pleasures of gossip — and so he creates a fiction that will celebrate two of its marginal types: virgin and gipsy, in a 'world's-end night' (87) which embraces the taboos that gossip only flirts with.

It is important to appreciate the effect of Lawrence's style in this enterprise. Kingsley Widmer, in a very good chapter on Lawrence's parables of regeneration in his *The Art of Perversity*, speaks of the 'odd combination of harsh realism and lyrical fairy tale' in *The Virgin and the Gipsy* and finds 'awkward changes in tone' in the prose.[15] The effect seems to me, however, rather different. Here is the beginning of the story:

> When the vicar's wife went off with a young and penniless man the scandal knew no bounds. Her two little girls were only seven and nine years old respectively. And the vicar was such a good husband. True, his hair was grey. But his moustache was dark, he was handsome, and still full of furtive passion for his unrestrained and beautiful wife.
>
> Why did she go? Why did she burst away with such an éclat of revulsion, like a touch of madness?
>
> Nobody gave any answer. Only the pious said she was a bad woman. While some of the good women kept silent. They knew.

What is happening here is that Lawrence with not altogether comic malice is parodying the gossip he describes. The first sentence has mock-horror in it, the second mock-pity, the third mock-incomprehension, mock-sanctimoniousness. There is treacherousness in the way that Lawrence exposes the 'spurious sympathies and recoils' of a gossip which would profess itself to be 'on the side of the angels';[16] for although the story sets out to disturb our imagery of piety and goodness, Lawrence has nothing fixed, nothing determinate to put in their place. The dangerous swerve of the question in the second paragraph embodies perfectly the unpredictability of the energies to which he appeals. It is not a destination but a journey to which the story calls us. 'If life is a great highway, then it must forge on ahead into the unknown. Sidetracking gets nowhere. That is mere *anti*. The tip of the road is always unfinished, in the wilderness.' [17] The pious lie and the good remain silent but Lawrence hints at the truth disturbingly; for *The Virgin and the Gipsy* is a tale told by a man whose imagination is committed to danger, and it is the potency of his authorial voice that prevents the tale from settling down into the realistic manner. Indeed, realism in Britain, as exemplified in the *tout comprendre tout pardonner* of a novel like *Middlemarch*, is one expression of the Victorian liberalism that Lawrence wanted to smash. His tale is etched in malice. If anything, it resembles a fairy-tale but a fairy-tale for adults, with a happy ending designed to assault rather than to reassure them.

For Lawrence's point is that the taboos which govern modern bourgeois life are irredeemably sham; they no longer make for real community, and therefore the contradictions which it is their social function to mask must be brought into consciousness and dealt with. Indeed, the taboos he depicts are the agents of a moral hygiene that actively works against human connexion. So, for example, the rector preserves in his heart 'the pure white snow-flower' of his former wife, whilst at the same time his senses seem occasionally to pick up from around him 'a rank, evil smell of selfishness and degraded lust, the smell of that awful nettle, She-who-was-Cynthia' (7). There are two consequences of such splitting: first, the loss of the outer world, of 'the danger of instability, the peculiarly *dangerous* sort of selfishness' (8) that characterised the real glamour of the woman; and second, the loss of the inner world, of the dangerous vigour of desire which shrinks to the kind of furtive passion that the vicar had felt for his wife. 'Our ideas of dirt', Mary Douglas reminds us, 'express symbolic systems';[18] but the images of hygiene and pollution that link inner and outer worlds in bourgeois society express a system which is impoverished and breaking down into open self-contradiction. Lawrence uses the real cleanness of the gipsy encampment to expose the dispiriting

and spurious hygiene of life at the rectory; and his point is that
the morality of rectory life is grounded in nothing other than an
aesthetic of disgust and approval — an aesthetic laid down,
it would seem from the language he uses, at the time of infant
toilet-training. We remember, for instance, the awful smell of
sewage that Yvette seems to detect at the rectory, and the awful
green rages to which Aunt Cissie submits as to explosions of
methane gas. Lawrence is determined to expose the contradictions of bourgeois culture, to bring home its real dirt to its
boasted cleanliness. He sees, of course, the social function of
its contradictions: the safe preservation of the status quo.
Behind the purity lie is the money lie, as he observes in
'Pornography and Obscenity'. But he sees too the high cost that
these contradictions exact: the hidden madness of the mature
who comply and the deep mystification of the young who rebel.

Lawrence's assault on taboo is direct: he goes for the family
— for the family as it falls victim to its own idealised self-image
of respectability. 'If we could once get into our heads — or if
we once dare admit to one another — that we are *not* the
picture, and the picture is not what we are, then we might lay a
new hold on life.'[19] But the Saywells are not the Do-wells;
a cowardly compliance traps them in 'the lie of purity and the
guilty little secret', they dare not admit either their own desires
or their own anger. The family therefore draws a symbolic
boundary around its own collusion and projects its own bad
qualities outside: purity within and danger without.

> Outside the family, what was there for them but danger and
> insult and ignominy? Had not the rector experienced it, in his
> marriage? So now, caution! Caution and loyalty, fronting the
> world! Let there be as much hate and friction *inside* the family,
> as you like. To the outer world, a stubborn fence of unison. (9)

But the hate inside the family is not honest either. It is a coded
expression of inner fears for the self, virtually inaccessible —
and hence dangerously mystifying — to others. Lawrence has
given us a perfect picture of what is now called a schizophrenogenic family, ruled over by the inner madness of its older
members; its real dangers lie within, in the need to feel itself
respectable and normal.

The rector's failure in manhood is at the heart of the story,
and the dissociations of his character are vivdly traced.

Lawrence shows emblematically how it is the clergyman who is the 'utter unbeliever' with 'no core of warm belief', 'no pride in life' (30). It is the head of the family who is the natural slave. It is the loveless father who pretends to be the 'soft-hearted, indulgent old boy' (8). It is the conservative in behaviour who is at the deepest levels of his thought an anarchist.

> As he said himself, he was a conservative anarchist; which meant he was like a great many more people, a mere unbeliever. The anarchy extended to his humorous talk, and his secret thinking. The conservatism, based on a mongrel fear of the anarchy, controlled every action. His thoughts, secretly, were something to be scared of. Therefore, in his life, he was fanatically afraid of the unconventional. (68)

The rector's habitual jocularity of conversation had successfully deceived Yvette into thinking him unconventional; but the apparent interplay between law and lawlessness in his talk is in fact illusion. No real interplay takes place — only a kind of ghostly simulacrum as befitting the half-life to which he has become confined. For the rector has no creative imagery of wildness. To him all wildness wears the face of danger; and when he feels the safety of his conversational half-life threatened by the actions of others, he himself becomes wild — but wild only 'like a cornered rat' (68). He thinks 'unspeakable depravities' (69) about his daughter and feels 'convulsions of sadistic horror' (70) at his own mental pictures of illegal love — an inner corruption that makes his courage in self-defence craven and his anger abject. It is the man who most values the purity of Yvette, Lawrence tells us, who leaves her 'deflowered and humiliated' (31).

Aunt Cissie shows a similar self-dissociation in her dismal struggles between those contradictory desires in herself which she calls self-sacrifice and selfishness; and every evening the unpalatability of her own virtue confronts her in the shape of that 'single lonely and naked boiled potato' (11) on her plate. Lawrence shows brilliantly how the family conflicts are both displaced and reenacted in the arena of the tea-table — how, in Winnicott's words, Aunt Cissie is 'using doubt about food to hide doubt about love.' [20] For the symbolic value of food and eating is well-known: food brings the comfort to the body that love and affection bring to the mind, whilst the shared experience of eating reinforces the individual's bond to his social group. But Aunt Cissie, we read, characteristically unable to keep her maid-servants and thus obliged to do the cooking herself, hated eating and 'hated the fact of eating' (12). It is clear how tightly around herself she has drawn the symbolic boundaries of purity. As Sheila Macleod wrote in *The Art of Starvation*, describing the will to purity in her own experience of anorexia nervosa, 'one can reject all foreign substances, for which food is a metaphor, and subject them to one's will. This is power indeed.'[21] It is the power of the mind intent to purify itself of the body, making taboo all the objects of the body's legitimate desires. But it is a vain tussle for Aunt Cissie with her endless supply of chocolates. The bitterness of all that she has lost — the comforts of youth, beauty, sex, food, sleep — will irresistibly flare up at times, as if in her body, with jealous hatred of others; 'and at such times', Lawrence says, 'she was insane' (9). Hence the extraordinary affair of the Window Fund, instigated (poignantly enough) to commemorate the men of the parish killed in the Great War. Yvette's insouciance about the money she has raised provokes a 'green tumour of hate' (30) to burst in her aunt, followed by a 'filthily ridiculous' (33) outburst of maniacal temper. The dam will burst, for better or worse, even as She-who-was-Cynthia had burst away; for the pollutions of dirt and disease that exist within the very shrine of purity create contradictions too great to contain.

Over Aunt Cissie and rector alike is the usurping matriarchal figure of Granny, ruling the household in 'the static inertia of her unsavoury power' (18). Lawrence honours her 'mottled majesty' (38) in a series of malicious phrases shaped with all the relish due to her iconic status in the story. For she is imperturbably bogus; in her aspiration after respectability and her gross physical complacency, in her sentimentality about her dead husband and her utter selfishness in all living relationships, she is the epitome of sham. Truth cannot touch her. Whilst the rector 'would never dare to face the fat worm of his own unbelief' (31), and Aunt Cissie would never dare confront 'the helpless tumour of her rage' (32), Granny's complacence is absolute. She has only to lie to believe herself. Thus it is that she seems in her blindness 'some awful idol of old flesh, consuming all the attention' (15). All that remains of past unhappiness, unconscious anxiety and unsatisfied love in her is the deep unsavouriness of her greed. Her strategy for survival is, of course, the opposite of that which her daughter was to develop: she does not want to repel the foreign but to consume it, she does not want to sacrifice her body but to satiate it. Her greed is both physical (for food) and spiritual (for gossip), a parasitism on the lives of others like that of the toad outside the beehive in the second section of the tale, swallowing up each generation of new life in the moment of its issuing forth. Melanie Klein defined greed as 'an impetuous and insatiable craving, exceeding what the subject needs and what the object is able and willing to give.'[22] Its interest in others is imperial not reciprocal, that is, and hence it breeds resentment. Granny is one of those people who, as Lawrence wrote elsewhere, 'hang on, and hang on, into a corrupt old age, just because they have *not* lived, and therefore cannot let go',[23] and the challenge facing the youngest generation of the family, Lucille and Yvette, is to grapple with the anger and resentment they feel in the face of such parasitism, mystified as it is by all the parade of respectability.

It is a difficult challenge, for Lawrence shows clearly in the tale how successfully bourgeois society enfeebles the opposition it creates. His picture of post-war youth, with its motor-cars and bicycles, its dances and parties, its slang and endless flirtations, is a paradigm of dreary emptiness. It is a life without significant image of desire, without significant image of rebellion. The trivial quarrelling over whether the window should be open or shut in the rectory parlour is emblematic of this; for Lawrence draws our attention to windows and doors throughout the story to remind us of the vital importance of those thresholds at the margins of our culture which prove to be entries into the significant life of the normally prohibited — the dangerous, the wild, with which our sense of the worth of life is inextricably interwoven. The girls, for all their open-air jaunts in Leo's car, feel themselves locked up in their lives. Where are the thresholds to be crossed? Where are the images of desire that open the gates to other worlds? 'It is very much easier to shatter prison bars than to open undiscovered doors to life', says Lawrence (19). Foucault has written beautifully of the ways that the bourgeois world since 1650 has placed all deviant and oppositional behaviour under the taboos of prison or madhouse, and of the consequent impoverishment of language and imagery that we all of us have suffered. Of madness he writes:

> It entered a phase of silence from which it was not to emerge for a long time; it was deprived of its language; and although one continued to speak of it, it became impossible for it to speak of itself. Impossible at least until Freud, who was the first to open up once again the possibility for reason and unreason to communicate in the danger of a common language . . .[24]

Lawrence's aim in *The Virgin and the Gipsy* is the same that Foucault ascribes to Freud; and his first step is to bring to consciousness that which is unconscious in taboo — the unpalatable truths of desire, anger and fear that masquerade as respectability. But first we must suffer with Yvette who, when she thinks at last that she has found in the Eastwoods an imagery of desire and alternative life, is threatened by her father with 'a criminal-lunacy asylum' (70). She comes indeed to fear that she might be 'one of the semi-criminal abnormals' (70). Purity has cast her out utterly . . . Against such pressure it is hard to articulate resentment. Lucille responds in familiar fashion by succumbing to a frustrated half-life of nerviness and irritability; but Yvette, the virgin of the title, has another strategy.

3. The Virgin

> . . . the *naïve* or innocent core in a man is always his vital core, and infinitely more important than his intellect or his reason.
> (D.H. Lawrence: 'Review of Cavalleria Rusticana')[25]

Lawrence's creation of Yvette, little Eve, woman-in-the-making, is perhaps his most remarkable achievement in *The Virgin and the Gipsy*. Yet it is a success that has persistently been sanitized by a kind of paternal sentimentality in critics. Leavis, for instance, wrote: 'The tale is a tenderly reverent study of virginal young life. As such it seems to me unsurpassable, and it has certainly never been surpassed. The freshness, the inexperience, the painfully conscious ignorance, the confidence and the need to believe in life are touchingly evoked.'[26] Julian Moynahan relates the story to a long British tradition which is concerned with the figure of the virgin girl and 'her *rites du passage* into full womanhood', and in which the virgin represents 'an ideal of the freshness and fullness of unimpeded life.'[27] But what is significant about Lawrence's story is its revision of the familiar literary treatments of virginity. It has something new to say because of the clarity with which it sees through the defensive social function of our sentimentality to the dangerous ambivalence which in real life marks our response to virginity.

Yvette is a virgin in a sense quite different from Lucille. The word itself belongs to the title of the story and does not pass the lips of any character within it — a fact that should alert us at once to the sense of taboo with which it is charged, the unnameable desires which its function is to control. For the concept of virginity signals both purity and danger — a paradox noticed by Kirsten Hastrup when she wrote that 'what is "dangerous" (ambiguous) at one level may be seen at another level as an expression of purity.'[28] The paradox, of course, expresses the ambivalence that always gathers around taboo. Purity has no meaning if divorced from danger — and virginity *is* dangerous, ambiguous, a something-yet-to-be, capable therefore of disturbing existent social and sexual categories and of overthrowing taboo. Its 'iron gates' (in Marvell's phrase) open out always upon the unimaginably new. It is thus a marginal category, charged with that energy which Mary Douglas found in each society in 'its margins and unstructured areas'. One function of that preoccupation with female virginity which Julian Moynahan noticed in our literature has been to regulate and socialize this energy, to subdue it to male power; and it is against such social control that Lawrence's tale is active. He speaks of Yvette as a virgin to indicate not only a particular kind of purity and potential in her (by the side of her father, for instance) but also to draw attention to the disruptive force she exerts on those around her — on men especially, from Leo Wetherell to the gipsy and her own father, but also on women too, as the tribute of Aunt Cissie's hatred shows. The demands of purity are laid so strictly upon her, therefore, because of the danger to the bourgeois world of the gifts she bears in her body.

But of course the body is only the book in which the far more potent virginity of her mind may be read. What is really provocative about Yvette is the state of undifferentiated dreaminess in which she lives — a state of mind to which adolescents often revert and which is commonly found in the children of schizophrenogenic parents but which Lawrence prefers to leave altogether unexplained. For to speak of adolescence or borderline states of mental health would be to valorize an image of social maturity which *The Virgin and the Gipsy* aims to subvert. We might make the point another way by saying that Yvette is not a particularly nice girl. The words that gather around her do not flatter: spoilt, unscrupulous, wayward, perverse, contrary, irritating, obstinate, inconsiderate, outrageously rude. Her dreaminess of manner enables her to be all of these things — not only unconsciously but consciously too, for she is not without cunning — and yet to remain finally unimplicated by them. It is a defensive strategy: her vagueness protects the vital naïve centre of her mind as an 'unstructured area' where energy may still reside and growth occur. Julian Moynahan saw something of this when he commented how 'her carelessness, frivolity, and apparently selfish indifference to the pseudo-feelings of her elders' was in fact nicely calculated 'to preserve the free flow and interchange within herself of natural impulse, feeling and conscious thought.'[29] For Yvette needs protection. She is at risk from that impoverishment of the language and imagery of love that makes cynicism seem finally inevitable, given the impossibility of the infinite prolongation of her strategy of deferment. Have a good time until you're twenty-six, then settle down . . . and underneath it all, as the rector's anarchy underlay his conservatism, a great disgust at the mere thought of connexion with men. The old patterns of hygienic dissociation reproduce themselves in the younger generation, caught once more between the purity of love and the dirt of sex. Lucille tries hard in the best modern way to *work* herself out of this contradiction towards an independence of her own, but effort only leads her into a deeper entanglement, an increased frustration and fatigue. It is to be Yvette, her vagueness and indeterminacy protecting the naïve core of her feelings, who will in some measure succeed in confronting the mystifying contradictions and taboos of her life.

But her vagueness carries its own particular perils — perils of narcissistic self-absorption; and Lawrence accordingly traces her passage from girlhood to womanhood in a series of images which embody the familiar transition of youth from love of self to love of others. As Eve in *Paradise Lost* gazes upon her own fair image in the pool of the Garden of Eden, so Lawrence's little Eve in her new blue dress (the traditional virginal colour) gazes upon herself with a blithe and infuriating narcissism in the mirrors of the rectory parlour. But the mirror is no door to another world for her; and neither, it seems, is the landing window to which she is always so hungrily drawn, until suddenly today the gipsy comes into sight. As Eve was aroused from self-absorption by the troubling reality of Adam, so is Yvette aroused in imagination by the troubling presence of her gipsy. Yet there are perils in imagination too, as Lawrence indicates by reference to *The Lady of Shalott*, that little nineteenth-century parable of a woman's life lost in the web of a work where all experience is vicarious, imagined. Tennyson's poem seems always to have been vivid to Lawrence; as early as *The Witch à la Mode* he had his hero say lovingly to his woman: 'Ah, yes, you like me for a crystal-glass, to see things in: to hold up to the light. I'm a blessed Lady-of-Shalott looking-glass for you.' [30] Neither the mental work that goes into narcissism nor the work that goes into fantasy will do for Lawrence unless it makes for living contact with others. His hostility to *The Lady of Shalott* epitomizes his rejection of a whole nineteenth-century cultural tradition in which the impingements of reality upon artistic and sexual fantasy were either dreaded as a kind of death or longed for as a *Liebestod*. Such fear, such nostalgia seemed funk to Lawrence; and it is no surprise that when Yvette sees not Sir Lancelot but the gipsy with his horse and cart from her window, she flies downstairs to meet him at the door.

To turn to the gipsy is to turn away from the rectory towards the margins of her society and the source of her own true power. It is to enter upon that metamorphosis in which the virgin indeterminacy of her mind will become committed. Three forces act upon Yvette to bring about this change which is, in fact, the true subject of the story: the gradual emergence of her own desire, her growing hostility to rectory life and, finally, the grace of circumstance. Leavis has described the first point beautifully — the way that Lawrence succeeds in his task 'of vindicating desire in the sense of compelling a clear and clean and reverent recognition.' [31] One of the loveliest things in the tale is the way in which the grey shapelessness of that dreary expedition in section III suddenly takes on colour, contour and excitement from the form of the gipsy's body, up there in that most marginal of places 'on the top of the world' (22). The word 'desire' itself is won out of all the mystificatory froth about fun, sex, love and marriage in section VII, and it retains the purity of its subversive force until the end of the tale. It is the word around which the possibilities of change, newness and energy cohere.

Yvette's hostility to rectory life reaches its head in that appalling scene with her father, when she is overcome by 'cold deadness' (70), a sense of universal futility and terror at her own desires. 'It seemed to wound her heels as she walked, the fear' (72). It is the signal of Eve's fall that the serpent should bruise her heel, and suddenly Lawrence's little Eve has been brought to that fearful experience which all the vital characters in the story reach — 'a numb, frozen loneliness' (71), as though buried alive. She has been brought to that moment which forces her soul to its crisis, that moment of death or resurrection in which the self learns of its own defeat or triumph — or, as in Yvette's case, of its own capacity for a running guerrilla campaign against the world. What saves her amidst all the mystification she meets is a 'calm, virgin contempt' (71) for her father which rises to a kind of joyous vindictive hatred when faced with Granny. Fear, desire and anger which had been taboo have now been brought to consciousness; and Yvette finds herself able after all to play a game inside herself, to play off the creative inner realities of her life against the compliant outer pretence. This new sense of life as game — the sense perverted into *gaming* in *The Rocking-Horse Winner* — expresses her relish of the dance of danger, the vitality that is to be found in risk. And yet still she cannot bring herself to make a real move in the real world, to respond to the gipsy's invitation to visit him. 'Be braver in your body, or your luck will go' (76): the gipsy woman's words to Yvette remind us that luck has its responsibilities.

Finally it is the circumstance of the flood that provokes her to act — and not just the flood but the man, the gipsy, awakening her from the trance of fascination in which she watches the great wave bear down upon her. I shall consider the detail of this world's-end night later. For the moment I simply want to draw attention to the great unanswered question that it raises for even the least prurient reader. Kingsley Widmer is convinced that Yvette loses her virginity, whilst Julian Moynahan is equally convinced that she does not. Does she or doesn't she? We may refer the question to the requirements of censorship if we wish, but I suspect that Lawrence's silence is part of his purpose. Confronting our own baulked curiosity, we should come to see that, as in *Comus*, it is not the physical but the spiritual aspect of virginity that counts. The great climax to *The Virgin and the Gipsy* is not the physical but the spiritual embrace of that which had been taboo; and I want now to approach the meaning of this embrace through a brief consideration of the role of the gipsy in the tale.

4. The Gipsy

> A real panic comes over me, when I feel I am on the brink of taking another house. I truly wish I were a fox or a bird — but my ideal now is to have a caravan and a horse, and move on for ever, and never have a neighbour. This is a real after-the-war ideal. There is a gipsy camp near here — and how I envy them — down a sandy lane under some pine trees.
>
> (D.H. Lawrence, Letter of 12 March 1918)[32]

Lawrence in his search for an alternative to bourgeois life could always be compelled by the image of the gipsy, even in his earliest days; and the reminiscences of Sarah Walker, recalling a time when Lawrence was in his late teens, deserve to be quoted in full on this subject.

> You remember I mentioned gypsies, well Bert had his eye on one of them girls. Vinny, her name was. She had a brother Rolo and they came to school with us for a week or two. Bert used to help teach them, big children did in those days — it helped the teachers out. That Vinny was a caution though, she didn't care for anybody, teachers or Lord God on high. She were a law unto herself that one, proud as a peacock. I don't know what her and Bert were up to in that hayfield but he got nits in his hair and how his mother carried on. We all caught nits that summer but it was common enough in those days. Vinny's brother Rolo, he was like devil incarnate, black curls, dark skin, beautiful teeth like pearls, not like ordinary clumsy lads that we knew. They held such mystery for us, we couldn't keep away. We used to sneak

up and watch them through the bushes although we'd been
warned time and again to keep away. We used to look out for
them every year.[33]

The irresistible mysteries of forbidden gipsy life: no better
illustration of the ambivalence surrounding taboo could be
found, and it is this ambivalence that is the subject of *The
Virgin and the Gipsy*. I hesitate to disagree with Judith Okely's
sense of the tale as merely one work amongst many 'exotic and
erotic projections'[34] in which the dominant culture portrays
gipsy women as impossibly glamorous or sinister and gipsy men
as dangerous abductors; yet it seems to me that such projections
form the subject-matter of the tale. For we see the gipsy
typically through the eyes of Yvette, either directly or indirectly
through Lawrence's sympathy for her. We see him with the spell
of glamour projected upon him; and hence of course the crucial
meaning of the final page of the story ('And only then she
realized that he had a name'), when the glamour is dispersed
and the taboo is able at last to enter the normal life of
consciousness.

Such subjective projections as they come and go are an
inseparable part of *all* our imaginative and intellectual lives;
they constitute the illusions and delusions at the heart of our
capacity to form relationships and value. They are thus
necessary to our well-being, necessary to save us from a sense of
our own futility; and Lawrence evokes them here in all their
dangerousness with full consciousness of what he is about. They
are, after all, his own self-projections too. *The Virgin and the
Gipsy*, that is, as it reaches the benign disillusion of its closing
sentence, has enacted the programme that Lawrence had
outlined in *Fantasia of the Unconscious*: that we should become
increasingly conscious of that which is unconscious within us,
not to control but to learn to respect the deepest movements of
our desires, fears and angers. 'Man thought and still thinks in
images', writes Lawrence;[35] and it seems to me that, in their
different disciplines, both Lawrence and Judith Okely are drawn
to the imagery of gipsy life as a source of value because it
represents the one ethnic group in Britain which has a fully
developed counterculture antagonistic to bourgeois life and
ideology. Both find, that is, in their different ways that the real
sustains the subjective projection. It was by virtue of what they
really were that the gipsies offered Lawrence an imagery of

undomesticated wildness, seeming to safeguard the subversive-
ness of desire in its running battle against bourgeois life — most
particularly against the bourgeois pieties of labour, property and
the family.

Gipsies traditionally reject wage-labour in favour of 'self-
employment and occupational flexibility';[36] and it is clear from
The Virgin and the Gipsy that Lawrence was deeply attracted to
the alternative forms of labour that they practise — labour
which, whilst economically dependent on the larger world,
nevertheless confers a measure of economic independence on
the labourer. There is nothing of the commonly alleged idleness
of gipsy life here. The gipsy, like Lawrence himself in real life,
is self-supporting. He works in his own time and his own place
for reasons both commercial and artistic; it is a craft as well as
a business that he practises with such absorbed intensity and
delight. The occupational flexibility and the travelling life so
prized by the gipsies entails an alternative view of property too
— a view again attractive to Lawrence who loved to travel light.
In a tale whose climax is the wholesale destruction of a property
which had been so oppressive throughout, the well-cared-for
possessions of the gipsies bring welcome relief. Horse, cart,
caravan, tools, implements for cooking and eating . . . all have
a simple clarity of purpose beside the mystifications that gather
round money and possessions in the rectory. Nor should we
forget the relation between the physical and spiritual aspects of
the rectory in the tale. As Lawrence had written to Catherine
Carswell in 1916, 'Christianity is based on the love of self, the
love of property, one degree removed.'[37] It is not only property
but all the institutions that support property that are symbolically swept away in the flood at the end of the tale: religion, law,
morality . . . and, of course, the family, emblematized in that
last brief glimpse of Granny's wedding-ring. The gipsy encampment has its own kind of family structure, kept secret from us as
from Yvette; and it is fascinating to watch her try to familiarize
herself with it, in defence against the danger of the gipsy's
challenge. ' "How many children have you?" ' she asks (13),
anxious to categorise, to reassert the domestic pieties that mark
the boundaries of the imaginable for her. But gipsy men, as
Judith Okely observes, not unencouraged by their wives,
consider that 'Gorgio women are fair game';[38] and the gipsy's
answer here is masterly. ' "Say five", he replied slowly, as he

looked up into her eyes'. All that Yvette has known of
bourgeois certainties dissolves before such calculation. What can
the family be where the man has such dangerously unaccount-
able power and the wife (if wife she be) colludes in procuring
for him?

These alternative attitudes towards labour, property and the
family that characterise gipsy life must inevitably tend to arouse
such a thrill of panic in the minds of bourgeois observers, for
they are the taboos that constitute ethnic difference. They
define the margins of the permissible, and everything that exists
at or beyond those margins seems touched with unnatural
power. Hence, of course, the magical attribution of precognition
that has been turned to such good account by gipsy women in
their fortune-telling. The vagrant dwellers tucked away in that
wild secluded scene of the quarry represent everything that is
foreign to Yvette; and their wildness is not valued as by
Wordsworth in *Tintern Abbey* for its harmony within an
agricultural landscape but for its unrelenting hostility to the
industrial landscape below — a hostility made still more
implacable, Lawrence says, by the gipsy's experience of
enforced conscription in the recent war. It has always been
possible for the fact of their economic dependence to be
perceived by the gipsies themselves in terms of a predatory
ideology of spoil (for this too reinforces their sense of ethnic
difference); but now since the war 'even the old sporting chance
of scoring now and then was pretty well quenched' (58). The
rules of the game have tightened; and hence to the gipsy and
his family, despite their wariness, the value of Yvette as a score
is high.

But the gipsy does not want only to score off Yvette, he also
feels a real tenderness for her; and here we come to an insight
at the heart of the story, the insight vouchsafed to Yvette in her
relationship with her father: that 'feelings are so complicated'
(72). There is anguish here in the complexities indicated by this
simple sentence, in its recognition that between culture and
counterculture the individual mind may be torn irreconcilably.
There is something of the Byronic hero about Lawrence's gipsy
'with that air of silent and for ever-unyielding outsideness which
gave him his lonely, predative grace' (74). His solitary defiance
is both joy and affliction to him. His insolence is that of the
tribe of the humble, his purity that of the sneer and his pride

that of the pariah. Contradictions mark his life as much as the life of those whom he opposes; and they do so precisely because of that opposition. Lawrence, however, does not depreciate this hatred 'which is almost a joy' (73): he authenticates it for its creative force in both the gipsy and Yvette. So he writes of Yvette: 'her heart, in its stroke, now rang as hard as his hammer upon his copper, beating against circumstances' (74). Yet Lawrence's celebration is not sentimental, and it is his perception of the *cost* of such anger and hatred which is chiefly responsible for the story's freedom from romantic nostalgia. He shows clearly the contradictions into which they lead the soul, so that Yvette and the gipsy alike are capable equally of love and of a dishonest use of one another for the purposes of private hostility against bourgeois civilization. Insofar as they feel anger, they find it also an affliction; and insofar as they feel tenderness, they feel it only in one of their many selves. Yvette's initiation at the end of the tale is into that which is contrary; and whilst without contraries is no progression, their co-presence in the soul spells painful self-division. It is the nature of this painful and incomplete initiation that I now wish finally to consider.

5. The Initiation

> Can England swirl round, re-born at the touch of Merlin?
> (H.D.: *Bid Me to Live*)[39]

The Virgin and the Gipsy takes its shape from traditional romance material, whether oral as in ballad and fairy-tale or literary as in the countless novels and poems that trace the *rites de passage* of a young girl into womanhood. At its heart is that theme so characteristic of romance, that regeneration is by that which is contrary, marginal, coming from outside: so, for instance, the wildness of nature might make good the imperfections of civilization. In certain kinds of romance — in *Sir Gawain and the Green Knight*, in *Paradise Regained* or *Heart of Darkness* — the confrontation with that which is contrary is perceived as a test. But, of course, no test is simply a matter of saying no; there is something to be learned, something of the foreign to be experienced and introjected, to the strengthening and perhaps also to the saddening of the romance hero. In other kinds of romance, most notably in Shakespearean comedy, the contrary — be it folly, madness or love — is to be embraced in the temporary grace of holiday; and here too a certain melancholy attends the reconstitution of normality at the end of the plays. Jessie Weston argued in 1920 in *From Ritual to Romance* that the great romance traditions of our culture originated in secret ritual practices whose aim was to secure the springtime regeneration of a waste land by the commission of an act that would at other times have been taboo — the ritual killing of a god or king, for instance, or the sacred 'marriage' of someone hitherto chaste. Whatever the historical truth of these speculations, they served to establish a connexion interesting to writers of the following decade between the literature of romance and religion, and to imply that the nature of that connexion lay in their common search for the powers latent at the margins of all societies and tapped only by the ritual embrace of that which is normally taboo, either in the embrace of struggle (the test) or in the embrace of acceptance (the carnival). A society must be in creative touch with its own antithesis, we might say, even if that contact is marked by a melancholy awareness of its own inevitable incompleteness.

The Virgin and the Gipsy is best approached as a variation on the Waste Land theme, in which Lawrence went as far as literature permitted him in order to recover for romance the powers of its ritual origin. By 1926 he had perhaps wearied both of the practical futility of re-creating primitive religions, as he had done for example in *The Woman Who Rode Away*, and of the factitiousness of inventing his own, as he had done in *The Plumed Serpent*. Henceforward, here as in *Lady Chatterley's Lover*, his effort was to find an unfamiliar religious language by which he might shock the modern world into new self-recognition. *The Virgin and the Gipsy* is a rite of spring; it is not a piece of descriptive realism but a romance which intends to initiate the readers into the same powers invented for Yvette where Lawrence had already found them — at the margins of his society. The clearest evidence of Lawrence's aim lies in the way that the story makes good the gipsy woman's prophecy: ' "Listen for the voice of water" ' (76). Novelist and gipsy speak with cognate magical powers; they share the same prophetic talent, speaking together with one voice from the margins of their society — with Merlin's voice, we might say, if we share H.D.'s sense of Lawrence as a writer. The actual connexion whereby once in primitive ritual a ceremonial 'marriage' led necessarily to the freeing of the waters and the springtime restoration of the land has now been replaced by a symbolic connexion. Here it is the freeing of the waters which leads to that ceremonial 'marriage' between opposites which is the climax of the tale. Yet this coincidence of circumstances coheres in the deeper symbolic pattern; and Lawrence invokes the language and imagery of religious ritual in order to valorize the powers at work in the sudden sacralization of the taboo. He has a much better insight than Frazer or Jessie Weston into the ambivalence that accompanies taboo; and it is this dangerous energy into which he wishes to initiate the readers. Dare the forbidden thing . . . this is a romance not of test or carnival but of subversion, in which the enemy embraced will prove to be an ally. It is not a romance that aims to confirm the actual or ideal order of society (as romance commonly does) but to overturn it; and its self-divisions of feeling and tone are accordingly not those of melancholy (which belongs to the sense of lost vitality) but of anger.

The gradual process of Yvette's initiation begins when, unlike the other girls, she crosses the threshold of the gipsy caravan to have her fortune told. The caravan is the holy of holies, a secret place which we are never allowed to enter. Nor will Yvette tell us what happens there: we only learn the mysteries of the gipsy woman's words much later on when the narrator authorizes them (but not their duplicity). Deliberately Lawrence makes the occasion mysterious. He has Yvette pause for a moment on the threshold of the caravan so that we can see clearly in her the wild timidity of the doe that has become her totem during this section of the tale. Such animal images work throughout the story to enhance its fabular quality and to devalue that most valued of things, the human personality; for it is, as the bestiaries suggest, our deepest passional nature rather than our personality that reveals us most truly. It is a wolf and a deer that meet in the gipsy's caravan; and time seems to stop and light to fade until Yvette re-emerges on her 'long, witch-like slim legs' in 'a stooping, witch-like silence' (28). The starting of the car's engine and the switching on of its lights finally break the rhythm of the charm; but we have seen Yvette begin the long process of her metamorphosis into something unimaginably new.

A similar pattern recurs when Yvette returns for the second time to the gipsy's caravan on that most magical of days, a Friday. Once again a sense of ritual is everywhere. She goes entranced to the encampment as though led by the tapping of the gipsy's hammer; and when she has arrived, everything that is done and everything that is touched — from the cooking implements to the cup of coffee — enjoys a ritual sanctity. It is a strange and strong piece of writing, during the course of which Yvette finds herself slipping away from her old personality — as though once more she were about to metamorphose into some quite new being. And once again at this critical moment the trance of the story is interrupted by the sound of a motor-car.

The arrival of the 'Eastwoods', as we have seen, entails the resiting of the moment of Yvette's initiation from caravan to rectory, and thereby reconstitutes the genre of the tale. But its immediate effect is to provide her with an alternative imagery of rebellion to that provided by the gipsy. As soon as she meets this new couple, Yvette is captivated by them. She is quite content, in one of her selves, to leave the gipsy to explore this new rich imagery of unconventionality — imagery not only of the nature of sexual attraction but also of practical domestic arrangements. The Eastwoods too, in their 'small modern house near the moors and the hills' (60), have sought and found a life at the margins of their society; and they too in their extra-marital relationship have made something new of the old bourgeois pieties of labour, property and the family — or at least for a little while in a little way they have. They will play something of the role of alternative parents for Yvette: a second mother who also had two small children and a husband whom she deserted for a penniless younger man, and a father with whom she may feel a genuine sexual warmth.

The most interesting feature of the Eastwoods' relationship, as Lawrence conceives it, is that they too — like Yvette and the gipsy — are presented as opposites: he snow and she fire. The sense of antithesis which is felt throughout the tale is particu-larly forceful here, emphasized by the repeated colorations of red and white. Without contraries is no progression: Lawrence is addressing himself subversively to the much debated question of what constitutes a 'good match'. But of course not all unlike people complement one another and not all opposites are counterparts. We sense at once something anomalous about this couple, something both moving and incomplete about the limited connexions between them; and we sense it particularly in the imperfect variations they play upon the theme of anger which is at the heart of the story. For anger is perhaps the most heavily tabooed emotion of our culture. Mrs. Fawcett's resentment at her unconventional situation, and her curious mixture of defiance and wistfulness at the sight of the virgin Yvette, spring from an anger which she cannot altogether appropriate; and as her anger is impure, so with precise correspondence is her love threatrical, willed. Even her honesty, admirable as it seems amidst the furtive secretiveness of the world around her, has nevertheless a rigid rationality about it which suggests a mind fixed and insensitive to its own impulses. She is Mrs. Force-it indeed, a bourgeois wife unable wholly to break away and corrupted by that which remains compliant within her. Lawrence's emblem tells it all: a naïve child almost lost inside that wealthy fur coat 'which seemed to walk on little legs of its own' (59).

Major Eastwood, on the other hand, indulges an anger 'of the soft, snowy sort, which comfortably muffles the soul' (65). He seems a man who has been hurt and who retains 'a curious indignation against life, because of the false morality' (61) — an indignation that lies at the heart both of his tenderness for Mrs. Fawcett and of his dissociation from all the other connexions of life. It is the comfortable inertia of his isolation, however, that prompts Yvette's final dissatisfaction with him (and that has perhaps prompted Lawrence to give him so provincial a name). For the bourgeois opulence of hearth and table have combined with his own muted sensitivity to muffle his capacity for work. Unlike the gipsy he cannot, for all his washing up, turn his anger to creative account by the processes of his labour. Neither Jewish nor Danish stock, it seems, can match the expectations they raise in Lawrence himself of pugnacious oppositional cultures surviving at the margins of their society; for they have now been absorbed into the apparently seamless uniformity of bourgeois life. Their vitality is diminished. Lawrence put it this way in 1925 when he described the Jewish unconscious to Trigant Burrow, employing the same distasteful language of stock and breeding that he prefers in *The Virgin and the Gipsy* to a language of social culture:

> Nothing springs alive and new from the blood. All is a chemical reaction, analysis and decomposition and reprecipitation of social images. It is what happens to all old races. They lose the faculty for real experience . . .[40]

And yet the uniformity of bourgeois life into which the Eastwoods have been absorbed is only apparent. Their role in the story is in fact a complex one. They bring it a *variety* which also *diffuses* its hitherto single narrative purpose — and thus they image both the extent of resistance to bourgeois convention and also the imperfection of all individual attempts to overturn it (which are simultaneously, we have seen, attempts to overturn oneself). Yet also, like good parents, by articulating for Yvette the legitimacy of her own desires they point her towards the future in which she may surpass them; for she will be an exception to Lawrence's own observation that 'very few people surpass their parents nowadays, and attain any individuality beyond them.'[41] Like adepts, that is, they bring their novitiate as far as they may in the way of her initiation, until finally she must proceed alone with the imperfections of her own particular adulthood.

Yet still Yvette cannot bring herself to make her move; still with the passivity of young bourgeois womanhood she sits and yearns. Her yearning, however, interests Lawrence: it seems almost a second sight that functions as a summons, an invocation, expressing the witch-like powers that she holds in common with the gipsy woman and that the story ranges against the dead Christianity of the rectory. Sympathetic magic, prophecy, totemism, *rites de passage* . . . throughout *The Virgin and the Gipsy* Lawrence draws upon the language and imagery of primitive religion to invoke those imaginative powers normally restrained by taboo in the bourgeois Christian world which he wished to overthrow — and the most powerful image of them all, of course, is the flood with which the story ends. It has the same Dionysiac quality that Yeats found in tragedy which is, he says, 'a drowning and breaking of the dykes that separate man from man' and upon which, he adds, 'comedy keep house.'[42] The collapse of the modern dam, undermined by an ancient mining tunnel, enables Yvette and the gipsy to meet upon new terms, as man and woman free temporarily from personality and the everyday taboos of moral and social hygiene — he commanding and she obedient, according to Lawrence's own peculiar views of sexual polarity. Yvette's first reaction to that 'shaggy, tawny wave-front of water' (80) bearing down upon her is to gaze with impotent fascination: 'she wanted to see it' (80) in all its insane horror — 'as if the flood was in her soul' (81), we might add. It is the arrival of the gipsy that awakens her, transfiguring all her dread into the desire to fight back. The flood is thus an image such as Yeats said those spirits called Gates and Gate-keepers lead men to; for, he writes in *Autobiographies*, 'they have but one purpose, to bring their chosen man to the greatest obstacle he may confront without despair' — 'the Image which is the opposite of all that I am in my daily life, and all that my country is.'[43] The flood, that is, considered emblematically in the light of the passions it rouses, is — in Jungian terms — the Shadow of the Persona; it is the anarchy that our civilization has made for itself and that Lawrence now brings it to confront. This is the moment of danger, when opposites meet and the marginal becomes central. Yvette and the gipsy struggle against their panic and fight for the hall door; and when they open it, they bring about not only their own salvation but also the drowning of Granny and the swamping of the house in which she had acted out the grotesque comedy of her life. It is a terrible cleansing, a Last Judgment in which the good and the not-good-enough are separated according to their deserts; and it is here that the image of resurrection comes fully into its own.

The hour proves the man: the gipsy — already once 'a resurrected man' (67) after his experience of pneumonia in the First World War — struggles to his feet after being mown down by the waters and is fiercely determined upon his own survival, together with Yvette. He shows a brilliant resourcefulness which suggests to me the force of Yeats' dictum: 'genius is a crisis that joins that buried self for certain moments to our trivial daily mind.'[44] To the gipsy, we might say, the flood is a recurrence of the Dionysiac outburst of the war; it brings his soul once more to that crisis in which it may know itself by its desire to live or die. For no resurrection is for ever; it must be reenacted at each great crisis, at each world's-end night of our lives. There is a problem here with Granny, of course, who no doubt also had the desire to live but not the capacity, and whom the gipsy and Yvette in the moment of their crisis are ready to let die. Kingsley Widmer argues that 'those momentous situations of self-revelation where rational and moral means lack relevance are the center of Lawrence's fictions';[45] and so they are. But we should also add that the fact of Granny's death, the desire that she should die or at least the acquiescence in her death, is part of the *anguish* that Yvette feels next day when the crisis is past. For the languages of fate, luck and responsibility are spun into a fascinating thread throughout the tale, creating a richness in which we can recognize both the variety and the contradiction of the ways in which we try to give meaning to our lives. Aunt Cissie's reaction is a paradigm: ' "Let the old be taken and the young spared! Oh, I *can't* cry for the Mater, now Yvette is spared!" ' (89) — and then she weeps gallons.

Yvette's resurrection — her restoration to human warmth after the 'frozen fear' (70) induced first by her father and then by the flood — is both decisive and of necessity imperfect. It is imperfect because it originates in only one of her many selves; and it is imperfect because she will keep it secret, certainly from her father and probably from all her family. As morning breaks, and ladders extend across the water that had washed the bridge away, comedy begins the long process of reoccupying its house. The ludicrous behaviour of the policeman in the bedroom, noticed so nicely by Leavis,[46] is emblematic of the restoration of all those taboos of propriety that had been swept away the night before; and in this world Yvette will once more learn to live. Yet she will live to herself differently from before. She has learned to be physically braver, to trust herself to her body more; she has tasted the precarious tenderness that sometimes lies on the other side of taboo; and so we are led to believe that she may formulate new standards of purity and filth. When finally she rises from her bed, her resurrection will empower her to continue confirmed in the course upon which she was set; it will empower her to continue to strike 'secretly on the inside of the establishment' (74).

What Yvette saw bearing down upon her was 'a shaggy, tawny wave-front of water advancing like a wall of lions' (80) — an image of *wildness* that expresses by antithesis the tameness of her bourgeois life at the rectory. Her mother, we remember, possessed a dangerous glamour 'like lions and tigers' (8). As the waters engulf her, Yvette loses her footing in 'a ghastly sickness like a dream' (81); and this experience must surely seem at first to us to be wholly destructive. But for Lawrence it was (to borrow the words he used to describe the work of the unconscious in dream) 'the death-activity busy in the service of life.' [47] The correspondent flood that Yvette feels in herself, that is, performs for her — by virtue of the gipsy's help — a cleansing function: 'As we sleep the current sweeps its own way through us, as the streets of a city are swept and flushed at night.' For our human creativity, Lawrence argued, consists in the quality of our daytime *resistance* to the *automatic* processes of nightmare, in the quality of our resurrected life after each death; and it is thus that he declared his opposition to the Freudian language of integration and sublimation. In his search for the authentic relationship between conscious and unconscious mind — that area in which we have so often been driven to fight out our understanding of alienation during the last hundred years — Lawrence's picture is Nietzschean rather than Freudian, aristocratic rather than democratic, celebrating the quality of those individual souls able 'to live with a tremendous and proud self-possession' [48] in the face of the destructiveness within and around themselves. The wildness he values is that which exists in *conscious* opposition to bourgeois society and which is to be found in its marginal figures like that of the gipsy; and the story he has told in *The Virgin and the Gipsy* is the story of the dedication of indeterminate virginal potential to the consciousness of determined opposition. He had written many years earlier in *A Modern Lover*: 'most folk had choked out the fires of their fiercer experience with rubble of sentimentality and stupid fear, and rarely could he feel the hot destruction of Life fighting out its way.' [49] *The Virgin and the Gipsy* traces the *rites de passage* of adolescent sentimentality and fear into adult desire and anger; and these are the twin modes of that spontaneous and potentially *cooperative* unconscious with which Lawrence tried to replace the essentially 'alien Unconscious' [50] of Freud. It is to the spontaneous movements of these emotions that he tried to cultivate a willed attentiveness as they impinged upon our daytime consciousness.

Here is the dangerous vision of creativity that *The Virgin and the Gipsy* serves, superseding Freud and Nietzsche alike in the valorization of the unpredictableness of 'the essentially religious or creative motive'[51] in men and women. Lawrence uses his knowledge of the great springtime fertility rituals that Frazer had collected to invoke that 'religious' motive so neglected in his own utilitarian civilization; and instead of the vanished framework of such primitive ritual, in which the community had been reconstituted, he substitutes the framework of romance in which the community is to be subverted. He writes to bring the souls of his readers to their crisis, to dare men towards the margins of the permitted (and maybe this conscious breach of moral decorum is directly or indirectly responsible for the variety of critical responses the tale has evoked).[52] For the proprieties must be smashed; and Lawrence writes to tempt us with an imagery of the wild. He acknowledges the danger that it involves and the anguish that it costs; but he is nevertheless determined to trust himself to desire and anger, even though they lead him (in Wordsworth's phrase of strongest disapproval) 'to touch/The ark'[53] and thus to tap those unknown powers that lie on the far side of taboo.

Notes

1   The ballad is traditional. I take my version from *Ballads and Ballad-Plays*, ed. John Hampden (1931), pp. 42–3.

2   D.W. Winnicott, *The Maturational Processes and the Facilitating Environment* (1965), p. 104.

3   Judith Okely, *The Traveller-Gypsies* (Cambridge, 1983), pp. 1–2.

4   Rudyard Kipling, 'The Gipsy Trail' in *Rudyard Kipling's Verse: Inclusive Edition 1885–1918* (1919), vol. I, pp. 240–2.

5   D.W. Winnicott, *Playing and Reality* (Harmondsworth, 1974), p. 27.

6   Arthur Symons, 'Gipsy Love' in *Poems by Arthur Symons* (1902), vol. I p. 41.

7   H.T. Moore, *The Priest of Love: A Life of D.H. Lawrence* (Harmondsworth, 1976), p. 111. Lawrence was speaking of *Lavengro*; there is no evidence he had read *The Romany Rye*.

8   George Borrow, *The Romany Rye* (Oxford, 1984), p. 79.

9   George Borrow, *Lavengro* (Oxford, 1982), p. 106.

10   *The Romany Rye*, p. 82.

11   *Phoenix* ed. E.D. McDonald (1936), p. 185.

12   My quotations are from the separate edition of *The Virgin and the Gipsy* (Harmondsworth, 1970).

13   Sigmund Freud, *Totem and Taboo* in *The Pelican Freud Library* vol. XIII (Harmondsworth, 1985), p. 85.

14   Mary Douglas, *Purity and Danger: An Analysis of the Concepts of Pollution and Taboo* (1984), p. 114.

170   D.H. Lawrence: Centenary Essays

15   Kingsley Widmer, *The Art of Perversity: D.H. Lawrence's Shorter Fictions* (Seattle, 1962), p. 181.
16   *Lady Chatterley's Lover* (Harmondsworth, 1961), p. 105.
17   *Phoenix*, p. 549.
18   Mary Douglas, *op. cit.*, p. 35.
19   *Phoenix*, p. 380.
20   D.W. Winnicott, *Through Paediatrics to Psycho-analysis* (1982), p. 40.
21   Sheila MacLeod, *The Art of Starvation* (1981), p. 70.
22   Melanie Klein, *Envy and Gratitude and Other Works 1946–1963* (1975), p. 181.
23   'Blessed are the Powerful', *Phoenix II*, ed. W. Roberts & H.T. Moore (1968), p. 437.
24   Michel Foucault, *Mental Illness and Psychology*, trans. Alan Sheridan (New York, 1976), p. 69.
25   *Phoenix*, p. 245.
26   F.R. Leavis, *D.H. Lawrence: Novelist* (Harmondsworth, 1973), p. 352.
27   Julian Moynahan, *The Deed of Life: The Novels and Tales of D.H. Lawrence* (Princeton, 1972), p. 211 and p. 213.
28   Kirsten Hastrup, 'The Semantics of Biology: Virginity' in *Defining Females: The Nature of Women in Society*, ed. Shirley Ardener (1978), p. 52.
29   Julian Moynahan, *op. cit.*, pp. 217–8.
30   *The Mortal Coil and Other Stories* (Harmondsworth, 1971), pp. 104–5.
31   F.R. Leavis, *op. cit.*, p. 355.
32   *The Letters of D.H. Lawrence*, ed. J.T. Boulton and A. Robertson, (Cambridge, 1984), iii. 224.
33   *Staple: A Magazine of Writing from the East Midlands* (Winter, 1983), p. 50. Sarah Walker was talking to Carol Herring. My particular thanks to John Worthen for this reference.
34   Judith Okely, *op. cit.*, p. 202.
35   *Apocalypse* (Harmondsworth, 1974), p. 50.
36   Judith Okely, *op. cit.*, p. 27.
37   Letter of 9 July 1916, *The Collected Letters of D.H. Lawrence*, ed. H.T. Moore (1962) vol. I, p. 460.
38   Judith Okely, *op. cit.*, p. 212.
39   H.D., *Bid Me to Live* (1984), p. 169.
40   Letter of 6 June 1925, *The Collected Letters of D.H. Lawrence*, vol. II, pp. 842–3.
41   *Fantasia of the Unconscious* (Harmondsworth, 1971), p. 31.
42   W.B. Yeats, *Essays and Introductions* (1969), p. 241.
43   W.B. Yeats, *Autobiographies* (1966), p. 272 and p. 274.
44   *ibid.*, p. 272.
45   Kingsley Widmer, *op. cit.*, p. 172.
46   F.R. Leavis, *op. cit.*, p. 356.
47   This quotation and the following come from *Fantasia* p. 163; I am referring in this paragraph to chapter 14 of that book.
48   Friedrich Nietzsche, *Beyond Good and Evil*, trans. R.J. Hollingdale (Harmondsworth, 1973), p. 226.
49   *The Woman Who Rode Away and Other Stories* (Harmondsworth, 1950), p. 226.

50   Charles Rycroft, *The Innocence of Dreams* (1979), p. 166. See chapter 9 of this book for a contemporary critique of Freud's theory of the unconscious along lines that Lawrence was in some ways feeling for in the *Fantasia*.

51   *Fantasia*, p. 18.

52   J. Middleton Murry considered the tale 'over-praised' and 'comparatively unimportant' (*Son of Woman*, 1932, p. 391), and Harry T. Moore finds it 'among the lowest of Lawrence's fictional achievements' (*op. cit.*, p. 424). On the other hand, the critics to whom I have chiefly referred here — F.R. Leavis, Julian Moynahan and Kingsley Widmer — clearly rate it very highly indeed. A tale that breaches decorum may always present problems of assessment — as *Lady Chatterley's Lover* shows most clearly.

53   See *The Prelude*, ed. E. de Selincourt and revised by Helen Darbishire (Oxford, 1959), p. 614. This phrase comes from lines 80–1 of the fragment quoted there.

I would like to acknowledge my gratitude to my wife Sue Gagg, and also to Gill Branston and John Worthen, for the care with which they read and commented upon an earlier draft of this essay.

Symbolic Seeing:
Lawrence and Heraclitus

MARA KALNINS

In the 'Foreword' to *Fantasia of the Unconscious* Lawrence acknowledges the influence of the pre-Socratic philosopher Heraclitus and expresses his belief that 'art is utterly dependent on philosophy: or if you prefer it, on a metaphysic . . . Men live and see according to some gradually developing and gradually withering vision. This vision exists also as a dynamic idea or metaphysic — exists first as such. Then it is unfolded into life and art'.[1] Lawrence's metaphysic, his doctrine of duality which developed and informed nearly all the work of his maturity, was originally derived from his reading of John Burnet's *Early Greek Philosophy* in 1915. But I am going to suggest that his interpretation of the ideas he found there underwent a striking change in 1929, the final year of his life, a change which, significantly, was precipitated by his re-reading of Burnet and the work of Heraclitus and the pre-Socratics in that year. The last poems, essays and in particular his final book, *Apocalypse*, far from being a tired attempt at re-statement of belief by a dying man as some critics have held, reveal a fascinating new direction in Lawrence's thinking about man and the universe which I believe would have had the profoundest impact on his life and art had these not been cut short by his death in 1930.

Lawrence called man 'a creature of duality' and as early as 1914 had envisaged human existence in terms of duality, of creation through opposition, a notion for which Blake's oft-quoted 'Without Contraries is no progression'[2] is an apt epitome. He first expressed this belief fully in portions of 'The Study of Thomas Hardy' where he criticised both Tolstoy and Hardy for having pitted their characters and their contraries against each other with tragic results, without the possibility of fulfilment and further growth. However, he argued, there

173

remained what he called a 'supreme art'[3] in which the
contraries *could* meet creatively for the enrichment of the
individual and he developed this belief in the story of the three
generations of the Brangwen family in *The Rainbow* and later in
the story of Ursula Brangwen in *Women in Love*. But it was his
reading of Burnet's *Early Greek Philosophy* in July 1915 which
gave him the philosophical foundation on which to build his own
doctrine, and the ideas on science, religion and human nature
he found there — especially in the writings of Heraclitus —
were to have the deepest and most lasting influence on his life,
mind and art. 'I shall write out Herakleitos, on tablets of
bronze' and 'I shall write all my philosophy again. Last time I
came out of the Christian camp. This time I must come out of
these early Greek philosophers'.[4]

His reading of Burnet's book inspired him in two ways: first,
he found in the writings of the pre-Socratics with their
conception of the cosmos — 'All things are full of gods'[5] — a
logically and consistently developed system of thought about
man and the universe which offered not only a rational and
scientific explanation of phenomena but one which seemed
equally satisfying to man's intuitive and emotional needs. It was
this combination of science and religion, which he felt Christianity and modern man had lost, that Lawrence found so
compelling and that helped him to define his own cosmology
and to articulate his understanding of humanity and the
manifestations of God as he saw them revealed in the
phenomenal universe: 'If we look for God, let us look in the
bush where he sings. That is, in living creatures' (*Phoenix* 708).
Of course the sense of a lost coherence is an illusion historically,
but it seems to match a profound psychological need in modern
man which Lawrence recognised and expressed in many of his
writings, the 'Foreword' to *Fantasia* being perhaps the best
known. In 'The Two Principles', for example, he noted:

> The religious systems of the pagan world did what Christianity
> has never tried to do: they gave the true correspondence between
> the material cosmos and the human soul. The ancient cosmic
> theories were exact, and apparently perfect. In them science and
> religion were in accord.[6]

Secondly, he found in Burnet's book the metaphors and symbols
with which to express his own growing understanding of human

nature, especially that part of reality which is inaccessible to logic and discursive language, that is, the realm of inner subjective experience, the life of feeling and emotion. For Lawrence recognised that human emotion cannot be dismissed as merely irrational; that, on the contrary, it is part of a complex fabric of experience and perception and possesses its own intricate pattern which finds natural expression in literature, music and the visual arts, through metaphor and symbol.

It is worth looking in some detail at several features of pre-Socratic thought which Lawrence adopted and to see how these helped to shape the ideas expressed in his poetry and prose. First, there was Heraclitus' notion of the One and the Many. Heraclitus taught that the universe exists only through duality, through the tension of opposites, but that these opposites were themselves part of what he called 'the One' or 'the Boundless' — that is, the primary substance out of which all duality emerges to form the universe, but which itself transcends all contraries. It was a concept towards which Lawrence himself had been moving. In a letter to Henry Savage of the previous year he had written:

> There is something in the Greek sculpture that my soul is hungry for — something of the eternal stillness that lies under all movement, under all life, like a source, incorruptible and inexhaustible. It is deeper than change, and struggling. So long I have acknowledged only the struggle, the stream, the change. And now I begin to feel something of the source, the great impersonal which never changes and out of which all change comes.[7]

And in July of 1915 he wrote: 'the Infinite, the Boundless, the Eternal . . . [is] the real starting point'.[8] Secondly, Heraclitus articulated what was to become fundamental to Lawrence's concept of creation: the law of 'strife' or 'conflict' as the primary force which causes all things to rise into being.

> Homer was wrong in saying: "Would that strife might perish from among gods and men!" He did not see that he was praying for the destruction of the universe; for, if his prayer were heard, all things would pass away. (*EGP* 136)[9]

Heraclitus had taught the necessity of the 'strife of opposites', that is the tension between opposites which holds all things in equilibrium or 'attunement' in what he calls 'justice':[10]

> Men do not know how what is at variance agrees with itself. It is
> an attunement of opposite tensions, like that of the bow and the
> lyre. (*EGP* 136)

In a kindred vision John Donne was to write in his *Paradoxes*
(also, significantly, acknowledging the specific influence of
Heraclitus): 'the Discord of extreames begets all vertues'.[11]

As we know Lawrence first developed these ideas fully in his
long philosophical essay 'The Crown', written in 1915, but they
are also present in some form in nearly all his subsequent work
and especially in the fiction, for Lawrence's conception of
human nature is based on this notion of duality and creation
through conflict. In 'The Crown' he links the creative potential
of 'strife' and duality in the cosmos explicitly with human
existence:

> There are the two eternities fighting the fight of Creation, the
> light projecting itself into the darkness, the darkness enveloping
> herself within the embrace of light. And then there is the
> consummation of each in the other, the consummation of light in
> darkness and darkness in light, which is absolute: our bodies cast
> up like foam of two meeting waves, but foam which is absolute,
> complete, beyond the limitation of either infinity, consummate
> over both eternities. The direct opposites of the Beginning and
> the End, by their very directness, imply their own supreme
> relation. And this supreme relation is made absolute in the clash
> and the foam of the meeting waves. And the clash and the foam
> are the Crown, the Absolute. (*Phoenix II* 371)

And in his novels he expresses this through the quest of his
principal characters to create themselves into new being through
the continual flux of opposition, to evolve or to destroy
themselves through the conflict of deep pressures both within
and without: 'And there is no rest, no cessation from the
conflict. For we are two opposites which exist by virtue of our
inter-opposition. Remove the opposition and there is collapse, a
sudden crumbling into universal nothingness' (*Phoenix II* 366).
Birkin and Ursula's quest for 'star equilibrium' expresses the
search for Heraclitean 'attunement' in human relationship:
'Couples are things whole and things not whole, what is drawn
together and what is drawn asunder, the harmonious and the
discordant' (*EGP* 137). And Heraclitus' dictum 'It
is the opposite which is good for us' (*EGP* 136) is

echoed in Lawrence's 'the fight of opposites is holy' (*Phoenix* 374).

Perpetual flux, then, is a necessary condition for existence, for all life is a continual process of becoming: 'The final aim of every living thing, creature or being is the full achievement of itself' (*Phoenix* 403). And this belief was also to determine Lawrence's exploration of the human psyche and how it achieves its own seemingly spontaneous and never-ending creation. His fascination with human psychology led him to read Bergson, Freud and Jung and to incorporate some of their ideas into his art, much as he had adapted those of the pre-Socratics, disclaiming a rigorously intellectual adherence to any one doctrine, but rather using the concepts he found to further his own developing ideas. Always central to his thought, however, was the notion that life 'is an unbroken oneness, indivisible. The mystery of creation is that new and indivisible being appears forever within the oneness of life' (*Phoenix II* 230). He was to develop his thoughts about the human psyche in the early versions of his *Studies in Classic American Literature* and in particular in the essay 'The Two Principles' and the early essay on 'Whitman' which contain, as Lawrence put it, 'a whole Weltanschauung — new, if old — even a new science of psychology',[12] transmuting literature and doctrine from the far age of the Greeks into contemporary significance.

Now it is not possible within the brief scope of a lecture to discuss fully the evolution of Lawrence's complex ideas about human psychology especially as he explored them in *Psychoanalysis and the Unconscious* and *Fantasia of the Unconscious*, nor to analyse here in detail the influence of Bergson, Freud and Jung. But his developing philosophy and his 'new science of psychology' remained in several important respects firmly based on the Heraclitean notions of oneness and duality: 'Life depends on duality and polarity' he wrote, and '*As soon as there is creation there is duality*'[13], so that the individual exists only by means of the interaction of conflicting elements. However this notion of duality in no sense implied a division between body and soul; on the contrary, Lawrence argued that the physical and the spiritual, the phenomenal and the imaginative, were and must be fused for the greater life, for the achievement of a balance and harmony between soul and body. He called the soul 'that forever unknowable reality which causes us to rise into being' [14] and spoke of the body as 'the flame of the soul',[15] a concept similar to Blake's: 'Man has no Body distinct from his Soul; for that call'd Body is a portion of Soul discern'd by the five Senses, the chief inlets of Soul in this age.'[16] Lawrence called this integrated self — soul and body informing each other — the 'physical psyche' or the 'psychic body' (*Phoenix II* 237); in *Fantasia* he calls it the 'biological psyche'.[17] And he resolved the apparent logical and semantic contradiction involved in such a concept by arguing that this integrated self is brought forth by a primal impulse, what he calls in *Psychoanalysis and the Unconscious* the pristine unconscious.

> At last we form some sort of notion what the unconscious actually is. It is that active spontaneity which rouses in each individual organism at the moment of fusion of the parent nuclei, and which, in polarized connection with the external universe, gradually evolves or elaborates its own individual psyche and corpus, bringing both mind and body forth from itself. Thus it would seem that the term *unconscious* is only another word for life. But life is a general force, whereas the unconscious is essentially single and unique in each individual organism; it is the active, self-evolving soul bringing forth its own incarnation and self-manifestation. Which incarnation and self-manifestation seems to be the whole goal of the *unconscious* soul: the whole goal of life. Thus it is that the unconscious brings forth not only consciousness, but tissue and organs also. And all the time the working of each organ depends on the primary spontaneous-conscious centre of which it is the issue — if you like, the soul-centre. And consciousness is like a web woven finally in the mind from the various silken strands spun forth from the primal centre of the unconscious.
>
> But the unconscious is never an abstraction, *never to be abstracted*. It is never an ideal entity. It is always concrete.[18]

Here Lawrence clearly defines his own sense of the unconscious although he would have been familiar with Freud and Jung's early and general use of the term to mean 'all that material of which the person is not aware at the given time — the not-conscious'.[19] Lawrence's 'pristine unconscious' would seem to be akin to Jung's concept of the 'libido' and Bergson's of *élan vital*, that is, a hypothetical energy of life which underlies all human growth and development. Jung defines it as 'a living power used instinctively by man in all the automatic processes of his functioning; such very processes being but different manifestations of this energy'.[20] Similarly Bergson speaks of 'this change, this movement and becoming, this self-creation, call it what you will, as the very stuff and reality of our being.'[21] Thus, Lawrence's notion of individual distinction and self-creation can be seen as a natural development from Bergson's belief that: 'the passage of consciousness through matter is destined to bring to precision, — in the form of distinct personalities, — tendencies or potentialities which at first were mingled, and also to permit these personalities to test their force, whilst at the same time increasing it by an effort of self-creation.'[22]

Although *Psychoanalysis* and *Fantasia* contain the fullest statement of this doctrine of mind and body interfused and of the creation of the soul, there are many examples earlier in Lawrence's work: Ursula's understanding of the oneness yet distinctness of life when she sees the uni-cellular creature shining under the microscope in *The Rainbow* (chap. 15), and her epiphany in *Women in Love* when she recognises that 'the body is only one of the manifestations of the spirit, the transmutation of the integral spirit is the transmutation of the physical body as well'.[23] It is important to recognise that Lawrence meant this integration of flesh and spirit literally (or, as he was fond of saying, 'scientifically') if we are to understand his developing conception of the nature of the psyche and his belief in its immortality. To see how Lawrence uses metaphor, symbol and analogy to express this belief we need to return to Burnet's *Early Greek Philosophy* which, significantly, he re-read in 1929 when he was writing the late poems and his essays on the Book of Revelation.

In his attempt to define the world of change from life to death, Heraclitus had argued that life arises from the delicate balance of fire and water in the soul; and he reasoned that what appears to limited human perception as death, as non-existence, is actually only an alteration in that balance which destroys the opposite tension that had created the entity but which also generates a new tension and thus creates a new harmony after the dissolution of the old. So we are told that gods and men, mortals and immortals are really one, each living the other's life and dying the other's death. Everything in the universe is the death of something else; the living and the dead are continually changing places: 'Mortals are immortals and immortals are mortals, the one living the other's death and dying the other's life' (*EGP* 138). To prove the scientific truth of this insight, Heraclitus taught that the universe is a balance of fire (or energy) and of matter, each changing places with the other. And indeed this concept of the transformation of matter and energy first conceived in the philosophies of Heraclitus and the early Ionians lies at the heart of our whole scientific western culture. It was an astonishingly bold metaphysical conception when Heraclitus postulated: 'All things are an exchange for Fire, and Fire for all things, even as wares for gold and gold for wares' (*EGP* 135). For example, what Heraclitus meant by 'exchange' can be illustrated when fire takes in fuel and gives out heat and light (*EGP* 135).

In the universal scheme of things, then, nothing is ever destroyed. The phenomenal universe exists in a continual flux of matter and energy and informing it is the creative mystery of life, perpetually unfolding itself in pure living creatures. Heraclitus' doctrine equally helps to illuminate Lawrence's notion of the soul and body in his late works and in particular suggests a possible interpretation of that puzzling tenth stanza of 'The Ship of Death' which has exercised many critics who have offered widely different interpretations. These have ranged from the Christian resurrection myth to some kind of metempsychosis, something akin to Pythagoras's notion of the perpetual migration of the soul to new bodies, a notion however which Lawrence would have ridiculed and for which there is no evidence in his writings. The last stanza, you will recall, reads:

> The flood subsides, and the body, like a worn sea-shell
>   emerges strange and lovely.
> And the little ship wings home, faltering and lapsing
>   on the pink flood,
> And the frail soul steps out, into her house again
>   filling the heart with peace.

In one sense of course Lawrence is using myth and symbol with poetic energy to articulate his belief in immortality so it would be a mistake to look for any rigorously argued philosophical statement on the immortality of the soul in the poem itself. As Graham Hough has pointed out, here he is 'beyond conceptual statement, in a realm to whose existence only symbol and image can bear witness'.[24] But that Lawrence had such an argument in mind is shown in one of the discarded drafts of *Apocalypse* where he offers a full and explicit statement about the process of death and the generation of new life out of that dissolution, which illuminates this stanza and suggests that his intuitive vision is supported by the philosophical reasoning of Heraclitus.

Remember that Heraclitus had called life the balance of fire and water in the soul (elsewhere he also uses the four ancient so-called 'elements' — fire, water, air, earth — to describe created being, as indeed Lawrence also does in several of the last poems).[25] Heraclitus argued that the soul itself is composed of the two opposite 'elements', fire and water, the dry and the moist, energy and matter, held in equilibrium. When one element predominates the result is a dissolution of the equilibrium, so that the soul will be now living and now what we perceive as dead. But this dissolution is never final; it is part of the eternal flux of things and is necessary before a new equilibrium can be generated from the disparate elements. And Lawrence adopted this notion, calling the soul 'that mysterious conscious point of balance or equilibrium between the two halves of the duality, the fiery and the watery'.[26] In the material universe, Heraclitus had reasoned, nothing is ever destroyed, everything is in flux and motion, creating and dissolving to recreate; in Heraclitus' scheme of things Mutability reigns. It was a vision naturally congenial to Lawrence and he assimilated this and other pre-Socratic teachings about the duality of the soul and the metamorphosis of being, and imaginatively adapted them to his own ends which were to show how that duality can create the third thing, the physical body itself. Admittedly, in the extract below, he rather confusingly uses the terms 'soul' and 'spirit' to indicate the two halves of the duality, of what he had earlier simply called 'soul', but nevertheless the point remains: the spiritual aspect of man is dual and it is that spiritual aspect which creates the body, literally causes it to come into being.

> In the old psychology, man considered himself really as a dual entity, a creature of soul and spirit, anima and animus, blood and "water". The body was a third thing, caused by the fusing of the blood and the "water", the anima and animus, the soul and spirit: and so, as the soul and spirit separate, the body disappears. In the "trinity" of the human entity, it is the body

itself which is the "ghost", being merely the manifestation of the "marriage" of the great "two", the blood and water, the moist and the dry, the soul and the spirit (*Apocalypse* 188–9).

He goes on to define the dissolution of this 'trinity' and its re-creation. When the two opposites come together once again, the new body is created: 'the resurrection is of the soul and spirit, and when these two rise and fuse again, new, the new body descends upon them — the new Jerusalem' (*Apocalypse* 189). Technically of course 'anima' and 'animus' was a distinction made by Jung, who saw them as the male and female parts, respectively, of the individual psyche which is in communication with the unconscious. But the idiosyncratic terminology notwithstanding, I would suggest that Lawrence symbolically articulates just this process of dissolution and re-creation in 'The Ship of Death'. And indeed, as early as *Fantasia* he had written: 'When any man dies, his soul divides in death; as in life, in the first germ, it was united from two germs. It divides into two dark germs, flung asunder: the sun-germ and the moon-germ. Then the material body sinks to the earth.'[27] The body, then, would seem to be an epiphenomenon of the soul, not the soul of the body as Lawrence had sometimes suggested elsewhere. Interestingly, Graham Hough had noticed, though not expressly discussed this, when he wrote of the late poems:

> And then, having followed Lawrence so far, it would perhaps be possible to go back to the beginning, to tread the same path again, tracing the same pattern, but giving a different value to the symbols — and to find that the flesh had never been the flesh in any common acceptance of the term, and that the frail soul had been there all the time.[28]

Now, it would be frustrating to expect a wholly sustained argument in Lawrence's late works on this topic. Certainly in some respects the value of Burnet's *Early Greek Philosophy* lay not so much in the rigorously developed philosophical doctrines to be found there but in the stimulus to his imagination. Nevertheless he felt that the ideas of the pre-Socratics were psychologically valid and enhanced our understanding of life, even if they were scientifically inaccurate in twentieth century terms, because they represent the human mind's attempt to understand and formulate its condition.

He writes, rather disarmingly, about the early Ionian conception of the cosmos in *Apocalypse*:

> This may seem all nonsense to modern minds. But it is the honest and passionate attempt of man to understand his own mysterious and complex nature, and I must say, it seems to me even now more satisfactory, more *dynamic* than our so-called science of psychology . . . if we really try to grasp the pagan symbolic psychology, in its great range and its great depth of understanding — symbolic understanding — (189).

Clearly literal truth and symbolic truth were equally valid and at times indeed interchangeable for Lawrence who was acutely conscious of the value of each mode, and his movement between the two kinds of truth accounts for much of what appears initially to be self-contradictory in his work. This brings me to the main focus of this lecture — the fascinating development in Lawrence's thought in the last year of his life on this topic. Just as he came to see soul and body as conceptually distinct but actually integrated, so a parallel development occurs in his thinking about man's way of perceiving the universe. He had always claimed that 'Man is a creature of dual consciousness' (*Apocalypse* 192), in perpetual conflict with himself, with the claims of emotion and instinct on the one hand, and those of the intellect and reason on the other, and that this was revealed in his two ways of perceiving the cosmos: 'Man has two ways of knowing the universe, religious' — which is to say poetic — 'and scientific' (*Apocalypse* 190), with a need to bring the two into harmony but often unable to do so, and never less so than in this age of scientific materialism. 'There are many ways of knowing, there are many sorts of knowledge', he writes in *À Propos of Lady Chatterley's Lover*, 'But the two ways of knowing, for men, are knowing in terms of apartness, which is mental, rational, scientific, and knowing in terms of togetherness, which is religious and poetic' (*Phoenix* 512). In his *Apocalypse* essays Lawrence sought to analyse this dual vision formally.

> At dawn we see the sun, red and slow, emerge over the horizon and beginning to sparkle: religion and poetry at once say: like a bridegroom coming forth from his chamber: or like the gold lion from his lair: something similar. But the scientific spirit says: What *is* the shining thing? Does it really rise up from behind the hill every day? — and if so, how does it get back behind the hill,

in order to be ready for the next dawn? How does it *work*? —
    There we see the two processes of the human consciousness.
Whenever I see the sun going down, I shall say to myself: The
sun is leaving us: he is looking back at us and departing: he is
setting over the edge of the world, taking his way into another
place. — That is the inevitable feeling of every man who looks at
the sun setting, be he the greatest scientist living. And it will be
the feeling of every man, while men remain men. It is our
immediate awareness of sunset. To remove or 'correct' this
awareness, we have deliberately to change our state of mind, and
say: No, the sun is not sinking. It is the earth which is turning
round and cutting with her sharp edge, called the horizon, over
the face of the really motionless planet, the sun. — There we
have our second or cognitive awareness of sunset: and we believe
the second awareness to be the 'truth'.
    But it is obvious there are two forms of truth . . . two ways of
consciousness. (*Apocalypse* 191)

I was struck by the remarkable similarity of this vision to
Tolstoy's in *Anna Karenin* where Levin, who has been caught in
just this dilemma of the conflicting claims of the intellect and
the emotions, experiences an imaginative, intuitive understanding of his place in the universe and his relationship with
mankind and God:

> Lying on his back, he was now gazing high up into the cloudless
> sky. 'Do I not know that that is infinite space, and not a rounded
> vault? But however much I screw up my eyes and strain my sight
> I cannot see it except as round and circumscribed, and in spite of
> my knowing about infinite space I am incontestably right when I
> see a firm blue vault, far more right than when I strain my eyes
> to see beyond it'.[29]

It is Levin's ability to integrate these two forms of knowledge,
through his imagination — what Lawrence called the poetic,
religious power — that gives him that sense of wholeness and
rightness, that gives form and ultimate meaning to his life and
his world. Significantly the novel concludes with these lines:

> 'my life now, my whole life, independently of anything that can
> happen to me, every minute of it is no longer meaningless as it
> was before, but has a positive meaning of goodness with which I
> have the power to invest it'.[30]

It was a hope which of course Tolstoy himself was unable to

sustain and his subsequent crisis of religious belief and his inability to reconcile the claims of the spirit and the flesh, the intellect and the instincts, left him until the end of his life a soul divided against itself. Lawrence never experienced the profound religious doubts of Tolstoy — he always retained his faith in a power which was manifested in the mystery and wonder and beauty of the universe. But like Tolstoy (and indeed Jung) he saw the human psyche divided in itself and, furthermore, balanced between the outer, phenomenal universe, and the subjective, inner world, with an urgent need to integrate the two worlds for its own growth and development. 'What man most passionately wants is his living wholeness and his living unison' he wrote in *Apocalypse* (149). He gave many names in his writings to the power that enables man to achieve this state of wholeness; for example, the rainbow, the crown, the holy ghost, the new Jerusalem. But it was always in essence an imaginative and religious action, a power which realised human potential and was indeed God incarnate in man: 'the clue or quick of the universe lies in the creative mystery . . . in the human psyche . . . the only form of worship is *to be*'.[31] The crucial question facing all men in every generation was always how to achieve this fulfilment and specifically how to bring the findings of science and the intellect into some kind of meaningful relation with man's emotional and spiritual needs: how to find a role that both interprets the world around us and sustains our being. He believed that these divisions could be transcended and that man could achieve wholeness through the cultivation and education of the imagination as it is expressed in the arts.

In his ever-deepening quest to understand the nature of human creativity Lawrence recognised that art is fundamentally the expression of human feeling. The arts we live with are formed by, and in turn help to form, our emotional experience and responses. Every culture seeks to give utterance to its felt life by giving form — whether literary, musical or visual — to its conception of the world, to enhance and comprehend reality. The philosopher Suzanne K. Langer has put it succinctly when she writes: 'What discursive symbolism — language in its literal use — does for our awareness of things about us and our own relation to them, the arts do for our awareness of subjective reality, feeling and emotion; they give form to inward experiences and make them conceivable. The only way we can really envisage vital movement, the stirring and growth and passage of emotion, and ultimately the whole direct sense of human life, is in artistic terms'.[32] Through art, then, we give form to feeling; we are able to imagine feeling and to understand its nature; and it is only through art and the creative imagination, only through symbol and myth (which are part of the language of art) that we can establish a connection with the numinous, with that which is beyond the merely rational. Lawrence believed that man is above all 'related to the universe in some religious way'[33] and that it is through art that he seeks to understand himself and to formulate that sense of vital connection. In one of the *Apocalypse* essays he wrote: 'essentially the feeling in every real work of art is religious in its quality, because it links us up or connects us with life' (155). It is through the imagination, then, that the human psyche can create those moments of intuitive understanding of itself and the world around it, that are its closest connection with the cosmos and with that greater power which all ages and cultures have called God.

Lawrence saw the whole purpose of human existence in terms of artistic creation; in his view the aim of one's life was 'to create oneself . . . create that work of art, the living man, achieve that piece of supreme art, a man's life'.[34] It is a belief similar to Keats' vision of the world as 'the vale of soul-making', and echoes Bergson's definition of the ultimate reason of human existence as 'a creation which, in distinction from that of the artist or man of science, can be pursued at every moment and by all men alike; I mean the creation of self by self, the continual enrichment of personality by elements which it does not draw from outside, but causes to spring forth from itself'.[35] In order to achieve this creation of the self men must develop what Lawrence called the poetic intelligence, by which he meant the imaginative rather than the merely rational faculty. Any expansion of our awareness, any extension of our sympathies is, in the deepest sense, a religious action. Lawrence called this extension of the intelligence: 'the essential act of attention, the essential poetic and vital act' (*Phoenix* 261) which puts us in touch with the heart of all things, which ' "discovers" a new world within the known world' (*Phoenix* 255). And he sought in his late works to show man how to achieve this act of attention.

He recognised that the essence of human imagination lies in man's ability to see and to understand the world metaphorically and symbolically — that is, imaginatively, as well as rationally. As a species we possess the seemingly unique ability of being able to see one thing in another — life in a candle flame, or time as a flowing river — and it is this *symbolic seeing* which gives coherence and meaning to the chaos of the physical universe around us. Mere scientific data about that universe is not enough. It is only when the intellect and the emotions are integrated through the power of imagination that the world takes on significance and seems ordered, beautiful and meaningful. This was Kant's definition of Beauty and Goethe's of Science. And this became Lawrence's vision in the last poems and essays where he achieved a new synthesis in his conception of human nature, overcoming the essential duality which had previously formed the basis of his understanding of human existence and perception. The late writings suggest a fascinating new direction in his thought: a recognition that the two ways of comprehending the universe — the poetic, instinctive, religious and the rational, intellectual, scientific — are in essence the same, both aspects of the act of envisaging reality which is at the heart of human activity and experience. He grasped that the two forms of knowledge which had always seemed to him such irreconcilable contraries, were actually both aspects of a primary imaginative faculty in man. Essentially both are the same in kind — both proceed from the poetic intelligence, by which he now meant the intellectual as well as the intuitive faculty in man. 'Men must develop their poetic intelligence if they are ever going to be men',[36] a belief akin to Blake's 'the Poetic Genius is the true Man'.[37]

In a discarded fragment of *Apocalypse* where he discusses this fundamental imaginative faculty Lawrence suggests that the process by which the great scientist or philosopher or mathematician arrives at his theory may be different from that of the artist or the poet, but that the power, the faculty itself is the same. And even the process is akin since thought moves from image to image; man thinks in symbols. Mozart affirmed that he could *see* his music, like a sculpture, in three dimensions; Darwin is said to have visualised his theory of evolution; Einstein to have dreamt he was riding a beam of light before waking with the theory of relativity formed in his mind; and we all know the story of Newton and the apple. 'Though the two streams of consciousness can never be identified with one another' wrote Lawrence, 'though we are divided between them, very often torn between them, still we are whole and integral beings in which the two streams can be harmonised and reconciled' (*Apocalypse* 192). He goes on to suggest that there is a power in man which generates both forms of consciousness, 'the way of affirmation' and 'the way of question' as he terms them, concluding: 'the point of all this is that there need be no quarrel between our two ways of consciousness' (194).

There had been suggestions of this integrated vision in Lawrence's work before (and indeed perhaps there is as much significance in the process whereby he explores the nature of the psyche as in any final conclusions he reaches). As early as the draft writings of *Studies in Classic American Literature* he had spoken of the possible 'harmony between the two halves of the psyche in approach towards a pure unison between religion and science'.[38] In *More Pansies* the poem entitled 'Thought' defines this concept as 'a man in his wholeness wholly attending'.[39] But I would suggest that it was not until *Apocalypse* and the last essay he wrote, a review of Eric Gill's *Art Nonsense and Other Essays*, that he developed this notion further and spoke of both states as part of that 'absorption into the creative spirit, which is God' (*Phoenix* 393), a belief again strikingly similar to Blake: 'The Eternal Body of Man is the Imagination, that is God himself'.[40] So it would seem that the dualities in Lawrence's doctrine had been but ways of distinguishing modes of perception and being in the human individual: that soul and body, reason and passion, intellect and intuition, life and death, were always aspects of a greater unity. And that in those last months before his death, articulated with poetic urgency in *Apocalypse* and the last poems, a complex, balanced and integrated pattern emerges, of dualities and contraries finally held together in the matrix of the imagination: a vision of radiant wholeness which Heraclitus, writing twenty-five centuries ago, had defined as the attainment of wisdom: 'to know the thought by which all things are steered through all things' (*EGP* 134), to achieve 'the perception of the unity of the many' (*EGP* 167).

Notes

1   *Psychoanalysis and the Unconscious* and *Fantasia of the Unconscious* (Harmondsworth, 1981), p. 15 (hereafter *Fantasia*).
2   *The Marriage of Heaven and Hell*, plate 3.
3   *Phoenix*, ed. E.D. MacDonald (1936), p. 516 (hereafter *Phoenix* in text).
4   *The Letters of D.H. Lawrence*, ed. J.T. Boulton *et al.*, (Cambridge, 1979–85) i–iii; ii. 364 and 367 (hereafter *Letters*).
5   John Burnet, *Early Greek Philosophy* (1892; 1920), p. 48 (hereafter *EGP* in text).
6   *Phoenix II*, ed. W. Roberts & H.T. Moore (1968), p. 227 (hereafter *Phoenix II* in text).
7   Letter dated 19 January 1914, *Letters*, ii. 137–8.
8   *Letters*, ii. 363.
9   DHL uses this quotation and others from Burnet, especially from the writings of Xenophanes, Empedokles and Pythagoras, in his 1929 Prefaces to *Birds, Beasts and Flowers*.
10 Compare this with the notion of 'justice' in DHL's poem 'The Primal Passions', *Collected Poems*, ed. V. de Sola Pinto & W. Roberts (1964), pp. 481—2.
11 *Paradoxes and Problems*, ed. H. Peters (Oxford, 1980), p. 21.
12 *Letters*, iii. 400.
13 *Apocalypse and the Writings on Revelation*, ed. M. Kalnins (Cambridge, 1980), p. 189 (hereafter *Apocalypse* in text).
14 *Fantasia*, chap. 11, p. 133.
15 *The Plumed Serpent*, chap. 19 (Harmondsworth, 1966), p. 314.
16 *The Marriage of Heaven and Hell*, plate 4. Cf. Donne's sixth paradox in *Paradoxes and Problems*, p. 11.
17 See David Ellis' article above on this concept.
18 *Fantasia*, chap. 6, p. 242. Earlier in 'The Crown' DHL had argued: 'The soul does not come into being at birth. The soul comes into being in the midst of life' (*Phoenix* 384).
19 'Introduction' to C.G. Jung, *Psychology of the Unconscious*, trans. B.M. Hinkle (New York, 1919), p. xi.
20 *ibid.*, p. xvii.
21 *ibid.*, p. xviii. The quotation from Bergson cited here is from *Creative Evolution*.
22 *Life and Consciousness*, p. 126.
23 *Women in Love* (Harmondsworth, 1966), pp. 215–6.
24 *The Dark Sun* (Cambridge, 1956), p. 214. Similarly, Sandra Gilbert, in her admirable study of the poetry, *Acts of Attention* (Ithaca, 1972) evades this puzzling stanza, stating only that DHL 'believed that to attempt an intellectual definition of what can only be known intuitively, through symbol and metaphor, would be an arrogant effort to comprehend "the incomprehensible" ' (p. 311).
25 See 'Salt', 'The Four', 'The Boundary Stone', 'Spilling the Salt', 'Walk Warily', 'Anaxagoras', 'Kissing and Horrid Strife', 'Strife' in *Collected Poems*, pp. 705–14. DHL also used ideas and terms derived from the generation of Ionian thinkers preceeding Heraclitus — especially

Xenophanes and Pythagoras — as well as those following him — in particular Empedokles and Anaximander. But it is important to understand that the beliefs informing these poems were, broadly speaking, common to the early Ionians and although thinkers like Empedokles sometimes gave different names to the forces governing the universe (names which DHL also sometimes used — for example Empedokles speaks of the four 'elements' and of two powers, 'Love', to unite, and 'Strife', to divide), it was essentially Heraclitus' doctrine of 'strife' which DHL felt best articulated the Ionians' conception of the cosmos and which he adopted for his own use.

26 *Etruscan Places* (1932), p. 100.
27 *Fantasia*, p. 162. Later in *Etruscan Places* he wrote: 'the soul itself, the conscious spark of every creature, is not dual; and being immortal, it is the altar on which our mortality and duality is sacrificed' (100). But this was before his re-reading of Burnet and the subsequent redefining and development of his ideas about the nature of death, immortality and life as he explored them in the last poems and *Apocalypse*.
28 Hough, *op. cit.*, p. 260.
29 *Anna Karenin*, trans. R. Edmunds (Harmondsworth, 1954), p. 835. It is significant, too, that Levin's lack of religious faith, which has been tormenting him, should be caused by his intellectual speculations. Like Hardy, Levin's intellect forced him into a rejection of the simple Christianity of his childhood and his adult life centres on a search to regain some kind of faith in which religion, which was an emotional necessity for him, could be reconciled with the intellect.
30 *ibid.*, p. 853.
31 *The Symbolic Meaning*, ed. A. Arnold (Arundel, 1962), p. 137.
32 Suzanne K. Langer, *Philosophical Sketches* (Baltimore, 1964), p. 82.
33 *The Collected Letters of D.H. Lawrence*, ed. H.T. Moore (1962), pp. 993–4.
34 *Letters*, ii. 299.
35 Bergson, *op. cit.*, p. 126.
36 Letter to Charles Wilson, 2 February 1928, cited in 'Introduction' to *Apocalypse*, p. 19.
37 'All Religions are One'.
38 *The Symbolic Meaning*, p. 138.
39 *Collected Poems*, p. 673.
40 'All Religions are One'.

Editing a Constantly-revising Author: the Cambridge Edition of Lawrence in Historical Context

MICHAEL BLACK

Textual scholarship is one of the oldest forms of literary study, and its long history inevitably shows changes of method and the development of new preoccupations. To a large extent these are the consequence of the different nature of the literary works which are the objects of study from time to time. The texts which first attracted attention were the Christian Scriptures and the classics of Greek and Roman literature. Two obvious features of these works are their great antiquity and the fact that they come down to us through centuries of manuscript copying. The editors of those texts may presume that they were initially composed as all works of any complexity are composed: by an author or authors who find that their attention is diverted by other occupations, so that the writing can only be completed over a long period of time, or who find that they cannot bring the work to completion in a single draft, but have to rework it through several stages of writing. Indeed, Horace proposed some such long process of reworking.[1] The relationship between the Gospels suggests that their authors, working in a formal tradition, were taking common material and refashioning it; and there are also books of the Old Testament where the scholar can detect as it were strata in the material, and repetitions which imply the assembling of preexistent material and draftings and redraftings by one or more hands. But any inference about the stages of composition must by definition be made by inspecting the texts themselves; there is little or no collateral documentary evidence, and to all intents and purposes the works have to be taken as finished. The emphasis has rather been on the immense time-span which separates us from the completed work, during which time it has been transmitted, copy after copy, over the generations. It became natural to assume an original lost archetype of the finished work as a single document. The manuscripts descending from this archetype can be related to each other as families and traditions. The scholar faced with these has essentially only two recourses open to him: he can either construct an eclectic text by choosing readings which he thinks authoritative from many manuscripts; or he can take a single manuscript which he thinks more authoritative, and attach to it an apparatus of readings from other manuscripts. The disadvantage of the first course is that it produces a text which never existed before, and which corresponds with no single text among all the witnesses. The disadvantage of the second course is that it does not break out of the tradition of the witnesses, which must all be presumed to be at some degree of distance from a lost original. That lost original is however the objective towards which the textual editor is striving.

When scholars began to study the early printed texts of our own dramatic literature, they found the situation was both similar and different, and more complicated. The notional advantage of printing was that it substituted the edition for the manuscript copy; an edition ought to be accurate; theoretically all copies in an edition are identical; and theoretically each edition may be more accurate than the last. But none of the theoretical advantages was realised — could not be, because of the limitations of early printing-practice. What we have in early printed texts is a complicated mechanical process of transmission overlaying a lost but inferred process of composition. We have almost as little evidence about the composition of Elizabethan drama as we do for earlier forms of literature: in particular we have very few manuscripts (no manuscript undeniably in Shakespeare's hand), few of the important documents such as letters in which an author might have left a record of his procedures and intentions (again, none in Shakespeare's case), very few proofs, very few records from the printing houses, and so on.

We do have some knowledge which can be usefully turned onto the problems, and it is of two kinds. We know a certain amount about printing-house practice; we do also have general knowledge about the ways in which theatrical companies produced the documents which transmitted the texts of plays through the stages of composition and publication. The limitation of our knowledge about printing-house practice is that it is general and theoretical, and there is no general rule which was not at some time broken by the particular practice of this printing-house or that. Such knowledge therefore lends itself to inductive reasoning of a dangerous kind: it must proceed via inference.[2] The same goes for what we know about the ways in which companies made and transmitted their texts. However, the two kinds of knowledge can converge. The bibliographical expert who analyses a sixteenth or seventeenth century printed text can point to features of it which allow him to infer with great plausibility that the manuscript which the printer used as copy was of a certain type: that it consisted either of the author's holograph foul papers, or of a fair copy, or of the copyist's prompt-copy prepared in the playhouse from those papers, or of a memorially constructed text, or of printed copy, or a mixture of these.[3]

This identification, I have suggested, is inferential, but it can be so plausible as to constitute the next best thing to the evidence of the actual lost manuscript. We seem now to be entering a stage in Shakespearean scholarship in particular where the inferences which can be made about the underlying copy lead scholars beyond the stage at which they merely feel contact at important cruces with a lost archetype, a completed work. They can now go on to a further inference; that they are in contact with processes of authorial revision. In short, they can go further than the classical or Biblical scholar; they cannot only posit an author who goes through what are after all the known and universal processes of composition itself, they can plausibly identify a certain amount of revision in the text.

It is with Shakespeare, of course, that these processes are most interesting and most important. It can now be hypothesised with virtual certainty that most of the 'good' Quartos of Shakespeare were printed from his own 'foul papers', which leave signs of him at work, and notably his loose-ends, lacunae, syntactical complications, and failures to resolve all the possible ambiguities of staging implicit in the text. The bad Quartos are printed from memorial reconstructions by an actor or actors, reporting their own parts well and others badly. It is hypothesised also that the later Folio texts mostly rest on theatrical copy annotated onto available Quartos. It can be reasonably inferred that this copy incorporates Shakespeare's own revisions, once he had seen, in years of performance, how the plays went in the theatre. It is plausible also to infer that he did not only react to the practicalities of performance, but that he thought further about what he had written, and refined his own conceptions. Comparison of some earlier with some later printed texts of Shakespeare therefore produces the hypothesis of a revising author. This view is so much a matter of common sense that it seems likely to prevail. It will have important consequences.

In the editions of Shakespeare now being produced we shall therefore shortly see a conflict played out between editorial tendencies. There will be a conservative, or self-styled conservative tendency which will in fact be eclectic. It will tend to act as if there was from the start a final Shakespearean intention, which was more or less corrupted both in the Quartos and in the Folio. It will continue the tradition which goes back to the editions of the eighteenth century, of producing an eclectic or conflated text, which incorporates readings from all the witnesses, chosen on grounds which are in a very general sense 'critical'.[4] The newer, more radical tendency will reject eclecticism, or rather it will narrow the grounds of emendation systematically. It will tend to argue that for instance the Folio texts of *Lear* and *Hamlet* represent Shakespeare's own substantial tightening and refinement of his earlier too ample or indeterminate draft.[5] Texts based on that assumption will cut some well known and much loved passages on the ground that Shakespeare himself cut them. That in itself will frighten some editors and more readers, but it is a necessary consequence of the view that Shakespeare himself took his plays through stages of composition, and that in doing so he both cut and amplified them. If this is taken to be a process of deliberate shaping, then Shakespeare's last stage of composition represented the play as he left it. The modern editor must hesitate to subvert that intention by retaining even substantial passages that Shakespeare cut. Nor can he be merely eclectic in individual readings. Rather he must be systematic: if he uses a presumed final state of the text as copy-text he can only introduce readings from other states if he can argue that they emend genuine corruptions in his copy-text. To do that, he will have to posit a composition and transmission sequence which places the known states of the text in a hierarchy.

The difficulty in the position of the radical modern editor of Shakespeare is the lack of direct evidence other than the evidence of the texts themselves — but this is the difficulty of the traditional editor too. If the radical editor wishes to contend that the Folio *Lear* represents a later more theatrically effective intention, he is forced to elaborate a partly critical argument, which — so far as it is critical — other readers may accept, but are not forced to accept. There is no letter from Shakespeare commenting on his progress with the work, and no manuscript in which we can see the deletions and insertions in his own hand. The case is circumstantial, or inferential from the bibliographical evidence, where it is not critical.

We have to come nearer our own time in order to find direct evidence from the author's own hand, or biographical support. If you take the case of Wordsworth, you see the difficulties with which a compulsively revising author faces a modern editor. The outlines of the case are well known: Wordsworth wrote his best work in the years 1798–1805. He feared and distrusted publication and withheld his work from it as much as he could. His compulsive tendency was to bring a work through successive stages in manuscript. The manuscripts of these stages have mostly survived. When he finally collected his work for publication he was not the young man who had written the best of it, and much of it was not the same work. The reader who wants the great Wordsworth has first of all to place in order the evidence of composition-stages and the bibliographical sequence of MSS and editions. He will tend to be most interested in the early work: he will want to follow it in the process of composition until it has reached a stage of maturity. He will then want as it were to freeze the frame: to rescue the text from the later stages in which Wordsworth made it safer or less disconcerting reading for the public of the 1850s.

Here too the basic case is critical. The fact that Wordsworth revised is not, as in the case of Shakespeare, plausible inference, but fact, since the MSS survive, and so do letters, Dorothy's diaries and much other biographical evidence. The critical element of the argument has been transferred from the notion of revision itself to the quite exceptional view that it is a mid-point in this process which we wish to identify and retain as the source of a truly critical edition.[6] However, this state is usually represented by particular manuscripts. If these are taken as copy-text, the states both before and after may be given in an apparatus, and the reader can see at all points what is the evidence for a particular reading, and can compare it with the hitherto standard text.

In both cases, Shakespeare's and Wordsworth's, what will be new about these modern editions when they arrive is the attention they pay to the fact that we are dealing with a revising, even a constantly revising author. It is also clear that this cannot be dealt with by any of the simple formulae hitherto advanced, such as 'giving the final intention', or using the last edition printed in his lifetime. These beg the most important questions, which are: was there a final intention; if so, how would it be identified; do we, in Wordsworth's case, want it; and did the process of publication constitute a faithful transmission, or a corruption?

If we come to our own century we find a number of important writers whose texts though printed under modern conditions were corrupt from the start. They present immense editorial problems because the process of composition was prolonged and complicated, and was either interrupted by partial publication, as in the case of Pound's *Cantos* or Proust's *A la Recherche*, or where publication can be said to incorporate a late stage of composition, but was at the same time a corrupting process, as in the case of Joyce and Lawrence. In all these cases, we are dealing with large, original or complex works, where in some respects the publisher or the typesetter were defeated by the unfamiliarity of the object they were dealing with. Before I come to the case of Lawrence, which is our interest here, I want to dwell at some length on that of Joyce's *Ulysses*, largely because the major edition of that work published in Germany in 1984 has an important 'Afterword' by the chief editor, Professor H.W. Gabler. This is a document of great importance for anyone concerned with the editing of modern texts. We on the editorial board of the Cambridge Lawrence approached it with some trepidation, but find to our relief that in the main it is describing magisterially and systematically something very like what we in our pragmatic way had evolved as a way of proceeding. Again, the central perception is that we are dealing with a work which evolved over a period of years, being transferred, as it evolved, from one document to another; and where in the last stages the processes of publication impinged on and complicated the processes of composition and introduced corruption. The 'documents of composition' themselves survive in quantity, and there are letters and other biographical records which give evidence about sequence and intention. This means that the editor can not only reconstruct virtually the whole process of composition; he or she also has for the most part the actual inscribed pieces of paper — notebooks, manuscripts, typescripts, proofs, printed editions — and can by ocular and mechanical comparison show their relationship to each other. Some lost stages can by these means be plausibly inferred and even partly reconstituted. What these documents demonstrate, in Joyce's case, is an extraordinarily painstaking and conscious method of elaboration, as if he were putting together a mosaic, piece by piece, in accordance with the vast preconceived scheme of his huge analogical structure in eighteen episodes ór movements. Even so, as he worked upon it, his own conception evolved. For a large part of the process, Joyce as composing artist was also the scribe. This inevitably involved the copying of each earlier stage even as he was amplifying and correcting it to create the next stage. He had a prodigious memory, but nonetheless sometimes as scribe introduced errors. As Joyce is seen to do this, the editor's task begins to crystallize: it is to follow forward the continuous process of composition, to identify readings lost on the way, and to distinguish those readings inadvertently lost from those superseded by revision. Documents of composition can be distinguished from documents of transmission, such as typescripts and proofs, and here it is the editor's additional task to filter out errors of transmission due to the hand of others as well as Joyce, yet to accept the genuine compositional changes which went on being made on these documents as well as the others. Gabler finds with Joyce, as we have found with Lawrence, that the author himself never compared one state systematically with the previous one, so that errors of transmission, including his own, are always a danger. This was not entirely inadvertence: for both authors it was as if seeing the work in its latest state presented the challenge to take it into the next one, rather than to look at the previous one. So Joyce, like Lawrence, took his work demonically through draft after draft — through six, eight or nine states for some episodes. Presented with an error — often his own error — the revising author is more likely to change it to a third state than to restore a first one. The editor following after him has to discriminate between error and revision, and has to resort to a rule — what Gabler calls the rule of invariant context. If the context has changed, one infers revision.

To reconstitute in his or her mind the entire process of composition and publication is for the editor the result of surveying surviving documents, establishing the relationship between them, and inferring the existence of lost documents — so that, properly ordered and understood, the documents themselves tell the story. Once they are so placed, they not only form a sequence, they form a hierarchy. It will become clear to the editor that the task is to recover or reconstitute the text which the author was by stages moving towards but never actually inscribed whole on one single document. One of the states of the text must be chosen as the base-text for the edition because it represents an ideal balance in terms of the progress of the composition itself, and the control of the author, and must then be emended to constitute the ideal text which is sought. It is inherently likely to be either manuscript, or in Lawrence's case more probably typescript with authorial over-lay. It is quite likely, but not certain, to have been used as printer's copy. It will stand at that point where it is possible both to look backwards and recover authoritative readings in earlier drafts, and to look forwards and admit authorial proof-correction; but where editor's interventions, printer's house-styling and typesetter's errors are not yet introduced. Typescripts are intrinsically dangerous: Joyce, like Lawrence, had his work typed by others with inconsistent practices who also introduced transmission errors; like Lawrence he had more than one copy made, did not mark them identically, and mixed the sheet-sequences. Nonetheless, the author's marked type-script usually incorporates late stages of composition, and is often the last stage to have been produced under the author's direct control and to have been marked by his hand.

Whether manuscript or typescript is used cannot, as Gabler points out, be decided in the abstract. What he has shown, as we are showing with Lawrence, is that there is no general rule that copy-text must be of a particular kind. The particular case has to be decided on the merits of the documents available, and in accordance with the compositional and transmission process which is revealed by comparing them. But while there are no rules of that specific kind, Gabler enunciates principles which seem to us to be cardinal in the editing of a twentieth-century author given to continuous composition. I might do well just to read here pages 1891 onwards of Gabler's 'Afterword', but can only recommend that you turn to those pages. To summarise them: Gabler takes as axiomatic that the first edition of the text was corrupt; the main purpose of the edition is to uncover and undo the first edition's textual errors. This is not done simply by taking the first edition and emending it. Itself (he says) the critical edition constitutes the ideal act of publication, producing an ideal text free of errors (or as free of them as is now possible).[7] It turns therefore to the documents of composition and documents of transmission, and traces the linear relationship between them, which, according to Gabler, enables the editor to 'define a continuous manuscript text for *Ulysses*, extending over a sequence of actual documents'.[8] This text, never actually written out as a continuous sequence by Joyce, becomes the critical text. This is essentially an ideal text, or a reconstruction: it is something that has never been seen before, even by Joyce. I think for a moment of those German Septuagint scholars who disapproved of the English process of constructing an eclectic text from the readings of several MSS, on the ground that it produced something never seen before. I think also of the radical Shakespearean textual editor today, who will not countenance a conflated text. What would they say of this? But what Gabler is proposing and has produced, and what the Cambridge edition of Lawrence is producing, is not an eclectic or conflated text where one simply admits a reading on alleged critical grounds (i.e. it reads better or fits a view of the meaning). Gabler's text, and our texts, are critical in the true sense. That is to say, the copy-text, or what we prefer to call the base-text, is emended on grounds systematically stated, and specifically to recover readings of authority or to emend readings without authority. That authority is conferred by our understanding of the successive stages of composition, or what Gabler calls 'the continuous manuscript text . . . , extending over a series of actual documents'. The documentary witnesses stand in a linear or chronological relationship to each other, and the status and authority of each can be stated, so that what each can contribute is logically determined. The editor must follow this logic in emending the base-text.

The concept of the 'continuous manuscript text' is novel, but examined it turns out to be a better formula for what used too simply to be called the author's final intention — 'too simply' because the intention was never realised, and may not even have been final. We have not, dealing with Lawrence, produced Gabler's term, or even that exact concept, but our procedures allow it to be implied. In practical terms it has led us to seek, in the continuously evolving text, that state where the author had nearly completed his development of the text, and had not inserted his last thoughts on his proofs, but where publishers and printers had not yet corrupted the text: to take that state as copy-text, and to emend it systematically. Our practice resembles Gabler's historical and theoretical exposition in that we both conceive of a critical text as the attempt to fix, as in a still photograph, a culminating moment in a long process before deterioration sets in. My analogy is inexact, for a photograph fixes what is there now before us and the ideal text is not there before us. Perhaps our effort is more like processing the film, where some things which have receded into shadow have to be brought forward, and some interferences airbrushed out.[9]

To turn directly to Lawrence: the Cambridge edition proposes to treat all the works in a series of uniform volumes, not, as with *Ulysses* to deal only with one huge work. There are important differences in scope and method. We have not used the computer, for instance, so ours may be one of the last important editions of this size to be done by hand and eye and pen and ink. Since we have not used the computer we have not been able to get it to print out the elaborately-layered text on one side of the page in the German edition: instead we have gone straight to a reading-text. We have produced a clear text only marked by line-numbering and the asterisks which lead the reader to explanatory notes. Entries in the apparatus criticus are not signalled in the text. The way we have designed these features of the edition has naturally attracted criticism. The ordinary reader dislikes line-numbering. However, if the text we have produced achieves the status we want for it, it will become the standard text, and to have provided also the standard lineation means that from now on all scholarly work on Lawrence is provided with a simple reference system, and that is a great benefit. As for the asterisks, if we had not provided them, we should also have been criticised for not helping the reader enough.

These are trivial features: what matters is the text. Here we hope to have provided — I will not say a definitive text, since there is no such thing, but an authoritative critical text which removes transmission error and corruption, restores deletions due to censorship and other interference, and above all springs from our equivalent of Gabler's concept of the 'continuous manuscript text' produced by the constantly revising author.[10]

Certain differences between Joyce and Lawrence leap to the eye. Above all, Joyce was an author who worked to a preconceived plan, even if in detail he amplified and revised as he went along. From 1914 to 1922 he worked laboriously on this one great structure. There is nothing exactly comparable in Lawrence: during a relatively short writing-life, say 1904 to 1930, he wrote what we shall be publishing in 30 volumes. He had therefore to work exceedingly fast, and one consequence was that once a book had appeared, its place in his conscious-ness was taken by the several he might be drafting next. Apart from poems and some essays and short stories published in journals, he never revised a work that had appeared in volume form: there was no collected edition in which he looked over his whole output and revised it. The books appeared in their corrupt texts, and they stayed in their corrupt texts.

The rapidity of his writing and this animal instinct to 'kick off an offspring as soon as it can go on its own legs' conceal the fact that he was an extremely careful artist at the stages of composition, and this despite his known principle that he could not plan a work in advance, as Joyce planned *Ulysses*. It *was* a matter of principle, since he wanted something to emerge 'unbidden from the pen': something within him that he did not know and could not therefore plan. When it came out, he read it to discover what it was and whether it felt right. If it didn't feel right, he wrote it again — and again until it was right. His usual method of composition, in the first stages, was therefore the whole draft, and he would write several if necessary. Readers are familiar with the three versions of *Lady Chatterley's Lover*, which have been published. They differ to the point where they may be considered three works. The writing which at one point split into the two novels *The Rainbow* and *Women in Love* went through eight discernible drafts, but the process was so complex that it is a bit arbitrary to segment it in that way.

Like Joyce, Lawrence never systematically and in detail compared one state with a previous one: if there was an oddity, he tended to change it to a third state. Like Joyce, he couldn't type — or rather, he hated typing — and was dependent on a number of friends, on people he paid, or on his literary agent. A first typsecript, revised by Lawrence, could be retyped and further revised, so that for many texts typescript inevitably becomes our copy text, and like Gabler we have to cope with inconsistent typing-styles, and the fact that when two copies were made Lawrence corrected them inconsistently, or in the case of *Women in Love* allowed Frieda to correct them, sometimes introducing her own corrections. Lawrence lived abroad after the First World War, and typically we find him in Italy or elsewhere, corresponding with agents and publishers in London and New York, sending them not quite identical copies of typescripts for publication in the two places, reading two sets of proofs at different times, and not managing to get the corrections on one set transferred to the other.

All this produces various kinds of transmission error and some textual variants of equal authority: from Lawrence as scribe failing to transcribe exactly all that Lawrence as author intended, failing to spot typing errors and lacunae, introducing inconsistent revision on to typescripts and so on. Above all, at every stage, to see a new state of the text placed before him was an incentive not to check and correct, but to revise, to carry the composition further. The texts are therefore unstable from start to finish of the composition process, as the joint effect of Lawrence's revision, and his and others' error.

It is also well known that over and above this instability there was more or less massive interference. From *The White Peacock* onwards, publishers were telling Lawrence that if he didn't remove this or that the circulating libraries would not order or the police would interfere. He wrote to live; he had to get published; he complied. At one stage Martin Secker professed himself willing to take out some sentences from *Women in Love* without even consulting Lawrence. He took the same liberty with *The Lost Girl* and with *Aaron's Rod*. *The Rainbow* was actually suppressed despite bowdlerisation, and Heseltine threatened a libel lawsuit over *Women in Love*.

While Joyce's text was therefore corrupt from publication largely because of its originality and its idiosyncrasy as well as Joyce's own infinitely complex process of composition, Lawrence's texts were corrupt from publication because of a mixture of complex composition, complex transmission, and editorial interference. The aim of the Cambridge edition is, like Gabler's, the act of ideal publication, that first true publication which for the first time produces an ideal text: or a text as free from corruption as we can now make it.

The Cambridge editorial board from the first established as its working principle that it would only recommend that individual editors would be given a contract to edit a volume if they produced a satisfactory draft introduction. 'Satisfactory' means here that it demonstrated that the editor had surveyed and was familiar with all the documents of composition and of transmission, and had placed them in an order which demonstrated that the whole history of composition was understood by the editor and could be stated as a narrative. As I said earlier, to place them in an order and to understand the relationship between them is also to place them in a hierarchy of authority, so that it would normally follow that one state of the text should be used as base-text, and that it should be systematically emended in ways which logic demands because they are enforced by our knowledge of the whole process of composition. So that if we did not evolve Gabler's phrase 'continuous manuscript composition' the concept once stated is familiar to us, and is the one we have followed.

Once an editor has had his proposal approved, he or she carries out in detail the plan which has been outlined. It goes without saying that as one gets deeper into the problem one's understanding changes, and occasionally there have actually been changes of base-text. This doesn't alter the important principle that the editor is working not eclectically, but systematically. Emendation is governed, indeed dictated, by one's concept of the composition and transmission processes, not by that form of critical judgement which amounts to saying 'I think it reads better this way'.

Since we are aiming to eliminate various kinds of interference or overlay produced especially by the printing stage of transmission, the texts which we are producing, particularly if they are based on manuscript, have numerous authorial characteristics, even inconsistencies. Lawrence's punctuation was inevitably house-styled by his printers: even his sentence-structure was tampered with. But his punctuation in its main elements is both characteristic and, often, expressive. Indeed we have regularly found that restoring his punctuation restores his sense. He was not minutely consistent however, and we have felt it right not to strip off one house-styling to impose another. The very careful reader will therefore spot small inconsistencies, which are Lawrence's.

We have had, for consistency in our own practice, to take a single line with editorial interference, especially deletions. Lawrence assented to house-styling as a normal practice. He assented also, with various degrees of good or bad grace, to the cuts which people imposed on him. Perhaps the most contentious of our restorations will be the paragraphs of *Sons and Lovers* which Edward Garnett cut. I understand those who say that *Sons and Lovers* is even now a bit sprawling, so that Garnett might have done well to cut more. It has been said also that Garnett was doing for Lawrence what Pound did for Eliot. We don't accept that: Eliot sought Pound's help, and was in later years as his own publisher uniquely able to undo Pound's work if he had wanted to. The analogy rather is with what Bentley did to Milton, or what Jonson would have liked to do to Shakespeare, who like Lawrence flowed too easily. Sufflaminandus erat. But if Jonson *had* edited Shakespeare, and the original MSS had survived, who would argue against the restoration of the cuts, even if, privately, one thought Jonson had exercised the best of neoclassical and personal taste? Great writers have to be allowed their mistakes of judgement, their disproportions and excess. They will make the most obvious of these in their early work.

I conclude by commenting briefly on criticisms of the plan of the Cambridge volumes. It has disappointed some readers that the introductions are so severely factual: they outline the history of composition, survey the documents available, and justify the choice of base-text. They also include a section on the early reception of the work, which usually makes depressing reading. The reasons for having this kind of introduction are implicit in all I have said above: these remarks are the fundamental justification of the volume-editor's whole procedure, and it is very important that they should be stated. Cumulatively also, these introductions will provide an accurate account of Lawrence's entire working life. We have added very substantially to the record, and made much clear which has been confused. I will confess also, as a writer of critical articles and books, that there is enough less-than-brilliant criticism already available. The Cambridge texts will make possible a new generation of critical writing about Lawrence, and this will follow, but it will take some years. Meanwhile our editors will sometimes confess that editing the texts is quite enough to be getting on with. I can add that the Cambridge texts are a resource which can be further used in many ways, and that the Press does have it in mind at some stage to issue cheaper editions with different editorial material. That might be the moment for critical introductions, reading-lists and so on.

Finally, notes. The critical apparatus is of course for the scholar who wants to check the justification of the text, and to see alternative readings displayed. Not many people use this material, but it is the ultimate check on the editor's work, both in its accuracy and its consistency, and it is a crucial part of the whole scholarly enterprise. We have evolved an extremely economical formula. The reader will see that we disregard printed editions after the first English and American printings, since they have no authority and there is no point in giving their readings. He will also see that we can only record variants from states in what Gabler would call 'the continuous manuscript text'. Early drafts which differ substantially from that text can only be commented on in the explanatory notes, or printed separately in appendixes. The Press is considering the publication of whole volumes of draft material — for instance 'Paul Morel', the draft of *Sons and Lovers*, and 'The Sisters', the draft of *Women in Love*. These drafts, if published, can be given their own textual apparatus, so that very early stages of composition can also be recorded.

As for the explanatory notes, here we have been much criticised and have accepted some of the criticism and modified our practice. A difficulty here is that for economic reasons we have attempted to satisfy as many kinds of reader as possible with one edition. At the top of the range, there are expert readers, probably middle-aged Anglo-Saxons with a traditional literary education. However, alongside them are serious, indeed expert readers of Lawrence with a European background, or indeed an Indian or Japanese background. These readers are less familiar with English dialect forms, or the common stock of classical or Biblical allusion, or British social habits in the era 1900–1930. For these readers some help is already necessary. At the other end of the range are all those people born since, say, 1965 who now study Lawrence for examination purposes, and who if they are not middle-class Angle-Saxons — or even if they are — inhabit a much changed cultural system. These people actually need a lot of help, but you will understand why in trying to help them we have offended some of you. Perhaps we should not have tried to cater for so many kinds of reader at once. But again, consider that the work that we are doing may have to last for fifty years or more. The reader of 2035 AD is much less likely to be offended.

We have modified our policy already, by deciding not to gloss any word or annotate any reference which can be easily found in a good desk dictionary or encyclopedia. I notice also as we go on that our annotations are tending to become less simply factual and to make cross-reference to other works by Lawrence. In this way a thematic interest, a critical interest is being developed.

Two things concern me here. One is that we have perhaps not annotated for the future reader some cultural intangibles. I mean by that, for instance, Lawrence remarking somewhere that Birkin went outside without a hat. It probably needs to be pointed out already that in the aftermath of the nineteenth century respectable people did not go out without a hat, and that the kind of hat you wore was a class-indicator. One reviewer [11] remarked that 'it is helpful to know' that in *The Lost Girl* Mr Houghton's scheme for turning the Endeavour into a full-time picture palace was part of a contemporary trend, and that before the First World War two men who shared a room could expect to share a double bed. These things, which are just 'in the air' at any given time will soon be, perhaps already are, as strange to the English reader as to the Japanese one.

The same reviewer said 'notes on the numerous parallels between Eastwood and Woodhouse are not very illuminating' — and here we touch a topic which has exercised the Board a lot. The volume editor feels bound to point out these parallels between places and people in the novels and in Lawrence's own experience. It is in danger of being both mechanical and reductive. In what sense 'was' Ottoline Morell Hermione Roddice, and so on? More interestingly, how can Gilbert Noon have 'been' both George Neville and D.H. Lawrence? My own view about this is that the volume editor cannot say nothing, and could not possibly say all that needs to be said. If a note is written which actually stimulates thought in the critical reader, that is a service. The reader will then embark on the whole topic — what is the relationship between this fact of original experience, which is being used, and the imaginative work which is neither autobiography nor reportage but nonetheless so often finds its starting-point in things which Lawrence actually experienced? From points like that one's whole understanding begins to develop, as it does from contemplating the actual processes of composition.

Notes

1   For reasons to do with the impossibility of controlling a text once it was released into the public domain. As Kenney says:

> . . . before submitting himself to a verdict from which there could be no appeal, an author would often try out his work on a smaller circle. There were good practical reasons for this, founded on the character of ancient publication. Once a book was in full circulation, there was no effective means of correcting it, let alone recalling it. Second thoughts therefore were likely to be unavailing; a corrected second edition could not be guaranteed to succeed the first. Horace puts the matter in a nutshell when he warns intending authors to show their work to competent critics and to keep it by them for revision for nine years before launching it into the world: *nescit uox missa reuerti* . . . (E.J. Kenney: 'Books and readers in the Roman World', in *The Cambridge History of Classical Literature II: Latin Literature*, 1982, p. 11).

This is an argument for assuming the existence of the 'lost archetype' mentioned below.

2   On these problems, see D.F. McKenzie, 'Printers of the Mind: Some Notes on Bibliographical Theories and Printing-House Practices' in *Studies in Bibliography* 22 (1969), pp. 1–75. McKenzie's great work *The Cambridge University Press 1696–1712* 2 vols. (Cambridge 1966) demonstrated from the unusually copious surviving records of a small working printing-house that every assumption about 'normal' general procedures made by theoretical bibliographers was breached in actual practice. P.W.M. Blayney in *The Texts of 'King Lear' and their Origins, vol. I: Nicholas Okes and the First Quarto* (Cambridge, 1982) exhaustively studies the repertory of types

used by one of Shakespeare's printers, and reconstructs the process of printing the First Quarto. In his second volume Dr Blayney will argue from the bibliographical evidence to the nature of the underlying texts in the Quarto and Folio versions. In his view some of the characteristics of the Quarto hitherto thought to prove it unauthoritative are a veil or overlay due to the printing-house, not to the scribe. The differences between Quarto and Folio, he will argue, are the result of intentional change, and show a revising author. There are two texts of *King Lear*, each representing a stage of composition.

3   'It was standard practice for the author to retire to the local tavern with the company and, reading his work from beginning to end, submit it to their criticisms. If the play was accepted, the dramatist would make a fair copy, accommodating as many of the actors' objections, no doubt, as his literary status and general temperament allowed. We know from contemporary manuscripts, and from the manuscript tradition which can be inferred from early printings of Shakespeare, that authors also introduced many revisions of their own at this point . . . The fair copy would then be marked up by the company prompter, or 'book-holder', usually after some transcription by a scrivener, to become a prompt-book. The sketchy stage directions characteristic of authorial papers . . . would now be filled out and regularised, and there might be some textual tidying-up . . . Once a text was established in a Book, it was ready to go to the Lord Chamberlain's office to be read and approved . . . [this produced a stage of revision demanded by authority] . . . Having won its license, a prompt-book would next be copied into 'parts' — rolls of paper written with each actor's lines and short cues — while a summary of it, known as 'the plot', would be pasted on stout card ready to be hung in the tiring house for the actors to consult during performance'. (John Kerrigan, unpublished lecture-course at the University of Cambridge. Lecture 1, fo. 6). Kerrigan points out that in rehearsal and performance it is discovered whether the play will work; and cuts and changes can be freely made, from this point on, to a text which has already gone through the elaborate process of transmission posited above. This is transmission *before* any kind of printing process. Kerrigan also points out that the instability of the text on the stage was then succeeded by the process of publication: Jonson and Marston replaced material cut in performance, added material, rewrote and generally polished their plays. Jonson re-revised for re-publication.

4   Kerrigan also points out the literary-critical consequences. Modern critical views of the meaning of *King Lear* are in effect the critics' response to a conflated text — have been since Bradley. If the play is re-edited to produce an unconflated text, it reads differently and needs to be interpreted differently. The critic is at the mercy of his text. He is certainly at the mercy of a defective text, and may expend ingenuity in accounting for features which the textual editor accounts for as corruption. He can argue back, however, that it is a *critical* judgement (in the absence of positive evidence that Shakespeare revised, and revised with this intention) that the difference between two texts reflects an author seeking for more dramatic concision, or eager to eliminate ambiguities.

These are critical issues; but the bibliographical evidence can strongly support this kind of inference or hypothesis.

5   An 'average' Elizabethan play has about 2500 lines. *Macbeth* is of this length, and the modern editor infers that it was *cut* to this length in performance. What must we have lost? The usual conflated modern text of *Hamlet* has 3535 lines. A drastic modern editor would shorten it by omitting Second Quarto passages cut in the Folio. This would lose about 140 lines, including the 'dram of eale' speech and the soliloquy 'How all occasions do inform against me'. See the Introduction by Philip Edwards, editor of The New Cambridge Shakespeare *Hamlet* (1985).

6   The Cornell Wordsworth Series presents through photographs, transcripts and apparatus criticus a complete account of every stage of the poems. So they can be traced through the whole process of composition. Cambridge University Press has committed itself to a critical edition by Jonathan Wordsworth which will take as the base-text for each poem 'the first completed version'. Jonathan Wordsworth explains this:

> When he finished a poem of any considerable length, Wordsworth had a fair copy made by his sister or wife (often in fact one by each), and it is these carefully made transcriptions on which the new edition should be based. For short poems there is sometimes no manuscript, but that is because they tended to be published much more quickly, and the first printed text has very much the status of the authorised fair copy.

Jonathan Wordsworth's statement of the basic position is useful:

> The final ("authorised") text of Wordsworth was published in his eightieth year, 1849–50. "Poetry, like schoolboys", as Coleridge once commented, "by too frequent and severe correction may be cowed into dullness", and not surprisingly the decline in poetic quality in successive versions of Wordsworth's printed texts is an important factor. Even more striking, however, is the damage to longer poems surviving in early completed versions. To the best of my belief *The Prelude* went through seventeen versions in the years 1798–1850; thirteen manuscripts survive (and several are lost) of *The Ruined Cottage*, on which Wordsworth tinkered for seventeen years before it was published as part of *The Excursion* (which was itself subjected to revisions until 1845); *The Borderers* and *Salisbury Plain* the poet kept in manuscript — and kept revising — for nearly half a century before publication; *Peter Bell* he held back for twenty years, and *The Waggoner* for twelve; *Home at Grasmere* he wrote in 1800; and revised extensively in 1806, 1816, and 1832, but it was still unpublished at his death.
>
> (Jonathan Wordsworth, unpublished proposal to Cambridge University Press, 1983, fo. 3).

7   *James Joyce. 'Ulysses': A Critical and Synoptic Edition*, prepared by H.W. Gabler, W. Steppe and C. Melchior (1984). 'Afterword', p. 1892.

8   Gabler: 'Afterword', p. 1895.

9   Analogies break down. The process of composition would need the cine-camera, since it extends over time. Too precise formulation in words is also dangerous. Gabler's concept of a 'continuous manuscript text' tends to reify

a process in time, carried out over many documents, some of which are not MSS, into a single notional document continuously inscribed in the author's hand. It is a very striking phrase, but needs to be received as a metaphor or analogy.

10   The phrase, and my title, are provided by a review by Professor Dieter Mehl for *Archiv für das Studium der neueren Sprachen und Literaturen* (1985). Professor Mehl kindly sent me a typescript. His review compares the Oxford edition of *The Tales of Henry James* and recent volumes of the Cambridge Lawrence. It is rather striking that Professor Aziz, editing the Oxford James, chooses as copy-text the *first* published version, though James later carefully supervised a corrected complete edition, which must, if words mean anything, represent his final intention. The argument for ignoring this would need to be similar to the argument about Wordsworth: a basic critical postulate that the final intention was not the best one.

11   Karen Hewitt, reviewing *The Lost Girl* in *Review of English Studies*, XXXV (1984), pp. 261−3.

I am grateful to John Kerrigan and Jonathan Wordsworth for allowing me to use unpublished material. My colleagues on the Editorial Board have seen a draft of this material, and I believe they agree with the main propositions, but the expression and emphases are my own.